Designing
World-Class
e-Learning

DESIGNING WORLD-CLASS E-LEARNING

How IBM, GE, Harvard Business School, and Columbia University Are Succeeding at e-Learning

ROGER C. SCHANK

McGraw-Hill

New York   Chicago   San Francisco
Lisbon   London   Madrid   Mexico City
Milan   New Delhi   San Juan   Seoul
Singapore   Sydney   Toronto

Library of Congress Cataloging-in-Publication Data
Library of Congress data has been applied for.

McGraw-Hill

A Division of The McGraw·Hill Companies

1 2 3 4 5 6 7 8 9 0   DOC/DOC   0 9 8 7 6 5 4 3 2 1

ISBN 0-07-137772-7

This book was set in Janson Text by V&M Graphics, Inc.
Printed and bound by R. R. Donnelley & Sons Company.

How to Contact the Publisher
To order copies of this book in bulk, at a discount, call the McGraw-Hill Special Sales Department at 800-842-3075 or 212-904-5427.

To ask a question about the book, contact the author, or report a mistake in the text, please write to Richard Narramore, Senior Editor, at richard_narramore@mcgraw-hill.com

For Annie, who helped me through the last book and then I forgot to dedicate it to her, so she gets this one, which is OK because she sustained me through both

Contents

PART IV

Assessing and Measuring e-Learning

Preface

The beauty of e-learning is that, in theory, it lowers and even removes the two biggest traditional barriers to a workforce's continuous learning and improvement: time and money. The hope driving e-learning is that every employee is now only one mouse click away from acquiring new skills that will propel his or her productivity to new levels. In reality, though, e-learning—like any learning experience—is frequently derailed by flawed methods and materials. But it doesn't have to be this way.

Drawing on my experience and the things my colleagues and I have learned designing cutting-edge, e-learning environments for companies such as First Union, Deloitte, GE, and IBM, and universities like Harvard and Columbia, this book will show you how to avoid the most common technological traps as well as how to create e-learning systems that will provide the highest-quality learning experience for you and your employees. Further, it will help you to anticipate the most promising developments on the horizon so that you can select the breaking technologies that will foster learning gains in the future.

We've Come a Long Way

In 1996, an earlier version of this book was published under the title *Virtual Learning*. At that time, e-learning was the Wild West of training. Some years earlier, I had founded the Institute of Learning Sciences at Northwestern University and directed its resources towards a multidisciplinary exploration of how, when, and why people learned and what role technology could play in pushing the envelope. We quickly uncovered the power of the computer as an experimental, learning-by-doing, teaching device, and we began to develop simulation software for training purposes. That hardly sounds radical now, but at the time it caused a stir. Mostly, it seemed to generate the fear that our goal was to supplant people with CPUs rather than to augment existing academic programs.

Despite the early resistance, the undisputed benefits of computer-simulated learning environments, wherein students could safely test out a variety of assumptions and scenarios to make faster progress toward learning goals, soon caught the attention of corporations. We formed the Learning Sciences Corporation (which later changed its name to Cognitive Arts Corporation) and became among the first to meet the incredible demand for custom-designed corporate training programs. Here, too, as in academia, we were met with some initial resistance and, perhaps, fear. Many in corporate training saw us as a threat to the established world of seminar leaders and training manuals. And with good reason. There had been some ill-advised earlier attempts to use computers in corporate training, an approach known as Computer Based Training (CBT). Basically, all CBT entailed was digitizing the existing training materials so that employees read monitors rather than a printed page. This misguided approach actually did replace people with monitors, as now the trainees sat in a computer lab and keyed in responses to dull questions rather than interacting with a master teacher in a classroom who could motivate interest and hard work.

So, when *Virtual Learning* was published, we were in the beginning stages of a bold experiment. Our mission: to prove that there was indeed a new, different, and formidable way to use learning technology. In particular, we wanted to get people excited about the potential of the computer as a social simulation device. We wanted to show that employees could best learn to sell by selling, manage by managing, and help customers by helping customers.

As you know, once upon a time that is exactly how new employees learned their jobs. They were hired and learned on the job. When training departments appeared on the scene, however, executives assumed they would enable new employees to "hit the ground running" by putting what they needed to know on the job in manuals and on tests. This was similar to the ideas practiced even now in schools. The premise is that telling people the facts of a situation can substitute for actually experiencing that situation. Unfortunately, nothing could be further from the truth. Learning on the job became anathema, learning in classrooms became the norm, and the actual learning curve lengthened.

Virtual Learning described our first attempts to build the "personal interaction" equivalent of the air flight simulator for business. We taught selling by creating simulated customers to whom sales reps could sell. We created artificial environment in which management trainees had to manage a team. We created simulated call centers where people learned to answer the phone by having simulated phone conversations, complete with wacky simulated characters and really annoying customer complaints.

But, unfortunately, as a book, *Virtual Learning* was somewhat ahead of its time. The Web didn't exist as far as training people were concerned, and training was still seen as a corporate backwater. Times have changed and e-learning is a major topic in corporations and in schools. While the intellectual premises for *Virtual Learning* remain the same (people still follow the same ineffective learning principles that they always did), the possibilities for learning have changed a great deal. Readers of this book will find the theory unchanged and everything else different. What we do is different and how we do it is different. Both the medium and the level of interest have changed, so there are a lot of new issues to talk about.

The New Web Phase

A few years after *Virtual Learning* appeared, the world of training on a computer got very hot. This trend was facilitated by the fact that the hardware was finally there: Computers were becoming more available and more commonplace at all levels of the corporation. This made it possible for far more companies to believe that they could afford to invent effective training simulations in order to make learning both enjoyable and lasting.

Things really started to heat up when companies discovered the Web. This was such an exciting idea that a new buzzword was coined: e-learning. Those who embraced it most fervently believed that all learning could be on the Web. Convinced that this experiential, learning-by-doing job training was both fun and significant for productivity as well as a cost saving in the long run, companies of all sizes set up e-learning initiatives. Suddenly, businesses began to believe that they could create high-quality training and deliver it via intranets and the Internet. Now, the Web isn't really a bad thing to discover, although it isn't entirely good either if you don't understand it— and few have been able to leverage its true value.

Most of the time, cost has been the Web's trump card. Web courses are cheaper to deliver. They are also cheaper to build, but only because, for the time being, people are so eager to get Web-based systems running that they're willing to settle for very little. Training departments that were trying to improve training suddenly find themselves pressured to deliver all their training on the Web. Faster and cheaper rarely means better, in training or in any other arena. If faster and cheaper means more "telling" and less "doing" in the classroom, then we can't be very surprised by the initial results that say that e-learning is boring and students are dropping out.

e-Learning *is* cheaper, not because it allows you to put your training manual on a Web page, but because it allows many students to experience training that was built once and then continually delivered. The savings is in the lack of need to do it again and in the ease of access. The savings should not be achieved by failing to spend time on devising good training procedures. The more corporations fail to get the results they anticipated using Web-based training programs, the sooner they'll be ready to try some of the ideas discussed in this book.

What's in This Book

Designing World-Class e-Learning examines the components of good training and helps you apply it to your learning environment. We consider how the Web prevents and enables good training. We talk about how to build high-quality training and how to use the Web effectively. We discuss how to deal with executives who want cheaper training but also who want good training. We examine the future of training and education in general. Although the initial euphoric bubble created by e-learning has now burst, e-learning will be with us for some time. Despite the shortsightedness of some executives, the future of e-learning is so bright that we may all have to wear shades

Acknowledgments

I want to thank Todd Thompson for helping me with this book, Bruce Wexler, for helping me with the original, and the whole Cognitive Arts team, without whom there would be so little to say. I want to thank Jeannemarie Sierant, Clark Starr, Steven Walsh, and Chip Cleary for guiding our corporate e-learning solutions. Also, key members of the corporate teams were: Tom Hinrichs, Karen Henke, Laurie Levin, Rob Dickey, Todd Hoyer, and Bob Kaeding, Jennifer Greene, Ruth Schmidt, Katherine Sargent, and Jonathan Smith.

I want to thank David Cohen, without whom there would be no Columbia University e-learning courses, and Paul McNeil, who has worked tirelessly with us. I also want to thank Frances

Boyd and David Quinn of the Columbia University American Language Program. Ray Bareiss, Chris Riesbeck, Gregg Collins, Alex Kass, and Kemi Jona are the key members of the Columbia Interactive team at Cognitive Arts. In addition, I want to thank Sheri Handel, Suzanne Furlong, Carol-Anne Chang, George Ganat, Carol Crehan, Jennifer Wright, Svea Volke, and Samina Sami.

e-Learning
by Doing

Get Smart: The Problems with Traditional Training and Education

Why can't people seem to do their jobs properly? Think about how many times you have interacted with people who are supposed to be providing a service but don't seem to have a clue as to what you really want or any idea of how to provide it. Do these employees know how to deal with complex situations? Did anyone ever think to teach them to do their jobs in a meaningful way? Was their training simply about following the rules of the organization they work for? This lack of knowledge isn't limited to people in low-level positions. Organizations are filled with employees who haven't been doing their jobs long enough to have really mastered their intricacies. Even the CEO is often barely aware of what is going on in the organization. He or she may not even know what his or her employees are supposed to do and certainly wouldn't know how to do most of the jobs he or she manages.

The result of all this: A day doesn't go by without customers being sent the wrong products, service reps providing callers with inaccurate information, deadlines being missed or overlooked, and someone pushing the wrong key on their computer terminal and mucking up a critical system. And these are just the visible problems. Many screw-ups go undetected at first because it's hard to keep track of everyone in a large organization. (Plus, if people are expert at nothing else, they're expert at covering up their mistakes.) A little knowledge, imparted properly, could go a long way to solving the problems in these three areas. Unfortunately, it's not being imparted properly.

Why Do We Spend All That Money on Training?

Theoretically at least, training should solve the problems just discussed. It's perfectly reasonable to expect an organization's often sizeable investment in training to pay off in competence, and top management has a lot riding on this. Slowly but surely, managers are recognizing training's critical role, not just as a cost-of-doing-business necessity, but as a way to gain competitive advantage. All of which makes it even more frustrating when training fails to meet its objectives.

The amount of unnecessary or useless training that goes on in companies today is staggering. Perhaps the most egregious examples of this practice involve computer training. Companies routinely spend millions of dollars and thousands of work hours helping their people learn how to master new software—spreadsheet, word processing, and other common computer functions. Such training is a waste of time and money for three reasons:

1. People's minds can't absorb the avalanche of information that typically comes with these courses—trainers can drill people like demons, and trainees still won't correctly label and store fifty-seven commands for future use.
2. Because the systems are new, there's no body of experience and expertise to draw on. Without the knowledge of where the failures are likely to take place and what might be done to avoid them, learning won't happen. It will only happen when trainers lead people into the places where they're most likely to fail on the job—when training does that, the unconscious mind gets interested and remembers.

3. Most importantly, this training is unnecessary because people will learn how to use the software on their own.

Training Versus Learning by Doing

"But wait," the defender of the training faith might be saying. "We use state-of-the-art, multi-media-based e-learning." We send our people to executive development programs at the top business schools. We have our own in-house teaching university. We have tests that measure what people in our training programs learn, and they generally test quite well."

To these defenders I would respond: Training won't teach your people to do their jobs as well as my grandfather did his when he apprenticed as a watchmaker. During his apprenticeship, grandfather learned by looking over the master's shoulder and trying his hand at his chosen trade. I am sure he screwed up a few watches while he learned, but eventually he learned the job through trial and error. There's no substitute for natural learning by doing.

Learning by doing works because it strikes at the heart of the basic memory processes that humans rely upon. We learn how to do things and then learn how what we have learned is wrong or right. We learn when the rules apply and when they must be modified. We learn when our rules can be generalized and when exceptional cases must be noted. We learn when our rules are domain bound or when they can be used independently. We learn all this by doing, by constantly having new experiences and attempting to integrate those experiences into our existing memory structures.

Intuitively, we all know this is the case. The more experience someone has with a given situation, the more effective he or she is in that situation. It follows that the best way to teach an employee is to let him or her work on a job that requires the skills you're trying to teach, and eventually that employee will pick them up.

This process by which people fail and practice and fail and practice until they get it right works especially well when:

- A system or process is new, and there's no available expertise with which to structure training.
- There's time for people to learn on their own, and they can fail without any significant, negative consequences for the organization.

- A de facto apprenticeship process is in place to help people gain the job skills they need over time.

The head of a shipping company for whom we designed training systems called requesting help. After discussing his situation, I suggested that he didn't need new training systems and that the apprenticeship approach to training would work for him. On a boat, novice sailors have the time to ask questions and look over more experienced seamen's shoulders. Because of the close quarters and cultures of learning on a ship, it's easy to learn from the experts. And there are plenty of mechanisms in place to ensure that a neophyte's mistake doesn't blow up the ship. Classroom training, or even e-learning, would have been an expensive and less-effective solution to this company's problem.

Disadvantages of Learning by Doing

What, then, is the role of training? Why not teach adults by letting them loose on the job and having them learn by doing? Here are a few reasons why this can't always work:

1. **Learning by doing can be dangerous.** The best method for learning to defuse bombs or fly jet fighters is certainly to learn by doing. But it is imperative that trainees practice in an environment where failure, which is a key element in learning by doing, doesn't mean death or serious injury.
2. **Learning by doing can be expensive.** Not all trainees are best used in their intended capacity right away. Even if using an inexperienced employee in a real job is the best way to train that employee, and even if no physical or grievous financial danger could be caused by the poor performance of the trainee, there is still a very good chance that the trainee will fail to be very useful while he or she is learning. In cases where it takes a long time to gather the relevant knowledge on the job or where employees tend to not stay in the job for long, the whole idea of prolonged training is absurd. But when failures cost money, either by damaging an expensive piece of equipment or by losing business by behaving inappropriately, it's best to allow failures to occur in practice sessions.
3. **Learning by doing can fail to provide relevant cases.** Training on the job may keep an employee from ever expe-

riencing all that he or she needs to learn. Real learning by doing can occur randomly in a varied environment. In general, not much breadth of experience is likely to occur in an actual job environment, in spite of everyone's desire that it happen.

Why the Educational Model Pervades Companies

In the right situations and given enough time, people are great on-the-job learners. But often, organizations don't have the time to recoup from novices' mistakes. When time is a critical factor, training may be preferable to letting people learn on their own.

So what's wrong with training? Everything that's wrong with training can be stated in four words: *It's just like school.* The educational model in school does not work. That fact, however, hasn't deterred business from adopting this model, which is based on the belief that people learn through listening. Memorize the teacher's words; memorize the training book's policies and procedures.

It's at this point in my public talks that audience members rise up in protest. Some claim that they learned a great deal in school. To them I ask: If I were to pull out a biology test from high school, how many questions do you think you could answer correctly?

School isn't really about learning; it's about short-term memorization of meaningless information that never comes up later in life. The school model was never intended to help people acquire practical skills. It is intended to satisfy observers that knowledge is being acquired (for short periods of time). Our major universities—the ones which parents dream about their children attending—were originally created to produce theologians. The rich people who went to Yale and Harvard often went into the family business rather than becoming theologians, but their training in the classics was not intended to provide them with business skills. The classics were taught to create liberally educated gentlemen who presumably would learn what they needed to know about real life somewhere else. The idea has persisted into the present that school should provide a "general education."

I was on the faculty at Yale for fifteen years. When I was chairman of the computer science department I was asked (along with the heads of other departments) to speak to incoming freshmen about the advantages of majoring in my discipline. Other department heads talked grandly about how they would broaden students' worldview and create well-rounded young men and women. Instead I said, "Major in computer science and you'll get a job." You would have thought that I had committed some terrible sin (which perhaps I had). "We're not a technical school," the university leaders criticized. "We offer a classic liberal arts education." (I was chairman from 1980–1985. Most of our computer science graduates in that period went on to work for Microsoft, where they became very wealthy.) This educational model in use today in high schools was actually designed in 1892. To put this another way, while the real world has changed a lot in that last hundred years, the subject matter has not changed at all.

Education should be about preparation for living in today's world. That should mean gaining job skills, personal skills, and mental skills. "Teaching students to think," the mantra underlying a classic liberal education, is of course a wonderful goal. The question is whether memorizing some facts about Chaucer does indeed teach people to think. The problem is less a matter of subject matter than it is one of method. One can learn to think, reason, argue, persuade, imagine, and be creative in nearly any domain of inquiry. The classics can serve a student well in this regard if, and only if, they are taught properly. Our education system has reduced most intelligent inquiry and argumentation into test preparation. We are worried about getting a good grade, memorizing the right answer, and performing well on multiple-choice tests. This educational model is failing a whole generation of students. More and more corporate training seeks to imitate this clearly flawed system.

There are other objections to my argument against the traditional training and educational model, of course. People tell me that philosophy or some other course taught them "how to think." Didn't they know how to think before they took philosophy? A good deal of cognitive dissonance is at work here. Because people labored so diligently at school for so many years, they convince themselves that there must have been a lot of learning going on. Although these people might admit there are problems with schools, they attribute those problems to sex, drugs, and rock and roll. The basic model is sound, they believe. As a result, they replicate it in work situations.

They're able to replicate it because the people who did well in school tend to be the heads of companies or to occupy other powerful positions. What worked for them should work for others, they reason. Only it doesn't. (And it worked for most of them because they were grinds or had good memories; it's debatable whether a Harvard grad has more work skills than a high school drop out.) We end up with Motorola University, Intel University, and Quaker University—with instructors trying to tell people how to work using the same lecture-and-memorize techniques.

Obstacles

What's scary is how top executives raise objections and concerns about new training approaches. It's scary because these objections prevent organizations from addressing critical mass problems. Managers at most organizations recognize that their current training isn't working, but they resist the notion that their training model is fatally flawed. As a result, they look to variations on the training-as-telling theme. They'll use computer-based learning methods to train their people; they'll implement intensive workshops that compress learning; they'll train employees as part of teams; they'll bring in various gurus who are experts at motivation, learning, and leadership. But when you strip away all the bells and whistles, they're still trying to tell people what they need to know, and it's doomed to fail.

Even so, organizations are afraid to try new approaches to training. See if the following fears are familiar:

- **Alternative approaches will take too long and cost too much.** After presenting my learn-by-doing approach to training before a group of managers, many of them will ask the same question: "Can we do it faster and cheaper?" The old educational model provides the false comfort of definable time and cost expenditures: It will take one week and $100,000 to teach 100 employees Manual X. A learning-by-doing approach isn't so easy to define. Many jobs are complex; they take awhile to learn. "Do we really have to do all that?" they ask. People get crazed about the time and money they have to spend on the training of many things, which brings me to my next point.
- **Alternative approaches to training are not effective.** For many good and bad reasons, people would rather stick with the old system of training they're comfortable with instead of trying something new.

- **Alternatives to training can't be measured.** In other words, they want it to be like school with a series of tests that measure progress and success. Organizations that use traditional training can at least test employees and see how much knowledge they retained from a course—not that it means anything, since facts memorized are facts quickly forgotten. In reality, real learning is difficult to measure through competence tests. How do you measure if a service representative is more empathic or if a manager has developed the ability to prioritize? By asking them to state the ten rules of empathic listening that you had them read?

The Good News

As bad as our training has been and as mistake-prone as our workforce is, there is opportunity for organizations to reverse this situation. Most organizations harbor experts in various areas who possess priceless knowledge. The key is to transfer that knowledge to employees in the right way at the right time. This transfer can be facilitated if we accept some basic premises of learning.

First and foremost: When learning isn't engaging, it's not learning. The movies, for all their faults, usually get this idea right. In the film *Dead Poets Society*, Robin Williams plays a teacher who jumps on top of desks, makes the class laugh, tells great stories, and gets the class involved in what he's teaching. The educational establishment at the school hates the way Williams teaches, based on the premise that if students are having fun, something must be wrong. Listening to lectures and memorizing countless facts and figures aren't engaging activities for most people. Minds wander; real goals take over. Good education means having real human goals and educational goals aligned. Students have to really want to learn what you want to teach.

When you are trying to do something, you are usually concerned with doing it properly. Doing is interesting. Education that involves doing is engaging. As ensuing chapters will demonstrate, training that is on a computer, on the Web or not, must involve a simulation of some type. People need to do in order to learn. Role playing offers people the chance to participate, to make mistakes, to take chances, to challenge themselves, and to learn.

To make this revolutionary notion a reality, however, managers have to ask themselves some tough questions about training:

- What do you teach?
- Why do you teach it?
- How do you teach it?
- Are you sure that's what you want to teach?

For now, let's talk about the first question. Most of us know the low-level skills and tasks we need to teach employees. It's the more complex skills and tasks that stump us. And, whether we like it or not, the modern workplace is filled with complex job responsibilities. People need to know how to manage a team in which five people are at each other's throats. They need to develop improvisational skills to satisfy a customer when the answer to a question isn't obvious. On top of that, organizations have grown so large that employees are dealing with a mind-boggling number of products and services and a complex system of processes and policies.

The subject matter expert who's best equipped to help these people may not be available to do so. The expert in any given product or situation may be stationed in London or may not even be with the company anymore; you can't just run down the hall and ask a question or learn by looking over his or her shoulder. And yet the need for capturing and delivering this expert knowledge effectively is great. This is an opportunity for e-learning. You can't fly all those experts to your training headquarters, but you can videotape their best stories and get them into an easily accessible e-learning course.

This is a great way to gather interesting tasks.

But let's return to the "what" question. What managers want people to learn isn't limited to subject matter or clearly definable skills. Attributes and values are also crucial. It's fine to teach salespeople what they need to know about the products they're selling; but trainers also need to teach them how to communicate with customers. That doesn't mean instructors should give them a lecture or workbook listing the ten rules of communication; rather, trainers must create simulated situations where they can practice communicating. Those salespeople also need to practice active listening skills, time management techniques, and ways to interpret body language. None of this is as easy as just lecturing about the obvious skills, but it's absolutely necessary.

The good news is that most of this is doable. Even though some learning may seem daunting, it can be accomplished if the right learning environment is created. A good analogy has to do with teaching people to program a VCR. No matter what advice you give them or how much they study the instruction manual, the task just seems too complex. But when you create an environment that allows them to practice and fail at VCR programming, with help when needed and in a situation where they really want to master the skill (perhaps their all-time favorite movie is on), eventually they'll master it.

The only learning that's not doable is when something is completely new and no experience or expertise exists to guide the learning. Organizations sometimes tell us they're launching a new system of some sort, and they want us to build a training program to go along with the system. That's very difficult to do. Without the knowledge of mistakes made and solved, without real expertise to guide us, we would be designing training in the dark. Effective e-learning requires real experience for use as a guide. We learn best from reality.

Most of the time, however, the issue is raising the level of expertise on existing systems. This is exacerbated by the increased movement of people from one organization to the next—by the time someone learns a job well, he or she's off to the next job. It would be nice if we could afford to let these people learn on the job, if we had the luxury of letting them make mistakes like my apprentice watchmaker grandfather did. But in our highly competitive business climate, mistakes are too costly. Still, we persist in throwing people into situations they haven't been trained to handle and hoping against hope that they can "get the hang of it." This false hope is the reason so many star athletes fail as managers—their experience has only prepared them to play, not to manage. It's also why I get so nervous whenever we elect a U.S. president who wasn't previously vice president—being governor of a state isn't adequate training. It takes a good year or two before any new president learns the ropes; they all learning by failing, but in their case failing can be quite costly (not to mention dangerous).

There's a better way to prepare people to do a competent job, and as the following chapters will demonstrate, it's a way that all organizations can use to deal with the major problems they face. The goal of effective e-learning must be to re-create as well as possible the breadth of experience an employee needs in an intense, danger-free, inexpensive, and timely fashion. E-learning should look and feel exactly like the job the learner is being trained to assume.

The Secret to Success: e-Learning by Doing

We all know that we learn by doing, but while we pay lip service to this idea, implementing it is easier said than done. John Dewey recognized this conundrum way back in 1916 when he complained that schools insist on telling students what they need to know despite research clearly demonstrating that we have difficulty retaining and can rarely use information that we are told. Not much has changed in eighty-five years except that the business world has decided that copying schools' methods of teaching would be a clever idea. Most organizations invest the bulk of their training dollars in lecture-and-memorize methods, as if lectures and manuals contained magical words that turned novices into experts overnight.

What's particularly galling about this situation is that the computer has made learning by doing a realistic goal for any organization; e-learning opens up myriad possibilities. One only has to look at the development of the air flight simulator as a training tool to grasp the possibilities.

You would think that organizations desperate to gain the competitive advantage of a highly competent workforce would capitalize on learning by doing. They fail to do so partly because of the reasons detailed in the last chapter. But the cause of their reluctance is also that managers don't understand e-learning or the possibilities it presents as a new way of looking at education and training.

So let's consider learning. We can start by viewing the process through the eyes of a child.

How Kids Learn

Small children learn to speak through mistakes and corrections. "Kuk!" the child screams when she sees Dad holding a cookie. "Yes, it's a cookie; do you want a cookie?" he responds. Dad does not give her lessons on pronunciation; he doesn't sit his two-year-old down and say, "Now I'm going to teach you how to ask for a cookie properly."

"Papa carry you," my daughter used to shout, raising her arms to be carried. "Papa carry me," I corrected. She insisted on saying it her way for three solid months. It didn't matter what I said to her. But now she no longer says this. Of course, she is now twenty-nine years old.

The point of these stories is that we accept our children's failures as part of the learning process. We don't become hysterical when they make mistakes, and we don't try to talk them out of these mistakes. We trust they will eventually learn how to ask for what they need. When you try to tell your two-year-old to do or not do something ("Don't hit Johnny," "Share your toys with Billy," "Play nice"), there is a good chance your child will ignore your advice. Children learn to share and be nice through experience; they (hopefully) realize that they have a better time with other kids when they don't smack them (and get smacked back).

Underlying all learning is a goal, whether it is to make the world conform to your wishes, to get people to move, or to be carried in someone's arms. If you have a goal, you are interested in learning so that you can achieve that goal. You're willing to be corrected for your mistakes and accept "try this, do that" advice in order to achieve your goal. Remember, though, that goals only work this way if they're your own rather than someone else's. My daughter learned how to ask to be carried not because her objective was to learn proper English (my goal for her) but because she wanted to be carried. Employees' goals revolve around doing their jobs better (and reaping the personal, financial, and career rewards that come to high performers). Unfortunately, most traditional training fails to help people meet their goals.

How Do You Get to Carnegie Hall?

It's not that the business world abhors learning by doing. The lower the skill level, the more likely that a company is training people through some sort of learning-by-doing method. People learn to operate a piece of machinery by looking over an expert's shoulder and then trying to do what the expert did. Organizations are usually not so foolish as to try to train forklift operators in the classroom.

But when it comes to "people" skills—sales, customer service, managerial training, and executive development—companies revert to the school model. They use in-house universities, guest lecturers, elaborate manuals, and tests to impart knowledge. Some companies boast that they offer their people 1000 different courses. Executive development and leadership programs abound. Organizations justify their programs by saying that they inspire people, they catalyze new ways of thinking, or they introduce people to new policies and procedures.

Terrific. I'm all for encouraging people to try new things. But no matter how inspired and enlightened people are, two principles of learning remain:

- Nothing anyone tells you (no matter how eloquent the speaker or insightful his or her words) will do any more than inspire you. You must *internalize* procedures to do a better job. To do this, you must try them out and receive help when you fail.
- Even if you could learn to do a better job by hearing about a marvelous new management technique, it still wouldn't matter: If you don't practice that technique over and over again, you won't remember it for long.

Wine School

To understand this idea better, let's go to wine school. Not a real wine school, but a wine school that resembles most corporate training programs. First we hand out four binders. One would be a geography binder including information about where Burgundy and the wine growing regions of the United States are, and about Virginia, New York, and Texas wineries, for example. The second would be an agricultural binder with information about the various grapes, where each is grown, and why; it would discuss soil conditions, climate issues, optimal grape picking times, and so on. The third would be about the wine-making process. Fermentation, storage, blending, and the like would be included, as well as a discussion of the wine business, such as who owns which chateaus. The fourth binder would include historical data, answering such questions as: What kind of wine did the Romans drink? Who invented the cork stopper? How were issues of proper storage discovered? Why do the British prefer to drink Bordeaux? Which wine-growing regions of France flourished in Roman times?

After instruction in these various areas, we would begin testing. What was the best year for Bordeaux in the last thirty years and why? Who owns Chateau Margaux? When did Mouton-Rothschild achieve first-growth status? What grapes are grown in Oregon and why? What was the first French-American joint venture in wine growing? Can you identify the Chateauneuf du Pape region of the Rhone valley on a map?

What is wrong with this picture? When facts drive the curriculum, people lose sight of the original purpose. The goals of the students, which presumably had something more to do with a desire to drink wine than with the desire to acquire facts, are ignored. Such a school would be unlikely to stay in business long—students would vote with their feet. If students in training programs could vote with their feet in analogous situations, they would flee the classroom as quickly as those feet would take them.

A successful wine school would not be likely to deliver lectures about wine. Teaching about wine means drinking wine, not memorizing facts about wine. Drinking with some help from someone who knows more than you do means that you will learn something. Being able to compare one wine to another, having many different experiences to generalize from, lets you create new cases (a particularly great wine would be remembered, for example) and new generalizations (such as seeing a common property that all wines from a certain place or year have in contrast to others from different places or years).

It took me a long time of wine drinking before I began to wonder about Rhone wines or the British preference for Bordeaux (they used to own that region of France). I know approximately when

Chateau Margaux changed hands because the quality changed dramatically (down and then back up) the last two times that occurred, and because I really like Chateau Margaux and need to know which years to avoid. I visited the famous Chateau Margaux and really appreciated the place and the wine I tasted there. But I would not have if I hadn't liked the wine in the first place (a shrine isn't a shrine unless it means something to you). I know where Bordeaux is now because I had to find it on a map in order to get to Chateau Margaux. I drank Bordeaux for years without really knowing any more about the region of Bordeaux than that it was somewhere in the southwest of France. All these facts would have been meaningless and easily forgotten had I simply been told them at the wrong time. The right time was when I wanted to know them, a time that could only have been determined by me and not a teacher.

Do We Know What We Know?

At first glance, learning seems to be a conscious process. We know what we know. We can tell people what we know, they hear it, and they learn it. But do we really know what we are learning when we learn by doing? Most of what we know of any importance to our daily lives is actually nonconscious. We can learn to say "fruity with a great nose" when we taste a wine, but really the taste is not describable. We just know we want to drink more of it not why it tastes good, and to some extent we may not care.

To design effective e-learning, we need to have a handle on what learners should experience. But most current conceptions of knowledge imply that we know what we know. Somehow we think that we can teach that knowledge by simply telling people what we want them to know. To some extent this is true. For instance, we learn multiplication tables by memorizing them. But memorization doesn't provide much knowledge of real value. Proponents of learning by doing (as opposed to learning by being told) have long lamented the school system's lack of understanding that people learn primarily by doing.

Learning by doing teaches nonconscious knowledge, the stuff we don't know we know. Learning by being told teaches conscious knowledge. What's the difference? A manager has to deal with people who are having trouble at work all the time. When do you fire the person and when do you counsel him or her? How do you know if an employee is telling the truth about his or her situation?

How do you know if a problem is temporary or will persist? Any experienced manager will tell you that he or she develops a feel for these things. The manager may cite a rule of thumb he or she made up about such situations, but mostly it's "gut feeling" kind of stuff.

Now, "gut feeling" may not seem very scientific, but the truth is that the manual of official human resources (HR) rules is what lacks human validity. Those rules were made to take the pressure off, to eliminate subjective judgment. But in reality subjective judgment is all we have. A good learning design allows learners to experience things and begin to see new experiences in light of old ones. Good teaching, in the context of e-learning, means creating the experiences that a learner has. If the virtual experiences are good, the learner will form the "gut feelings" that you want him or her to have.

For example, in an e-learning system we built for Walgreens that teaches how to manage a pharmacy, situations develop that create angry customers. Anyone who has waited on a seemingly interminable line for a prescription they badly needed knows what I mean. In one of the scenarios we designed for Walgreens a man comes in on crutches, all bandaged and in obvious pain. He is told to wait for the pain killer that he says has worn off since the first dose given to him at the hospital. Policy says that you must fill prescriptions on a first-come, first-served basis. Common sense says otherwise in this instance. Learners who see the customer in terrible pain, but then make him wait his turn to fill his prescription are reprimanded by the simulated supervisor for blindly following policy. This leaves the learner a vivid emotional impression that will help to form gut reactions to customers (which are, after all, based on experience) in the future.

How We Understand

When we attempt to understand anything, we do so by being reminded. The reminding process enables us to compare new experiences to old ones, helping us to make generalizations by looking at the two experiences together. The reminding process is not always conscious, however, so we are not always aware that we have made a new generalization.

One of two things happens during this nonconscious comparison process. Either our minds recognize that the new experience is significantly different from the one we have compared it to, or that it is really very much like it. (I will ignore gray, in-between cases here.) When a new experience is found to be different from our prior closest memory, we must create a new case for it. For instance, we can use our prior knowledge of trains to help us out on our first airplane ride; but we soon realize that, while the comparison may have been helpful for initial processing, airplanes are really cases of their own. Eventually we treat them as a new thing entirely.

By our tenth airplane ride, we will have long since forgotten that comparison. Instead, in trying to compare airplane rides to each other, we will have created an airplane "script" in our heads that reminds us what airplane rides are like in general, including not to expect much of a meal. This is, of course, the other aspect of the comparison process. Finding a new experience to be a lot like an old experience allows our minds to build expectations. When those expectations fail to be realized, we remember other experiences with similar failures and create a new set of expectations. Expectations (and especially the failures of those expectations) are the basis for learning.

Four Steps to Take *Before* Creating an e-Learning Course

Now think about a particular skill of your own job. Did you master it because of the company's training program or because of a course you took in business school? Neither. You mastered that skill through months—no, years—of practice. By gathering experience, recovering from failed expectations, explaining what happened to yourself or others, and dealing with hundreds of cases, you gradually learned the subtleties of the job that aren't easily taught. No one can tell you how to handle a particularly difficult customer; you can't just read a manual about how to manage subordinates fairly but firmly. You need to jump in and learn what works firsthand. That's how leaders learn to lead. Reading all those books on leadership won't do it. Only when you find that your management approach results in low morale and high turnover are you motivated to be a different, more effective leader.

Similarly, when you see that you have inspired your subordinates, when you see their improvement and know that you are partly responsible, you feel secure that you know what you are doing. Ironically, you may not actually know what you are doing in that you may not be able to clearly state what it is you just did.

These are all quite good! This is a process for gathering worked examples/methods.

But you will become confident in your own intuitions about what to do, and that is very important.

When I lecture, I tell my audience that lecturing is silly because "none of you will remember much of what I'm saying." In a few days or a few weeks, listeners forget just about everything I tell them. The value of lectures—and the value of school and traditional training—is to get people started in the right direction. It is, in fact, the value of this book. If I'm sufficiently provocative, funny, and insightful—in other words, if I'm entertaining enough so you don't tune me out—I may induce you to think about what I have said (a kind of mental doing) or, even better, to give my ideas a try. But I can't do for you what you need to do yourself. You need to practice, and for that you need practice environments—places where people enjoy the freedom to experiment using e-learning. For instance, managers of a restaurant chain we worked for wanted us to train all the managers; so I said, "Fine, let's build a simulated restaurant."

Naturally, that would have been an ambitious undertaking; so the managers responded as many organizations do: "That's so complex and expensive, can't we start with something simple?"

Many organizations want to start simply. That's not always possible, but let's consider four easy steps you can use to get a feel for the e-learning process.

Step 1: Start with a Job in Your Organization That Requires Well-Defined, Repeatable Skills

When organizations tell me they want to start e-learning using something simple, I ask them to name a job that's easy to perform. The aforementioned restaurant chain managers told me that that would be their hostess jobs. "Anyone can be a hostess," they said. Well, maybe they can, but training a hostess in a meaningful way would be quite a complicated undertaking. Some jobs that appear simple require complex skills that are difficult to teach. A hostess has to deal with a wide range of human issues—drunks, obnoxious customers, people who become ill, and so on. Though anyone is theoretically qualified to be a hostess, the reality is that doing the job well demands certain intangible skills.

A job that the restaurant chain thought to be much more difficult—that of bartender—is actually much easier to train for from an e-learning perspective. The restaurant felt that bartending was difficult because there were so many drinks and mixing procedures to memorize. From a computer perspective, though, it's an eminently simple job to simulate. A simulation for bartenders is relatively fast and inexpensive to build—learning how to make one drink requires the same skills as learning to make another. It is the practice that introduces the complexity.

The point here is that if you want to start building simple e-learning simulations, pick a job with well-defined, repeatable skills.

✯ Step 2: Figure Out Your Most Pressing Training Issue

Organizations often want to start e-learning efforts where the hurt is greatest. Often, organizations start thinking about e-learning while in crisis—they're desperate to get people up to speed in some job, procedure, or process, and some smart human resources executive recognizes that traditional training won't suffice.

This panic reaction is fine, as long as you keep the following caveat in mind: Someone in your organization must have already done what you want others to learn to do.

✯ Step 3: Identify the Best Subject Matter Experts in Your Organization

"Roger, we want you to teach our people how to work within this great new process we're implementing." As I've stated before (and will state again), this is a common request, and it's one that's very difficult to fulfill. If you lack experts in a given area, you lack the knowledge critical to mastering that area. Who is going to tell you about the tricks of making that process work? Where will the stories about difficulties come from? What about exceptions to the rules? Whose tried and true behavior do you model? Better to get that process up and running before you try to train an entire organization in something no one really knows how to do.

The ideal circumstance is when a company has someone who can do a job perfectly, knows how to talk about what it takes to do the job well, and the problem is to create 1000 people just like him or her in a variety of locations around the world.

Step 4: Gather Stories

Why stories? Because that's where golden nuggets of organizational knowledge reside. In every organization, stories lay dormant in each employee's head. These stories are rarely told to other employees who have the exact same job and could benefit greatly from hearing them. I should emphasize that stories are usually far removed from the description of jobs created by HR departments; those dry documents only *hint* at what's important to learn in language that never inspires, such as "Job X has the following ten responsibilities. . . ." It's analogous to telling a beginning art student that Monet painted a lot of water lilies in a blurry kind of way. No matter what you say, you can't really learn what Monet is all about until you delve beneath the neutrality of the description.

In the world of work, war stories fill you in on what lies beneath the surface. Unfortunately, these stories are not included in traditional training. Often they are about the unofficial procedures, the things that really get the job done. To hear them, you need to go for drinks with a bunch of veteran employees or hang around the lunchroom. That's where you'll hear about how Sally needed to meet a number of tight deadlines and devised an ingenious shortcut inspired by a Seinfeld rerun. It's listening to some Management Information Systems (MIS) guy proudly detailing how he ignored his boss's instructions and figured out how to get the most out of a piece of software.

Every organization has thousands of stories. The problem is getting people to tell them. Sometimes the problem is that organizations are so large and spread out, people never get a chance to meet other employees who could tell them relevant stories. It's also possible that people are reluctant to tell their stories because the stories make them, the organization, or their bosses look bad. Or it may be that some people aren't good storytellers.

As a result, designers of e-learning solutions have to be clever to draw these stories out. Sometimes the interviewer can get someone started by asking, "Do you have a story about working here that you wish everyone in the company knew?" Designers often catalyze storytelling with a number of specific, leading questions, such as:

- What is the most interesting thing that's happened to you on the job?
- What do you like about your job?
- What about your job is hard to do?
- What difficult problem did you solve yourself?
- Do you recall a time when . . . (such as, someone wouldn't let you do *x* or tried to get you to do *y*)?

Once interviewers hit upon a promising response, they should become more specific in their questioning, trying to draw out stories about screw-ups, complexities, and crazy situations.

There are different ways to use these stories for e-learning, including creating "corporate memories"—collections of stories told by company experts easily accessible through computer systems. But for now, let's focus on how to use these stories in simulations.

Learning Can Be Simulating

Like a good novel, a good simulation asks your learners to suspend their disbelief. Whether you're creating a simulation on a computer or through role-playing, you want participants to experience the event as if it were really happening. Perhaps more to the point, you want to avoid evoking an unnatural response—a response someone wouldn't give in real life.

Since we learn from our mistakes, a good e-learning solution must also allow for the possibility of mistakes. You must be able to do it wrong, fail painlessly, and try again. When mistakes occur, all sorts of things can happen. An actor playing the role of the boss can criticize you for doing something wrong. An associate can come into the room and inform you that the employee you just fired has filed a discrimination lawsuit against the company. You might lose a major customer because you neglected to meet their delivery deadline.

Scenarios like these pack a punch. When learners goof up, it doesn't feel like it was just a computer exercise. It feels real. When failure occurs, the simulation is often designed to give users a number of options on how to proceed. A menu of choices appears, and users can opt for hearing an expert tell a story related to their failure. Learners may want to try the scenario over again. They may determine it would be helpful to do some research. Users may choose to call upon a coach to give them some advice. E-learning technology makes it possible to have these choices and to access everything from text to animation to video clips. It also makes it possible for the people in the scenario to react to users' statements and decisions in a realistic manner. If users are rude to a customer, for instance, the customer will respond with the verbal abuse the learners deserve for being bozos. Sophisticated systems also make it possible for trainees to navigate through a scenario in different ways. One learner may move through it more slowly than another. One person may prefer to ask the coach a lot of questions, whereas another may just want to keep going through the scenario until he or she gets it right. A good simulation can accommodate a variety of personality types and preferences.

Verisimilitude is created in many ways. Perhaps one of the most surprising ways—at least surprising to people schooled in right and wrong answers—is the ambiguity that must be built into a good simulation. In a program we did for the Environmental Protection Agency, for instance, the user receives a call from someone who complains that the ground is polluted in his area. An expert pops up on the screen and advises the user that if he or she doesn't feel the call is serious or significant—and if he or she is very busy—the user should move on to other things. Another expert, however, advises that the user treat callers like friends and attempt to work with them.

In other words, the program communicates there's not always one right answer. It invites trainees to learn to use their judgment rather than rely on someone else's—especially when the someone else isn't as close to the situation as they are. Organizations today are facing increasingly complex situations where there are many possible answers. Traditional training that insists on right and wrong answers disempowers the individual—it robs people of their decision-making ability.

That's not to say that simulations should always create ambiguous situations, since there are times when right and wrong options clearly exist. In a program we created for a British water utility, the simulation taught that it was wrong to frighten customers about possible pollution in their drinking water. We communicate this information only after the trainee actually does something like this. Then a story tells about a time when a customer service person actually panicked a customer, who then called the police and the health department and made things quite difficult for the company.

Sometimes simulations, like real life, need to throw some curves. In the EPA program designed to teach people to run public meetings, we have a priest appear on the screen and complain about sanitation in a poor neighborhood. Since the trainee is expecting a discussion of other issues, he or she has to learn to refocus the meeting on a very serious problem that is not actually an EPA problem. Dealing with the unexpected is a critical skill in a rapidly changing world, and it's a skill most training programs ignore.

Helping People Learn to Do Just About Anything

Simulations are effective in helping people learn to deal with change, take risks, value diversity, and many other amorphous skills. But the simulations are only effective if you're clever about constructing them.

For example, let's say you want people to learn to be less resistant to change. If designers create a program that telegraphs the punch—that sets up a situation in which it's obvious users are supposed to be scared by change—people will respond as requested and not learn anything. Trainees easily fall into "student-mode," parroting behavior that they know is wanted by the teacher. If, however, the designer builds a situation that causes learners to act naturally—to resist change reflexively—then the designer has produced the ideal simulation for learning. When people resist change unconsciously, the program points their resistance out to them, catching them off guard.

"Put your training on the Web" may be a mandate handed down by a chief financial officer (CFO) for cost reasons; but it is also a mandate for improved quality in training because it offers the possibility of *doing* over *telling*. These simulations can be a lot of fun and that means that people will want to use them. This matters a great deal. When you want to be in school, you learn more than if you wish you were somewhere else.

E-learning won't work if your people lack motivation. The simulation must help them achieve a goal they want to achieve. This is why I insist that simulations use *goal-based scenarios*. Think about this concept in terms of how children learn. Kids want to learn to ride bikes, and that motivates them to practice and fail until they achieve that goal. But do they want to learn the names of cities throughout the world? Probably not. But designers can create a computer simulation where the goal is to win a game by traveling to various cities for some purpose, and suddenly users learn because they need to do so in order to achieve a goal that they want to achieve (like see a movie that was filmed there.)

We created a simulation for a company that was designed to help the company deal with a certain type of customer. Although the simulation was for recent hires, a number of veteran employees asked to participate in the simulation. Why? Because they were eager to learn something that would help them perform their jobs better. There were cases in the simulation that they had never encountered, and they were worried about the right way to handle them.

No doubt there are some employees who don't care about how they perform—some are lazy, cynical, and just putting in time—and who lack the motivation to learn. But the majority of employees want to do well and hate the feeling of incompetence. Few things are more frustrating than not being able to do a job effectively because you lack skills and knowledge you know you should have.

Who Are the Best Candidates for e-Learning?

Everyone. There should even be chief executive officer (CEO) training courses, though the common view of CEOs as godlike figures makes it difficult for them to admit that they could learn a thing or two. In fact, it's always struck me as ironic that companies won't let low-level people learn on the job and insist they be trained, but are content to let high-level people learn while they work without the benefit of training.

As painful as it might be to admit, no one knows automatically how to do his or her job. It's difficult for corporate managers to acknowledge that their organizations are constantly hiring people for jobs they don't know how to do. How could they? Although people arrive on the job with certain skills—public relations, legal, MIS, and other types of expertise—they lack understanding of the job's unique aspects.

I once hired a chief operations officer for my company, a former president of a software firm. Although his experience indicated he was a good candidate for the job, he was far from an expert at this particular position. He didn't know much about my company's historical dealings with clients; he didn't understand my attitudes about different policies and procedures; and he couldn't have known about how to get the most out of the people who would be working for him. As terrific as his generic management skills were, he had a lot of specifics to learn. High-level executives need training, too. They too need to learn from experts and learn from failure.

Can we build e-learning systems for such people? The cost savings are less because the number of employees who will use the system is much lower. But this is where the corporate memory is. This is where the big decisions are made and millions are earned or lost. While it is unlikely that any particular company will produce its own e-learning system for its CEO, such systems are being produced. More and more companies will buy these products off the shelf as the big-name business schools build them.

Little by little e-learning systems will be "productized." Eventually, there will be large libraries of courses produced by prestigious universities, and the very best companies will train executives on various noncompany-specific issues in business. E-learning within an organization will then more likely focus on more company-specific issues.

e-Learning by Doing at IBM, A.G. Edwards, Enron, and Wal-Mart

Let's put all our training on the Web!

This stunning idea seems to be on the minds of many CEOs these days. Web-delivered e-learning is sexy right now. Organizations are scrambling to get their training up on the Net. Is this a brilliant financial strategy, an ingenious educational move, or yet another sign that CEO's don't know or care much about training?

The Web as Library

The Web is a wonderful information-delivery mechanism. It has lots of information (more and more—in fact, an overdose of information) and can get it to you fast. Web-based training *sounds* nice enough, but it's just that much more "stuff" posted on the Web unless there is some real value to it being there.

If a CEO said, "Let's put all our training in the library!" this wouldn't be considered such a genius move. But the Web is a kind of library, a storehouse of information where you go to get something to read and sometimes something to do. It is in some ways a brilliantly organized library: Type in some key words, and suddenly there appears some very relevant stuff. Or it can be quite the mess: You type in what you want and get everything but what you seek. Oh, what we might give for a good librarian who could just field your question and know where to send you.

To Web or Not to Web

The Web is about instantaneous access, while any course requires hours or days (not minutes) to complete. Why, then, is there such a push to put training on the Web? There are only three possible answers to this question:

1. **The people who are pushing for training on the Web haven't a clue about training or about the Web.** The enthusiasm for Web-delivered training carries with it certain dangers. In the bountiful crop lies the seeds of educational famine. In their haste to get in on the action, too many organizations are simply converting their existing training manuals to Hyper Text Markup Language (HTML) and slapping them up on the Web. And what's the point of cheap and easy access to bad learning?
2. **There is something you can do on the Web that you can't do without it that makes the Web very important in training.** What exactly is so wonderful about the Web? It's convenient. Unlike CD-ROM–based software, Web systems are easy to update and maintain. You can make all your changes in one place and implement them simultaneously for everyone accessing the site. Web technology allows educators to seamlessly integrate new developments and current events, making the learning experience more dynamic and relevant. Such "updatability" sidesteps the infamous version-control problems present in much of the software out there today. And organizations love the fact that they can house different segments of training together (adding more modules as they are built) at one Web portal. Last but certainly not least, there's the potential for community interaction and collaborative learning that the communication capabilities of the Web will take to a whole new level.

But let's not get ahead of ourselves here. Since the Web is a young medium, Web-delivered training has a host of issues associated with the relative immaturity of its technology. There are always bandwidth considerations, and developing a system for multiple platforms can be a big headache. Except on local networks, video isn't a viable option on Web-delivered systems right now. This can be a problem because in certain situations it's paramount that the user sees the action unfolding before him or her in order to make the learning experience realistic and useful. Basically, because there's more machinery, there's more variables involved.

3. **Money.** This is the real answer. People within organizations who have pushed to have training available on the Web are usually interested in saving on the costs of airfares, hotels, and classrooms for their employees. This is, of course, a fine idea; but it's a reason to do e-learning in general, not to insist that all e-learning be on the Web. The Web is a delivery vehicle for e-learning, but so is a CD-ROM. It's certainly faster and cheaper to post a training site and give out the Uniform Resource Locator (URL) and password than to burn, that is, copy thousands of compact discs (CDs) and ship them all across the world. But is the cost of overnight delivery so expensive as to cause us to sacrifice the emotional impact of in-your-face video and seemingly real characters and situations with which to interact? As long as students can receive and access the course the day after they enroll, it makes sense to build the best possible course you can and not let the delivery mechanism impact its quality.

It is also less expensive to build Web courses than it is to create full-scale video-based simulations. They are not better educationally (with the exception of well-built Web-mentored classes, which I will discuss in Chapter 12), but they are cheaper. Cheaper is of course good. The question is: Is the trade-off worth it?

So education on the Web is currently a bit of a mixed bag. Will organizations that are putting their training manuals on the Web and calling them "e-learning" eventually switch to e-learning solutions that are all about learning by doing? Our experience says they will. To see the power of learning-by-doing simulations in an e-learning environment, let's look at some programs I have built. Since good teaching requires well-told stories, I will now tell some of my e-learning stories.

e-Learning at IBM

In 1997, IBM CEO Lou Gerstner commissioned research to find out which qualities separate the best executives from the rest. A year later he initiated a similar study for managers. In both cases, the ability to effectively coach employees turned up right at the top of the list as an essential skill for good management. Because IBM is highly dedicated to training and executive development, the organization immediately began looking for ways to improve its managers' coaching skills. After all, IBM wanted its managers to be the best, not the rest.

IBM bought into a coaching methodology created by former race car driver Sir John Whitmore, as laid out in his book, *Coaching for Performance*. Whitmore's model consists of four stages (GROW.), including (1) setting *G*oals, (2) doing a *R*eality check, (3) identifying *O*ptions and alternative strategies, and (4) determining *W*hat needs to be done, when, and by whom. For a while, IBM delivered this information to managers through training workshops. But eventually the organization came to believe that this wouldn't be enough. Coaching isn't something you can learn entirely from a book, no matter how good the book is. You need practical experience.

IBM's e-learning consultant was familiar with my learning theories from his grad school days and was happy to discover that I had founded Cognitive Arts (CA). Thinking that a Web-based system to supplement the classroom coaching training would be a good first project for their online training effort, he recommended that IBM consider working with us. Of course, this was our first Web project as well. We may have been flying blind, but we were flying blind together.

The project was also IBM's first major attempt at international training. In writing scripts for an international audience, the content team had to avoid any confusing Americanisms and colloquial language but still make the interactions original and interesting. Another concern was that bandwidth in remote international locations is sometimes limited. There were people halfway across the world who would be accessing the system from their eight-year-old Think Pads. So both video and audio were out of the question.

Playing to Two Audiences

IBM felt that completing simulations based on the GROW model would be valuable pre-work to get trainees up to speed on coaching before their classroom training. That way they could have shared (simulated) experiences and a solid point of reference when they got to the classroom. And we were more than happy to be able to work with a proven, concrete model like Whitmore's. Well-articulated models make the designers' and content developers' jobs easier because what the trainees need to learn is crystal clear; good models also reduce the team's reliance on the client for general content. What we had to decide was whether to incorporate the entire coaching arc into each scenario or to focus each scenario on one particular segment of the model. Eventually we chose the latter, because interactions in real life generally don't follow the model perfectly and making it realistic (and therefore useful in real life) was, as usual, of the essence. So we had to get some real-life situations from the client, then find ways to make trainees apply the model's concepts in those situations.

We conducted interviews across several continents to get stories, quotes, perspectives, and experiences that we then used to help shape the simulations. One challenge we discovered in talking to managers was that most of them think they coach just fine and don't need to be trained on it. To combat this attitude, we purposely designed the scenarios so that the user's choices don't always garner glowing, "all is right with the world" responses. This helps convince them that maybe their coaching skills aren't quite as impeccable as they thought they were.

The program was aimed at both management (the top 28,000 at IBM) and executives (the top 3,000), with a set of four scenarios for each group. Managers can go through the senior executive scenarios if they want to, and if they want to get ahead they probably will—the opportunity to play at being an executive is too tempting to pass up. Executives, on the other hand, probably won't go through the managers' scenarios; but they are much more likely to use a system that says it's for executives and caters to the situations they face. In actuality, the only real differences between the senior executive and manager scenarios lie in the details of the story lines. The decisions executives face are higher level, while the situations managers deal with are more hands on. Still, each scenario pits its users in common coaching scenarios allowing them to hone their skills.

I'll Be in This Weekend

In one of the manager scenarios, "I'll Be in This Weekend," Lisa, a new manager, is struggling with time management and meeting expectations. Her project team is frustrated by her inability to delegate and her tendency to micromanage. She risks burnout if she continues at this pace. Lisa dashes into the user's office and says:

"Sorry I can't make our meeting today—I need to leave early. My sister's in the hospital, and I've got to see her. But I'll be in this weekend. I left my notes with Anne, and she'll bring them to the meeting. If there's anything else you need, please page me. I may be in a little late tomorrow morning as well. But, as I said, I'm coming in again this weekend, as usual! Don't worry, everything will get done. It's under control."

In the first tasks of the scenario, the user must convince Lisa that she's working too hard and set up a meeting to discuss the situation. At the meeting, if the user notes that she seems to be under stress and asks how things are going on the new job, Lisa responds matter-of-factly (see Figure 3-1):

You caught me at a bad moment! Actually, I love the job, and I feel it's going well. I am a bit overextended now, but things are under control. The team's not working effectively yet, but things are getting done.

To help decide what to do next, the user can click on "Tips," which says to "Help Lisa examine the problems that she and the project team are experiencing" and provides two links to sections of the coaching model. The user can also access "Pros and Cons," which highlights the potential up and down sides to each approach.

Generally, the key to coaching is to ask open-ended questions you don't know the answers to (as opposed to asking questions for the sake of asking questions). The content team had to structure the choices so that the user couldn't just fly through the system by choosing an open-ended question choice each time. Coaching is a

Figure 3-1

lot more complicated than that, and it's important to drill this fact home to trainees. A user who knows to ask open-ended questions and wants to be helpful in light of her sister's health problems might want to "Ask Lisa if she is concerned about balancing her work and personal priorities." If the user chooses this, Lisa becomes upset (see Figure 3-2):

> **Not any more than the average manager! I mean, my sister being in the hospital is really a one-time thing. Aside from that, is there some reason you feel I'm not handling my job and personal life effectively?**

The user can learn from his or her mistake in any of several ways. The tutoring, of course, had to be very good, considering it

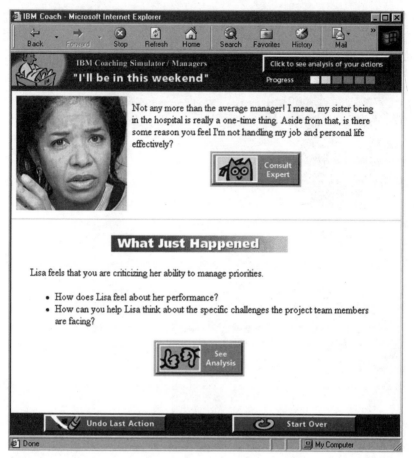

Figure 3-2

coaches the user on coaching. If the user is to believe the lessons the system is trying to impart, the tutoring must stick with Whitmore's model. One way that we chose to reflect Whitmore's ideas in the tutoring was to have it ask questions of the user. For instance, the "What Just Happened" tutoring summarizes Lisa's reaction and offers self-reflective questions the user can ponder as he or she tries again. The user can also click "See Analysis" to read a summary of the consequences of all the actions he or she has taken so far in the scenario or "Consult Expert" to read a story from an IBM coaching expert.

The IBM Coach simulations feature extensive branching, offering several different paths through the system that may eventually lead to the same result. For instance, three of the choices shown in the above screen shot move the user forward in the scenario, each to a different interaction. This approach accommodates the fact that, in coaching, there is sometimes more than one thing you can do or say that will work. It also allows the user to recover from nonfatal mistakes. Meetings don't stop when you say one slightly wrong thing—you have to recover from your mistake and get the interaction back on track.

Learning About Technology Barriers the Hard Way

Because this was our first Web project, we smacked face-first into several technology-related hurdles. In hindsight, the program was probably too advanced for the Web at that time. On Netscape, for instance, the system crashed constantly during testing; to get around the problem, we had to reprogram the entire thing and redesign the interface. The lesson here is that if a system works well on one browser, that doesn't mean it will work well on another. But, because we practice what we preach, we learned from our mistakes and found ways to climb over all the hurdles.

And it's a good, thing, too, because it allowed IBM Coach to be an immediate success. There were over one hundred thousand hits within the first three months. More people went back to complete the scenarios than to look at the Whitmore presentations. Two hundred to three hundred people were finishing the scenarios each week.

The more-human evidence was also positive. The head of HR at IBM stood up in a meeting, pointed to the program we built, and called it the future of training at IBM. One manager called the system the best training he'd ever had. IBM liked the system so much that it has re-purposed the design and solicited us to build several similar systems.

Lessons Learned

- E-learning can function well as pretraining to be undertaken before learners attend classroom training. That way learners have a shared point of reference in their simulated experience from which interesting and useful discussions can spring.
- With e-learning on the Web, the systems you build must be adaptable to the lowest tech specs a user might require. It's

quite helpful to know what these specs will be before building the system.

- Solid learning models (like Whitmore's GROW) make the work of creating quality simulations much easier.
- The main difference between training for managers and training for executives lies in the presentation and context of the simulated story's details. The management and leadership principles themselves don't change.

e-Learning at A.G. Edwards

In the fast-paced world of financial consulting, firms are constantly competing for high-performing brokers. As an incentive to lure new talent to work for them, many firms are beginning to offer online training that allows brokers to learn on the fly, in little pieces, without having to spend much time away from their clients and work. As a fairly conservative organization, A.G. Edwards was a bit skeptical of the e-learning revolution. But, wanting to stay competitive, it decided it had to get in on the action, too. Web-based training was attractive because of its "updatability"—it would be easy to drop in new content as tax laws and other investment information changes. Having worked with us on a CD-ROM project called *Client One*, A.G. Edwards asked us for advice on designing a Web portal for its training.

Most of A.G. Edwards' existing training was based around different levels of classroom seminars that form a corporate university, complete with 100-, 200-, and 300-level classes. The idea in coming to Cognitive Arts (CA) was that, instead of long and tedious seminars for each of these phases, the 100- and 200-level courses could eventually be replaced by online learning, to be topped off with more advanced seminars. As I've noted elsewhere, seminars are much more useful when trainees have gained experience by going through simulations beforehand. A.G. Edwards just needed to figure out where to start.

Solving the Mysteries of Financial Products

It became clear to us early on that there's a great deal of mystique surrounding some of the products A.G. Edwards offers. Financial consultants (FCs) tend to view these products as much more complicated than they really are. They're scared of the details and as a result sometimes tend to avoid selling these products.

The existing product training, previously delivered in the seven-week new hire curriculum, obviously wasn't producing the results A.G. Edwards wanted. Trainees simply weren't gaining the product knowledge they needed to do well in the selling portion of the curriculum. Case in point: During sales training, facilitators complained that they had to slow the class down to review product issues. So, in addition to being below snuff on its own, the product training was creating a domino effect by undermining subsequent portions of the new-hire curriculum. A.G. Edwards wanted its new FCs to arrive at sales training with a good command of investment options to recommend and discuss with clients. That means FCs had to be able to evaluate product options in terms of investors' needs by analyzing the associated risks and benefits of each option.

We saw this area as an important, relatively quick hit that could immediately help boost sales and suggested creating a training system on product knowledge as a pilot class. A.G. Edwards could add courses around more complex financial planning issues later.

We interviewed FCs and learned that, in financial consulting, there aren't necessarily right and wrong answers. The financial world is more complicated than that. If you open an individual retirement account (IRA), you're doing the right thing by saving for retirement. Whether you get a traditional or a Roth IRA is important; but choosing one over the other is not a mistake. The important thing here isn't to pick what's "right" over what's "wrong," but to take the best *approach*. This involves asking the right questions in order to uncover the client's needs, then mapping those needs to a potential product or recommendation.

So we set out to build a system that would teach FCs to analyze and act upon opportunities to recommend products and services based on client need. A.G. Edwards wanted to create ten scenarios around four product areas:

- Private Money Management Fundamentals
- Estate Planning and Trust Services Fundamentals
- IRA Retirement and Plan Distribution Fundamentals
- Client Choice and Account Choices

In each of these product arenas, the idea was to make trainees gather, then demonstrate product knowledge in a real-world environment. That way, the lessons stick much better than they would if the product information were presented in a vacuum. After all, these products are not *used* in a vacuum, but rather in the real world to help real people with real issues. In order to prepare learners for a wide variety of situations, the team created several fictional clients with varied situations and investment needs.

In each A.G. Edwards product training scenario, the user:

1. Reviews the clients' financial information
2. Asks questions to uncover the clients' short- and long-term goals
3. Researches and evaluates different alternatives
4. Answers the clients' questions about recommended strategies

The user can look at as much or as little documentation, and ask as many or as few questions, as he or she wants before making a final decision and justifying that decision.

Estate Planning for Clients Who Don't Think They Need It

In order to get a better feel for these simulations, let's look more closely at one of the scenarios in the Estate Planning and Trust Services Fundamentals section. In "Estate Planning for Clients Who Don't Think They Need It," the user must review and recommend estate planning solutions for June and Eugene Jonco, who aren't sure they really need to do any estate planning. They do, however, want to safeguard their irresponsible son's inheritance and make sure their wishes are carried out after they die.

First, the user has the chance to delve into some general issues to consider about estate planning. Then, he or she can review the client's financial information, including the net worth statement and key points. After looking at the numbers, the user can ask any of several questions of the Joncos to learn more about their situation, wishes, and plans (see Figure 3-3).

When the user is satisfied that he or she has learned enough about the Joncos' financial situation, the user reviews the client needs and selects the most important indications that they need estate planning. The system provides tutoring on incorrect

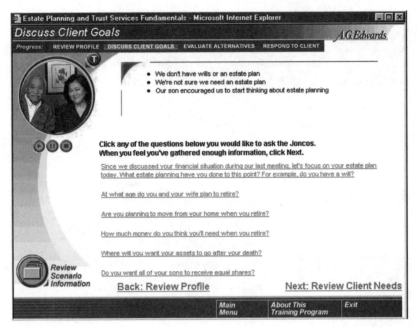

Figure 3-3

choices. Then, the user has the opportunity to explore possible estate planning strategies—including estate planning basics, expert stories, and vocabulary. All of these activities are done at the user's leisure—he or she can complete as little or as much research as necessary. Of course, inadequate research will most likely come back to haunt the user when he or she has to recommend appropriate strategies to the client. In that phase, the user sees four potential estate planning product recommendations and must decide whether or not to recommend each. Perhaps more importantly, the user has to provide reasoning for the decision (see Figure 3-4).

After the user submits all the decisions and their justifications, "What Happened Here?" tutoring pops up to tell the user what went wrong, then gives the user a chance to try again.

Before meeting again with the client, the user can review a graphic of the plan that has been decided on. Now, A.G. Edwards didn't want to teach how to couch these solutions to the client conversationally; in other words, strategic analysis is favored over what to say. So the questions that the Joncos come to the user with are all about estate planning products themselves. The

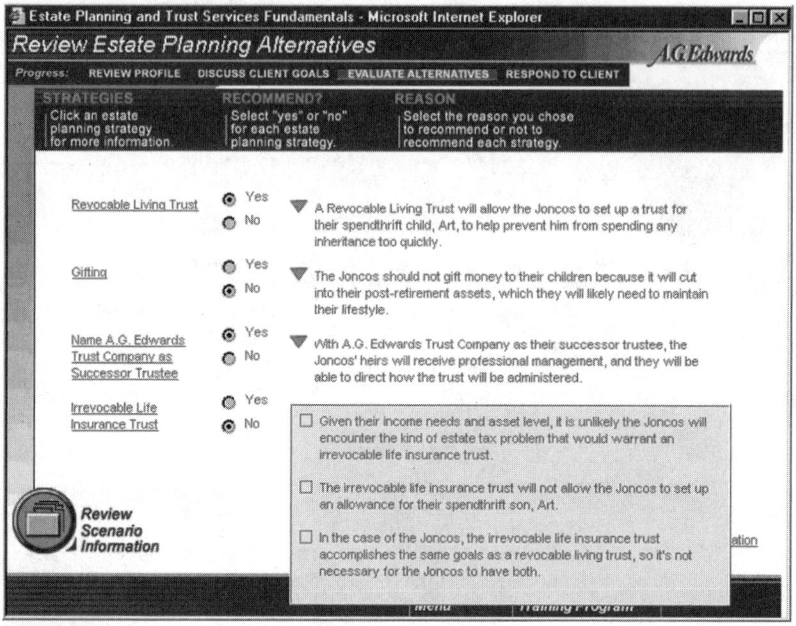

Figure 3-4

important thing is not how the user expresses the information, but rather that it's correct and useful for the Joncos, considering their needs and wishes. Mistake tutoring informs the user what went wrong (see Figure 3-5).

As the user finishes the simulation, a wrap-up screen provides tips for moving forward and summarizes what the next steps might be.

The original plan had been to use a similar design for each product area; but it turned out that the content for each area was different and had to be presented differently. Plus, each product area, the Subject Matter Expert felt that his or her particular content was the most important and didn't want to be pigeonholed into following a template design. It was a pain, but in the end they were probably right. Since content should inform design and not the other way around, we had to tweak the design a little for each course. Still, the basic design for each product section is similar to that of the estate planning simulation detailed above.

Each section also contains its own miniperformance support system that allows users to explore issues and brush up on basics. This resource can be accessed either outside the scenarios as a ref-

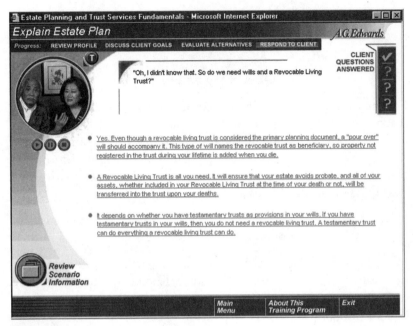

Figure 3-5

erence tool or during scenario problem solving. Used as a stand-alone tool, the trainee can search general product and service details, definitions, and informative text. Used as a reference during the simulations, the student can ask questions on topics relevant to the choices they're making as a form of proactive tutoring.

Lessons Learned

This is GREAT advice!!!

- The easy updatability of Web-based training is key for organizations whose content is constantly shifting.
- For first time e-learning ventures, start with a problem that—if you fix it—will have an immediate, recognizable impact on the bottom line.
- In order to keep learners' interest, and for the lessons learned to be useful, it's very important to connect difficult content to the human, real-world context in which learners will use it.
- When providing resources, allow users to do as much or as little research as they want; then make the subsequent tasks

much more difficult for those who haven't done their home-work.

e-Learning at Enron

Originally a natural gas pipeline company, Enron has expanded its reach substantially over the last ten years and now has its hands in multiple cookie jars, including energy and power, capital and risk management, the Internet, and broadband. A highly innovative company, Enron has grown into a huge organization with business units all around the world.

Communication Breakdown

With so much going on across so many departments, communication at Enron is as vital as it is difficult. Enron conducted a survey on communication and was concerned about the results. In particular, ratings were low in five areas:

- 59 percent of employees said decisions were not communicated well.
- 54 percent said they did not feel free to voice their opinions openly.
- 55 percent said the company didn't act effectively on employee suggestions.
- 70 percent said communication was not good across departmental lines.
- 61 percent said they were not encouraged to challenge established procedures and policies.

These results were particularly galling to Enron because it considers itself to be an organization of great communicators. Executives knew that, if its people couldn't communicate, they couldn't share ideas, and the organization would cease to be innovative.

So Enron embarked upon its first e-learning journey, asking us to build an interactive Web-based program to improve the communication skills of its employees at all management levels. The program had not only to give managers practical experience in communication, but also to show them how strong communication skills could help them achieve their business goals.

Enron wanted it on the Web because it wanted to stay innovative, and a great deal of innovations in e-learning these days are on the Web. Also, Enron's managers don't have an abundance of time or patience. The hassle of having to get their hands on a CD-ROM and install it was too much; they wanted to be able to just click on a link and play around in the system for 20 to 30 minutes at a time, whenever it was convenient for them. Plus, the training would be global, so it would be much easier to deliver on the Internet then by burning and shipping 5000 CDs all across the world.

Enron wanted streaming video in the system in order to better portray characters' communication breakdowns. But how could we both deliver on the Web and include high-quality video? Well, everyone at Enron has access to a T1 line or better, and Enron Broadband Services was willing to host the media. There was good bandwidth, with streaming from Houston, London, and Hong Kong. Employees at more remote sites could either use the text-only version or request a CD-ROM. So it made sense both economically and educationally to deliver the training via the Web.

Enron wanted us to fashion the simulations out of the five trouble spots in the survey. Of course, in the real-life situations that Enron employees face, these types of problems don't naturally or neatly occur independent of one another. We interviewed 132 Enron employees, including both executives and managers, to make their survey responses come alive through real-life experiences and stories about communication breakdowns within the organization. From this information we developed scenario overviews—rough sketches of simulated interactions. We showed the overviews to focus groups at Enron and asked them to identify where and what specific instances of communication breakdowns were actually happening on the job. And from there we wrote the scenarios.

We went through all this effort to get the details right in order to make the system believable so that the managers would buy into it. Enron's culture is not touchy-feely—it's all about business. Therefore, it was very important to structure the simulations in a way that presented to the user the consequences of how communication (or lack thereof) affects the bottom line. For instance, managers won't do the scenario on giving feedback because they're particularly interested in developing their employees. They'll do it because it hits them right from the start that if their employees aren't performing up to par, it could have negative consequences on their own jobs.

Simulations for Those Who Need It, When They Need It

In each scenario in Enron On-Line Communication, the user plays a different role within the company. Enron didn't want to make all its managers complete all the scenarios. Rather, each manager has a couple areas where he or she has encountered similar, upsetting situations or where he or she wants to improve communication. Often this depends on the manager's role within the organization. A manager, then, can just go through the scenarios that interest or impact him or her. It was also important to let the users do what they want, when they want because Enron doesn't set aside any specific training time to complete these simulations—managers just try to fit them in when they have time. Because of these time constraints, we had to resist the temptation to connect all the scenarios under one overarching story—independent scenarios are easier to get through and provide more value when training needs to be delivered in short spurts.

In each scenario, the user is presented with an overview of the situation, then has the opportunity to do some background research by pouring over scenario-specific resources. These resources include things like an employee's last performance review or notes about an idea an employee has come up with. Since the resources are available on an on-demand basis, the user doesn't have to do any research before jumping in and making decisions if he or she doesn't want to. Much like in A.G. Edwards Product Training, the scenarios are much harder for people who haven't prepared themselves properly. The resources are available throughout the scenario for those who want to consult them in the midst of the decision-making process. Throughout the scenario, the user can click on "What should I consider" to get a rundown of the situation, what needs to be done, and tips on how to proceed.

In interviews we found two common types of mistakes Enron's managers make in their communication: People (1) don't use the right medium for communication (e.g., too many e-mails), and (2) don't always effectively get across what they're trying to say when they do talk face-to-face with employees. To reflect this, each scenario in On-Line Communication features two different kinds of decisions. The first involves making a strategic choice about what medium to communicate in (e.g., phone, email, or in person). The user is asked to defend his or her reasons for picking that course of action and receives tutoring on both incorrect choices and faulty justifications. The second type of decision consists of actual interactions with fictional peers, with the focus on how the user communicates strategic decisions (e.g., what to say). If the user doesn't make the correct choice, he or she gets advice and tutoring, complete with links to a small performance support system full of tips, expert stories, and resources for effective communication. The user can also reach these resources independently from outside the simulations.

Meeting of the Minds

The order of these interactions changes depending on what the content of the scenario calls for. In "A Matter of Meetings," for instance, the user plays the role of a new lead on a project requiring collaboration from several different departments. The user's goal is to get the project team back on track by addressing its communication problems. The scenario begins when Asha Goyal, a team member, complains to the user about how the old project leader ran meetings. She gives an example of a failed and unfocused meeting:

". . . And you know, he hadn't told her anything! Rachel barely knew about the project. Rick had to do the cost breakdown and risk analysis, and he needed Joe's input on feasibility to do it. Not to mention the people in the meeting—they get off track, nobody gives any feedback . . . it's so frustrating!"

Before acting on the situation, the user can explore background information by reading an email from the previous project leader or by asking questions, each with video responses, from two current team members (see Figure 3-6).

When the user has done enough research, he or she can prepare for the meeting by sending out an email, deciding (1) whom to invite to the meeting, (2) what to focus the meeting on, (3) the goals of the meeting, and (4) action items. For each, the user must select the response(s) he or she feels are most appropriate; the system provides brief tutoring for incorrect or omitted choices.

After the user sends the e-mail, the simulation jumps ahead to the meeting. Here the user must do and say the right things to

Figure 3-6

move the meeting forward and effectively address the team's communication problems. When the user mouses over a strategy choice, "What this might sound like" text appears in a box onscreen, as shown in Figure 3-7, giving the user an idea of how each potential choice could be articulated.

Each choice leads to a video response from the team members at the meeting. If the user chooses to "Discuss past communication problems with participants" at the outset of the meeting, for example, an argument breaks out among the team members:

> MARION: "There are FAR too many e-mails. I'm getting them too late, and the deadlines are always concurrent with my department's. . . ."

> ASHA: "If people would attend, and take care of their own responsibilities, this project would be going more efficiently. . . ."

> MARION: "Hey, come on! We're trying to get past this—why do you have to keep bringing up old issues?"

> RICK: "I get my stuff done—don't blame me for that!"

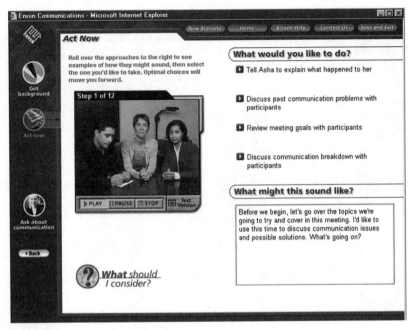

Figure 3-7

For incorrect responses, "What went wrong?" tutoring details the action the user chose, why the team reacted the way it did, and what a better approach might be. After the user gets through the meeting, he or she must then decide what strategic actions to take regarding team members who missed the meeting. For each step, the user must choose an action and justify it (see Figure 3-8).

When the user successfully completes the scenario, he or she goes to a reflection page that details where the user made mistakes in several key skill areas, including preparing for the meeting, focusing on meeting objectives, soliciting feedback, and following up on decisions.

Enron On-Line Communication was delivered in early 2001, and, at the time of this writing, the user-testing feedback has been very positive.

Lessons Learned

- Even if you have concrete information (e.g., survey results) as the basis for an e-learning project, you still need to talk to as many real people as possible to hear the stories, frustra-

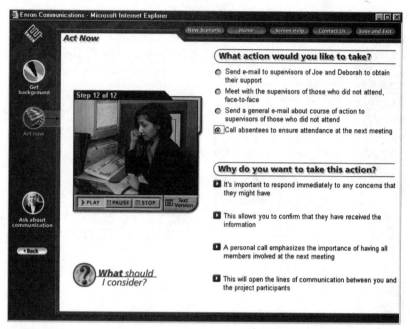

Figure 3-8

tions, and firsthand experiences from which you will create the simulations.

- Simulations should be built and presented with the organization's individual culture and working atmosphere in mind so that learners will use and learn from it.
- The types of decisions you give users should reflect the types of decisions they make and struggle with in real life.

e-Learning at Wal-Mart

There are three types of hourly supervisors at Wal-Mart. Department managers head up specific departments within the store such as Sporting Goods; customer service managers oversee the cash registers, the customer service desk, and layaway; and personnel managers look after a variety of human resources, payroll, hiring, and training tasks. They are all called hourly supervisors because they get paid by the hour; hence they are managers, but not really management.

Nevertheless, Wal-Mart wanted its hourly supervisors to think and act more like management. Supervisors often get so caught up in their own work that they don't think about how what they do affects other departments and the company as a whole. For example, if another department is short-staffed because two people call in sick, they are sometimes reluctant to lend one of their associates because they're too worried about their own department's sales numbers. Wal-Mart wanted its hourly supervisors to think strategically, better balancing the big picture—what's best for the entire store, for the entire company—with the operational, immediate concerns of the everyday job.

To bring about this change, Wal-Mart knew it would have to train supervisors to improve their communication skills—including mentoring, providing constructive and positive feedback, and listening skills. Wal-Mart also needed its supervisors to work smarter— that is, prioritize tasks, balance the needs of employees with the needs of the store, delegate when appropriate, collaborate with other departments on resource allocation, and react to change. Finally, the organization wanted its supervisors to feel empowered to make decisions to improve store performance, including customer service, merchandising, and associate advocacy.

In order to be effective, Wal-Mart knew it would have to present these new leadership skills in an understandable manner and within the context of current work practices. Consistency was important—the activities hourly supervisors did, as well as actions considered to be "best practices," varied from store to store. Training would also have to help standardize performance expectations across the company.

The existing supervisor training consists mostly of PowerPoint presentations and manuals slapped online—the only shadow of interactivity being to click the "next" button. This may ease the burden on the user's page-turning muscles, but it doesn't do much else. There are also online assessments that are basically multiple-choice tests meant to gauge employees' skill levels. The other problem with this training is that it was way too comprehensive. The content that trainees were supposed to sponge up included everything a supervisor could ever possibly do. And whenever you throw so much raw information at trainees, they are bound to forget all of it almost immediately, pretty much canceling out the entire training effort. Wal-Mart wanted to create new training for the Web, and knew there had to be a better way.

The Best Advice . . .

We visited thirteen stores and talked to sixty-six employees—from cashiers to store managers—about if and how leadership skills are used on the job. This helped the team learn how leadership skills are acquired and built in the Wal-Mart world, which in turn allowed us to design a system to fit the supervisors' needs and goals. For instance, we learned that the system had to be immediately practical and true to life, as well as easy to navigate and understand. We encountered the usual challenges in designing the training system: Training time is limited, it's hard to get supervisors to think strategically, and the audience has varying leadership experience and skills. But, most importantly, the training solution had to somehow be relevant to different supervisor roles that consist of different day-to-day activities.

In order to deal with this last challenge, we invented a unique design. Disparate learners going through some training scenarios might complain, "That would never happen to me." This is particularly a concern when, as in Wal-Mart's case, the daily work experiences of the target audience vary greatly. We solved this problem by designing third-person scenarios in which the user watches a common in-store situation unfold, then dispenses advice to one of the characters in that situation.

Learning to Lead, as the Wal-Mart hourly supervisor training system is called, is made up of three suites of four practice scenarios (for a total of twelve scenarios), each scenario focusing on a different leadership skill. After watching a situation, the user chooses from among three suggested approaches to the challenges, as told by an advocate for each position. The consequences of whatever advice the user chooses to give plays out on video, as well as in tutoring for incorrect choices. This approach works because the learner is not playing the target role, and therefore cannot reasonably say "That would never happen to me," since the simulation doesn't imply that it ever would. It also takes some of the pressure off the user: Since it's not the user actually taking action, but rather a third party acting on the user's advice, the user feels a little more free to play around. It's much easier to make mistakes when they're not your own, even in a simulated environment. And, as I've said time and time again, making mistakes is exactly how you learn.

The user can also ask questions about relevant concepts to get guidance from Wal-Mart senior leaders and experienced hourly supervisors. Each practice scenario also includes at least one "error recovery" task—this allows the user to make a mistake and continue forward with a chance to fix it in the following task. Mistakes in these simulations include things like not taking the big picture into account, assessing performance problems too hastily, and failing to delegate when appropriate. The system keeps track of the user's mistakes over the course of the scenario and delivers tailored feedback at the end.

Learning to Lead also includes a mandatory assessment scenario for each suite. The only difference between assessment scenarios and practice scenarios is that the assessments provide very minimal feedback along the way (as opposed to the readily available tutoring and expert advice in the practice scenarios). The system tracks each action taken in the scenario, and at the end uses this information to provide feedback and, if necessary, suggest remediation. This information is recorded in Wal-Mart's training administrative system to establish companywide baselines, recommend other training, and uncover trainee needs.

Hook, Line, and Sinker

A closer look at one of the assessment scenarios might be illuminating. In "Hook, Line, and Sinker" (see Figure 3-9), the user advises Calvin, a department manager in Sporting Goods. Gary, an associate working in Calvin's department, used to be a great worker, but lately he doesn't seem to be motivated. As the scenario begins, the user sees a video of Gary just pointing a customer who's looking for fishing gear in the right direction instead of taking him directly to the product he wants. The customer tells Calvin, who helps him find the gear. Later, Darrell, the assistant store manager, asks Calvin about the situation:

"...He used to put a lot of effort into his work, but not lately. He acts like he's not motivated anymore."

The user then has the opportunity to listen to three advocates, (see Figure 3-10), each of whom offers different advice. For example, one advocate says:

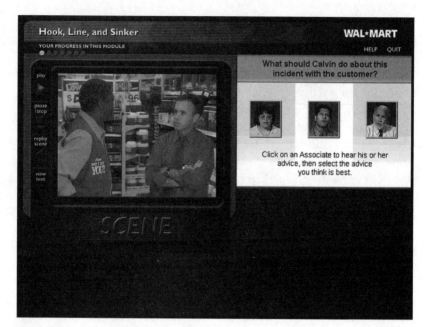

Figure 3-9

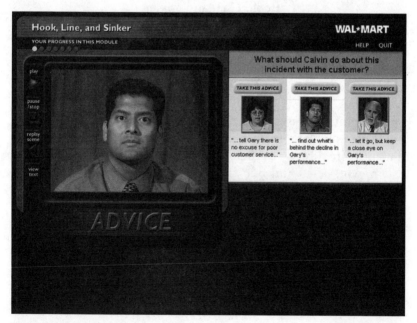

Figure 3-10

"Supervisors have to know when to get involved and when not to. Gary has been one of Calvin's best associates. His recent loss of enthusiasm is probably only temporary. Everybody goes through ups and downs. Calvin should keep a close eye on Gary's customer service and attitude. If it becomes a problem, then Calvin should intervene. But it isn't to the point yet where Calvin needs to say something."

The user must decide which piece of advice is best for Calvin. Whatever suggestion the user chooses to give Calvin plays out in another video clip, where the user learns from the consequences of this advice.

Eventually, the user learns that Gary is feeling unchallenged and wants more responsibility. Since he is an avid camper, Calvin puts Gary in charge of the camping section. He excels with the new responsibility, and even comes up with a great marketing idea. The user must advise Calvin about how to help Gary adjust to the challenges that come along with his new responsibilities. Later, the user has to help Calvin determine the best way to recognize Gary's continued success in his new role and mentor him as he seeks a promotion in a different department. When Gary gets the promotion and leaves Sporting Goods, the department is understaffed and swamped. The user must advise Calvin on whether he should leave his customers in order to do an interview. At the conclusion of the scenario, a reflective tutoring page summarizes what the user did to get there and notes opportunities for improvement based on mistakes the user made.

Learning to Lead also contains a performance support resource called Leadership Toolbox, which the user can access at the start or the end of each scenario. The Tool Box consists of fifty video clips, plus six clips of Sam Walton himself espousing the core competencies of leadership. This tool helps share best practices and adoptable solutions for common situations and offers role models who can relate practical experiences to hourly supervisors. The user can also access specifically applicable questions during individual scenarios.

Just Watch Me

Now, with a system architecture like this, high-quality video is absolutely vital. It's much more meaningful for the user to see things acted out in front of him or her than to hear or read a description of what might happen. And in this system, the user can watch the action and consequences play out more fully because he or she isn't an actual character in the simulation, but rather a third-party advisor. Therefore, the simulated conversations are rich and completely two-sided. Without video, these situations wouldn't be nearly as realistic, and the system might lose credibility among trainees.

Luckily, video was an option because the system is downloaded individually to each store's server. Streaming video runs off the store's server instead of from the home office or some other central location. It also helps that trainees complete the program in the store's training room so that there's never more than three or four people using it at any given time. This helps avoid the usual Web problems associated with too many people accessing a site at once. Plus, according to our programmers, Wal-Mart's computer systems rival NASA's. So we were free to build a very video-heavy system.

Learning to Lead is in its final stages of development at the time of this writing. So far, initial feedback from user testing has been outstanding. Users really like the realism of the system and how well we captured Wal-Mart's culture. Because the situations were very real to them, they really hit home. They especially liked watching situations unfold before them, then having a hand in the outcome of those situations. Some commented that this was entirely different from normal training—they were used to videos of gorgeous people all done up, doing the right things, with the customers smiling contentedly. Contrast that to the system we built, with real people and customers who get peeved at the drop of a hat. Users also liked screwing up because they thought it was fun to see bad things happen to other people. They were having so much fun they barely realized they were learning. And isn't that the whole point, really? *why is this true*

Lessons Learned

- If your training is too comprehensive (i.e., you try to pour too much information into it), trainees will be overloaded and won't come away with any new understanding.
- Creating third-person scenarios in which the user gives advice to someone else helps fight against the oft-heard "That would never happen to me" complaint. Learners are

also less afraid to experiment and make interesting mistakes if they're making them for someone else.

- In Web-based simulations where video is vital, make sure the organization has the technical capabilities to support it. If not, CD-ROM may be the best option.

Conclusion

Essentially, our approach to learning is the same regardless of how the product will be delivered—via Web or CD-ROM or a combination of the two. We start with a problem, then try to create the best possible and most realistic experience in which we can solve that problem. Cost, technology, and time don't enter into the equation until later. With the rate at which Web technologies are maturing, the possibilities are expanding almost as fast as we can think of ways to take advantage of them.

PART II

Instructional Design Principles for e-Learning

4

Expectation Failure: The Engine That Powers e-Learning

The *F* word (*failure*) is anathema to both teachers and CEOs. We punish students with bad grades when they offer the wrong answers on tests. We punish employees with negative performance reviews when they make mistakes. The bigger the failure, the bigger the punishment: Flunking and termination await those who fail frequently.

All of these negative consequences give failure a bad name, which is too bad because people need to fail in order to learn. Simulations offer people two possible ways of responding to failure:

- I don't know why I'm screwing up—help me.
- I know I'm screwing up, but I'll figure out what's going wrong myself.

Either response is fine. Your personality dictates which one you choose in a given instance. The point is that a good simulation is designed to give people opportunities to fail as well as opportunities to think about why they failed.

Done effectively, e-learning solutions emulate the natural learning process. Again, remember how kids learn: When they want something from mom or dad, they find extraordinary ways to fail in order to get attention. For each new learning activity, there are multiple failures. When they start dressing themselves, they put on their pants backwards. When they begin to talk, they say, "I goed to school." Small children are failure machines, failing hundreds of thousands of times before they learn the proper way to get their parents' attention, to dress, and to speak.

For adults, failure can take many forms. The first day on the job, the boss tells the employee to get to work, and the new hire's natural response is, "How?" It's a failure in the sense that we don't know how to do the job properly and have to keep asking for help so that we understand what to do next. Professors, like most people, are completely lost the first year on the job. All they know is their area of study. New professors don't know how to deal with the mind-boggling array of questions students ask, from "What should I major in?" to "Do you think this internship will help me get into graduate school?" to "What courses should I take?"

Failure can also translate into an inability to predict the outcome of behavior. A marketing analyst fails to realize that his or her lack of knowledge about an emerging market resulted in a lost opportunity for his or her company. On a larger scale, military and political leaders of the United States were unable to predict what would happen when the country became involved in Vietnam. Certainly, U.S. leaders learned from this failure, because every time Congress considers intervening militarily overseas, they're reminded of the Vietnam failure.

Expectation Failure

Failure means to mess up, to fall short of a goal, to strike out, to break down, to lose. Lots of synonyms exist, but from a learning perspective, they lack one key modifier. For learning to take place, there has to be *expectation* failure. In other words, an employee expects to make a sale but it falls through; he expects a new process to save money but it doesn't; he expects to meet a deadline but misses the target date. In one sense, expectation failure has a broad scope because it can encompass positive experiences: An investor purchased a stock thinking it might go up a few points, but she didn't expect it to skyrocket 50 points in a matter of days. This might look like success, but it's a failure in that she didn't expect it, can't explain it, and doesn't understand it.

What does all this have to do with e-learning? Consider what happens when learners' expectations are met. For instance, when they sit down at their desks, they always manage to land in their chairs. Because their expectations are met, they don't have to think about or explain sitting down. But what would happen if one day they landed on the floor, missing the chair? They would have to think about and explain this failure. These outcomes lead to two guiding principles of failure:

1. **Real thinking never starts until the learner fails.**
2. **It is easy to recognize expectation failures because people insist on explaining them.** When we start coming up with explanations for things (our favorite team's victory, election frauds, extraordinary culinary experiences), that is when an expectation has failed.

Thinking and explaining catalyze learning.[1] People who go through life repeating the same successful behavior, never trying anything new or different (at which they're bound to fail), learn precious little. Most of us don't have that problem. In a work environment, the vast majority of employees experience constant expectation failure, the only possible exceptions being those at the very bottom of the ladder. These people are often forced into routines, doing the same job the same way year in and year out. They hate their jobs. This leads to a curious point. In an odd way, expectation failure is fun—it makes life interesting.

Most people are swimming about in a sea of failure. You might think that they'd drown in our unrealized expectations. Discouraged and dismayed, they would simply give up and sink from sight (or furious and frustrated, quit or do something to get themselves fired). But most of us, in fact, work well in an environment of failure. We're able to do so because our mental life depends on expectation failure—it is the natural way our minds function.

---

[1]There has been a great deal of work done on learning in the fields of psychology, cognitive science, artificial intelligence, and related disciplines in the last thirty years that underlies much of what I describe here and in subsequent chapters. In the bibliography at the end of this book, I list some of my favorite readings in learning theory (some of which were, or course, written by me).

That Reminds Me of a Story

When people experience expectation failure, their minds create a reminding strategy. It takes that failure, gives it a name, stores it away, and retrieves it when they fail again in exactly the same way. The reminding strategy enables people to think about that old failure within the context of the new failure. This isn't done consciously; it's a natural mechanism that helps us cope with failure.

A personal experience will illustrate this process. A friend of mine requested my advice about which woman he should marry. He said that he loved one woman and she loved him, but added that he thought she might be crazy. He didn't love the second woman as much, but explained that she wasn't as crazy and he thought she'd be a good mother.

"Let me tell you a story," I responded. Something my friend said triggered a story I had labeled in my mind, a story revolving around a failure I had made in making a selection decision. A number of years ago, I had decided to hire a CEO to run my company so I could devote more time to being a professor. I interviewed someone who seemed eminently qualified for the job, and our interview went well. During the course of that interview, the candidate mentioned how he'd been going through a divorce and boasted about winning a heated custody battle that entitled him to both the kids and the house. I hired him, but a few years later we had a falling out over the fact that when he was placed in a difficult situation, he became vicious. His behavior was similar to his boastful description of his custody victory, I realized with hindsight.

To my friend who was trying to decide between the two women, I said, "Listen to what people tell you about themselves, because they mean it."

Now think about how I "found" this story to tell. The process my unconscious mind went through must have looked something like this:

1. I asked myself, "How do you predict people's behavior when they're telling you something bad about themselves?"
2. My failure to predict my former CEO's behavior became a label in my head.
3. My friend communicated that he was trying to predict the behavior of a person who he suspected might behave badly.
4. The words of my friend triggered the labeled memory in my head, and I told my story.

Now apply the point of this anecdote to learning. As people make mistakes and experience trouble, it would be nice to be reminded of all the right stories at the right times to help us deal with these problems. Sometimes, this is exactly what happens. When it occurs in a work situation, that reminding becomes expertise: Employees say to themselves, "I had that problem before; here's the solution."

But sometimes people lack the experiences to summon up stories they can learn from. To obtain those experiences and turn them into reminding stories, people need to fail on the job or in a simulation. Failure causes people to be receptive to stories. The job of an e-learning designer is to gather the best stories an organization has to tell and encourage failure in a simulation making learners eager to hear those stories.

The Results of Success

When I was a professor at Yale, an ambitious freshman approached me and asked me to tell him what courses he should take—at the time Yale didn't have any requirements. I advised him to take whatever interested him. "No," he protested, "I want to take the ones that will help me do well in my career. What courses did *you* take?" I listed the required courses that I was forced to sign up for years ago. "Okay," he said, "I'll take those, because if they made you successful, they'll make me successful."

Of course, those courses didn't make me successful. Yet the myth of success is powerful, and it seduces us into believing we need to avoid failure at all costs. In reality, people who never fail are bored out of their skulls and lack risk-taking ability and creativity. They can do one job competently in one specific way—for them, learning is a closed-ended process that doesn't allow for flexibility. Organizations may gain employees who can complete simple tasks effectively, but they lose the innovation and adaptability necessary to compete in a global marketplace. They may also lose employees who become bored with their success and leave for greater challenges elsewhere.

Learning from Exceptions

Failure-based systems prepare people to deal with situations where things don't go according to plan. When I consulted for an

Italian railway company, managers told me about a recent accident involving one of their trains. The company had just added some new cars that were larger than the norm. The computer that traced the routes for the drivers gave an "all clear" signal because it had used the old measure for the cars. The driver of a passing train got the "all clear." He relied on what he had been told by the computer. These larger cars' size caused them to stick out past the station platform, and an accident ensued. Following the railway company's procedures, the driver was watching his computer screen, which failed to alert him that an accident was about to happen. If the driver had only looked out his window, he would have seen the problem and been able to prevent it. No doubt, the driver will be alert to this problem in the future, failure being the good teacher that it is.

But what about other drivers? And what about other situations where the rules aren't applicable? The railroad company needs to build a simulation in which engineers experience exceptions to the rules, where they fail to deal effectively with problems using traditional responses. Given a chance to practice failing, engineers will learn what to do when things don't go according to plan.

When employees know only one script, they aren't particularly adaptable. If all that the training has taught them is the company-approved way to perform their jobs, they'll be completely lost when a job doesn't go according to the script. At a time when change is omnipresent in the work world, it makes sense to let workers experience a script failure during training. Out of this failure, they can learn to create a new script and adjust when things don't go exactly as planned.

To accomplish this, e-learning should systematically (though artfully) lead people toward the proverbial cliff, unaware of where they're going until they find themselves falling. Many trainers resist this path. When I tried a flight simulator and managed to crash the plane, I was told I was the first one ever to do so. If I were in charge of training pilots, I would make sure to fashion a scenario in which trainees had to navigate through severe lightning with one engine out and the others sputtering, the cabin filling with smoke, and the plane being tossed about. Better to have pilots experience this situation as a simulation for the first time than when they fly a real plane. Then if such a catastrophe happens in the air, the pilot will be reminded of the simulator experience and know what *not* to do.

It's hard for companies to grasp the notion of safe failure. Telling an organization that its training should encourage people to make horrendous mistakes can rub managers the wrong way. An analogy to learning how to drive a car can help reluctant CEOs understand. Besides the largely perfunctory driver's education courses offered by schools, teenagers learn to drive by almost killing themselves and others. New drivers fail in all sorts of interesting and truly memorable ways, and there's no question that if they survive the accidents and close calls, they become better drivers. Companies allow their new, inexperienced employees to have similarly horrific accidents on the job. If the employees aren't fired for incompetence, they probably grow to become skilled employees. Building expectation failure into an e-learning system is an alternative to this school of hard knocks.

Failing with Dignity

Most kids don't mind failing until they start school. As long as parents tolerate mistakes with good humor, children are perfectly willing to mess up time and again. All this changes when school begins and their failures become the subject of public ridicule—grades are posted for everyone to see, or a teacher chastises a student who does poorly in front of the entire class. The same thing happens in organizations when people who have made mistakes or taken risks that didn't pan out receive public tongue-lashings from the boss. This creates an environment where it's difficult to learn from failure—rather than admitting an error and seeking help, employees prefer to cover it up and avoid public humiliation.

Think about what happens when you mess up in front of a group. Say you've just completed a presentation, and your boss remarks negatively about the quality of your ideas. If you're like most people, you'll respond in one of two ways:

- **Blame the boss for your failure.** When an employee fails, he or she needs to explain that failure. Learning does not take place in this instance because the employee becomes convinced that the failure was the boss's fault. Rather than focusing on what he or she did wrong and storing it for future reference, the employee remembers blame and anger.
- **Blame yourself and feel embarrassed and humiliated.** Memory of an experience is corrupted by strong negative

emotions. The valuable lessons associated with failure aren't stored whole; the employee becomes so upset that it overwhelms his or her mind's capacity to label and store.

Trainees' reactions all reflect their motivation in training. If a company takes *all* the sting out of failure, it won't be memorable. If people view the failure as trivial or they don't have much of a vested interest in succeeding, the role-playing scenario won't stick. The motivation isn't there for the trainee's unconscious to file it in a properly labeled drawer. Of course, if failure goes too far in the other direction and feels like the end of the world, blaming starts.

Failure during a computer simulation, on the other hand, usually doesn't trigger our blaming impulse (of course, some people might blame the software for being too difficult or unfair, but that's the exception). The computer simulations offer three distinct advantages:

- **The failure can be controlled.** In real life, humans fail by accident. They don't plan to fail in exactly the right way so as to maximize learning. Sometimes novices fail at an esoteric task, and the knowledge gained from that failure will never be needed again. Trainers can design computer simulation failures so that the focus is on learning targeted skills.
- **The failure can be explained by experts.** When learners make blunders, their minds cry out for explanation. At that moment especially, trainees are open to suggestions. It's what the psychologists call a "teachable moment." In real life or in role-playing, people may be too upset to listen to an expert's advice. Or the advice may come days later, when learners are far past that teachable moment. In a computer simulation, the expert is programmed to appear *right when* people fail.
- **The failure is private.** Though learners may feel like idiots when they mess up an assigned task or become unhappy when a supervisor appears on the screen and explains they were wrong in their approach, people's feelings are cushioned because there's no one around to observe the failure. This cushion enables memory to label and store.

Failure in an e-learning environment works so well because users can fail in private. Ameritech had a standard classroom course designed to help people develop telephone skills. We created a computer simulation designed to do the same thing, and employees overwhelmingly preferred the computer simulation to the classroom. People commented that they were "embarrassed" to give the wrong answer in the classroom and were "afraid to take a chance." In private, they felt much more comfortable with taking chances and making mistakes.

These feelings arise because failure should be a private experience in which a learner has the opportunity to think about options not chosen. The computer doesn't care when someone makes a mistake; it creates an environment well suited to reflecting on one's mistakes.

Real Goals Motivate Learning from Failure

Many e-learning approaches assume that people naturally have the goal to learn: Put it on a Web page, and they will come. But if you've ever seen what happens when a teacher leaves a classroom or a boss leaves a meeting, you know that isn't always so. People have the goal of gossiping, of taking coffee breaks, and of making personal phone calls. They have other, nobler goals, but you have to recognize what these goals are and link them to learning. Otherwise, people will fail and learn nothing.

Failure, in and of itself, isn't a catalyst. Every manager has seen employees who have made major mistakes become apathetic or despondent. If people are not motivated by a goal, they'll get stuck in failure. To catalyze the self-explaining process that leads people out of failure, they need motivation. If it's there, they'll ask themselves the following three questions:

- How did I fail?
- How can I fix this?
- What do I have in my experience to help me?

Some employees, because of their particular personalities, won't self-explain. They'll fail and start to feel frustrated. To prevent this from happening, a good e-learning system has to have a way for learners to back up and ask for help. Now, this is not a traditional "help" button. It's a button that allows a learner to say that he or she doesn't know what to do next and wants a little guidance. Telling him or her what to do may not be the right thing at that point. It depends upon the situation.

Perceptive managers recognize the goals to which their people will respond. The goals may be obvious and financially related: promotions, raises, bonuses. They may have to do with approval from a boss or their peers. They may revolve around winning a competition or achieving a performance target. Whatever the goals, they need to be incorporated into learning systems or else people won't have the energy to figure out their failures.

Real Goals and "Unreal" Simulations

What motivates employees to learn in simulations when the learners know their failure has no impact in the real world of their organizations? There are a number of answers to that question. First, think of that pilot-in-training at the controls of a flight simulator. He makes a maneuver and is informed that if he were to do that same maneuver in a real plane, he would have killed himself and 148 passengers. The goal of keeping oneself and one's passengers alive would motivate most people to learn from this failure. The right sound effects (or physical effects if possible) can keep an experience real enough.

But consider a less dramatic situation. We created a computer simulation for Anixter Corp. in which salespeople arranged a meeting with customers to sell them the company's services. If the learner doesn't make an effective phone call to the customer, he or she doesn't get the appointment. If the learner fails to invite the right person to accompany the learner to the meeting, he or she has to start the whole process over again. These and other situations tap into common employee goals—the desire to do well in the simulation and the need to know how to deal with difficult situations that will arise in the field.

You can also motivate people with incentives. For instance, if someone successfully completes twenty simulations, he or she receives a promotion. Any tangible, valuable reward will do. What won't work are artificial goals, the equivalent of giving a student a gold star for a job well done. Most people will instantly recognize and disregard an artificial goal—that is, the first one to finish the simulation successfully gets a pin that reads, "I'm a good learner."

I don't want to pretend that simulations always prepare people to handle real situations effectively. There can be transfer problems, especially if you're relatively inexperienced in a given area. If, for instance, you're a young manager who has gone through a few simulations on decision making, that doesn't mean you'll be able to make all types of major, complex decisions effectively. Still, the "reminding" concept presented earlier in the chapter holds true. If a simulation is done well, it seems real and becomes a labeled memory that's triggered by a similar experience—we're reminded of it despite the fact that it's a simulation. The trick is to make the experience emotional. People remember strong emotions. They remember when they were afraid or upset or quite pleased with themselves. Simulations that evoke real emotions become real memories. A failure is a failure, and whether in a simulation or a work situation, if it feels real, it helps us learn.

5

Ten Powerful Design and Delivery Principles

Stories, simulations, goals, practice, fun, and failure are all critical to any e-learning system. But of course, change comes hard in the business world. So I understand that, despite what I say, there will still be a strong desire to make new e-learning systems look just like the old training that they are intended to replace.

The Rules

To help readers reject the old precepts, I'd like to do two things. Later in the book I will discuss a variety of e-learning systems that are radically different from the training that has gone before. Before we get to that, however, here are ten "rules" that can guide companies in their attempts to build e-learning solutions. They're not rules as much as thought-starters and misconception-breakers for people who are ready to lead the e-learning revolution.

1. You Remember Best What You Feel the Most

It is difficult to forget the first person who broke your heart or the car accident that broke your body. Intense feelings stick with people; anything that packs an emotional or visceral punch imprints itself on your mind. That's why dry, lifeless manuals and lectures are instantly forgettable. It takes the emotional intensity of experience—or a simulation of that experience—for stories to stick.

Which brings to mind sex education. Some of you may recall the old Monty Python routine in which John Cleese teaches sex education by making love to his wife. Contrary to what you might expect, the students aren't paying attention. Instead, they're dozing, throwing spitballs, talking amongst themselves, and generally ignoring Cleese and his wife. The lesson here is that even something intrinsically interesting can become dull if it is treated as a subject the learner has to learn and if it lacks personal meaning. There's not much emotion in watching someone else have an experience (and even prurient interest can be quashed if it's "required for the test").

In business, people remember highly emotional encounters: the time they blew an important business deal, getting chewed out by the boss, or finding out a project was being shut down after six months of hard work. Although it's true that simulations don't have the same impact as real work situations, they can engender strong feelings—crashing a simulated plane can be quite frightening. Good e-learning solutions are more than purely cognitive exercises; they evoke emotions.

In order to bring out these feelings, it is vital that simulations be realistic. The memory has trouble storing that which it knows to be a fabrication. The worst role-playing scenarios are ones that employees laugh at behind the trainer's back, the ones that set up situations that couldn't possibly happen in the real world of work. A lot of team training commits this sin—people know that real team environments are much more volatile and unstructured than those in training sessions. Scenarios always guard against scripting fake realities. In one coaching module, a scene called for a subordinate talking to someone two levels up from him about golfing together. It was completely unrealistic or at least rare for a junior executive and a middle manager to socialize in this way. Even minor flaws such as this one can cause people to reject the scenario and thus fail to store and label it properly.

2. Dumb Employees Aren't Born; They're Made

Organizations are constantly selling their people short. How many times have you heard someone say, "We have to simplify the training because we hire idiots" or some variation on that theme. Certainly, people do act like idiots at work, but only because they've been trained to act that way. A reporter in Chicago wrote a travel series in which he drove a rented car through forty-eight states. After racking up over 17,000 miles, he returned the car to the rental company. The only question the service representative asked was, "Did you put in gas?" Now that's an idiotic question given the mileage, but it's the one that all rental car company employees are trained to ask. It's as if organizations assume that their low-level people are only capable of memorizing five questions.

When I go to an airline counter, I sometimes ask, "Is the plane on time?"; the airline reps usually look up at the board and say "yes." Then I ask whether the incoming plane actually landed. That's when they're forced to find out the real answer to the question. These people are trained to look at the listing on the board because airlines underestimate the intelligence of both the passengers and their own staff.

What companies don't understand is that even people who don't seem that bright or did poorly in school are good learners. They have learned to function in the world, haven't they? They have learned to communicate in English, to recognize the parts and processes that make up the world around them. They usually have a natural impulse to help others and, in business, to meet customers' needs. That impulse is drummed out of people by companies that believe the way to get employees to do what they want is to make them into mindless robots who follow every rule they are told. This is not the way people learn, and it is certainly not the way to get employees to show initiative.

E-learning solutions that simulate situations an employee is likely to encounter, that allow him or her to make mistakes despite attempts to be helpful, will enable the trainee to accumulate sufficient experiences to be effective in a wide variety of customer interactions.

3. Deliver Training Just in Time
(Or When a Learner Has Just Failed and Really Needs Help)

Though this is typically difficult for organizations to do because they're locked into training schedules, it is a key advantage of e-learning. The old idea that 100 employees learn about a new sales tool over the course of a week because that's when a facility and the trainers are available to teach that tool is just that—an old idea. Those 100 employees will need the sales tool at different times—some may need it three weeks after the course while some may need it three years later.

But much of the ballyhooed e-learning is done the old way. Rather than take advantage of a software-based system's flexibility, organizations revert to the educational model: Everyone must complete x hours of training before going on; the learner must make it through every second of the computer program before being allowed to put the knowledge to use. This regimentation forces companies to lock into training schedules.

E-learning can train thousands of people all over the world simultaneously—a wonderful thing for a global organization. The problem is, the more people learning at the same time, the more likely the training will be a "one size fits all" operation. Or, to put this another way, the more people, the less interaction.

What e-learning has essentially been so far in its early days is a way to put a lot of distance between the conveyance of information and the time people really need it. Of course, this is true of education in general. People are always being taught things that they will "need for the future," things they typically will have long since forgotten when the future finally arrives. E-learning should decrease the depersonalization of training, not increase it.

The mind can only hold so much information for so long—when there's a lot of data, it should be conveyed just before it's needed. For a lesson to really sink in, you need to be failing and flailing for help. You need people actively asking questions rather than passively watching "educational" television.

Even more important, people need to be motivated to learn. If learners know they're not going to use the training information for months, learners won't have much of an incentive to concentrate. If, on the other hand, learners have a sales meeting with a lawyer tomorrow—and they screwed up the last presentation to a lawyer—they'll concentrate intently on training that occurs just before tomorrow's meeting.

4. Failure Can Teach Just About Anything

E-learning can be used to help people learn soft (people-oriented) skills, not just hard (widget-oriented) ones. Organizations are especially intent on teaching their people soft skills such as leadership, teamwork, and creativity, but they're doing so in ways that range from faddish to foolish.

Many executive development programs have an "adventure" component in which teams of executives are challenged to work together to raft whitewater rivers and climb mountains. The assumption is that these activities will help people acquire leadership and team-building skills. What they actually do is help people learn how to raft and climb. If trainers want people to learn to be leaders in business situations, the trainers have to put them in business leadership situations. Quarterbacks, who are typically great leaders, don't necessarily know how to lead a project through to completion on time and under budget. To teach a skill, you must teach it in a relevant context. Simulations allow for teaching just about anything that can be simulated. If you play a role that seems real to you, the learning will be real as well.

Categorizing and collecting stories about tough decisions leaders have had to make is a good start. Then simulations can be created where people are confronted with some tough (and realistic) decisions: Should I fire five senior people who haven't been performing up to snuff, or should I spend a good deal of time and money training them to perform better? When faced with these tough decisions, people are ready to hear how experts in leadership resolved similar issues. Even with the help of experts, it's likely that trainees will fail to make the right decisions at first. Leadership is not a simple skill, and the right decision for one won't be the right decision for someone else—personality type will influence decision making, and one person will lead by example whereas another will lead by strength of personality. Still, it's fine to let them fail and obtain an instructive memory for later use.

Companies are also making mistakes when it comes to teaching creativity. Perhaps the biggest one is assuming that people are naturally uncreative. This assumption leads to the development of all sorts of unusual tools and techniques designed to help people become creative—free association, lateral thinking, and so on. None of these tools, however, will overcome the real obstacle to creativity: negativity. In school and at work, people are constantly told that their ideas are bad. Teachers ridicule kids who make oddball suggestions (because they're not the right answers) and bosses reject ideas that they deem weird, risky, or at odds with traditional practices. All this stifles creativity. Such negativity is really too bad, because people are all naturally creative.

In fact, the few people who are considered "creative types" in organizations may not be any more creative than their fellow employees; they're often just the ones with the thickest skins. Perhaps 99 out of 100 of their ideas are mediocre, but they have the emotional armor to keep articulating them until a good one pops up. Creativity is best fostered by allowing people to fail without consequence. If you know you can try something out and see how it goes, with absolutely no down side to failure, where no one will know and no one will care, you are willing to try a lot of different things. This allowance for easy failure is the real value of a good e-learning simulation.

Given this negativity, the way to help people use their natural creativity is to enable them to practice being creative. This can be done on a computer when there are people connected to each other. So, for example, chat rooms that revolve around wacky issues can cause all kinds of good ideas to emerge; Ask what should be done with all the popsicle sticks in the wastebasket and encourage wacky responses. A lively discussion, even one that is mostly kidding, may cause interesting ideas to emerge that relate to company issues. Inviting people to formulate original conclusions (without making them feel stupid if they're not feasible) enables creative thinking to emerge.

5. You Will Teach Yourself Better Than the World's Best Trainer or Highest-Paid Motivational Speaker

Teachers tend to think that they are more important to the learning process than they actually are. People naturally teach themselves. When something goes wrong, people automatically ask themselves how they messed up and seek advice in order not to repeat the same mistake. This is especially true when we're learning complex tasks. When I started my first company (a complex task if ever there was one), I made many mistakes I would never make again. But I would have made those mistakes no matter how many books I read about how to start a company or how many consultants I asked for advice. Like everyone else, I had to learn the hard way. For instance, when I began it seemed like we had great cash resources and didn't have any money worries. Only the visceral experience of seeing how quickly money disappeared helped me understand the need for good financing and the need to produce products quickly.

Similarly, I started out wanting to be Mr. Nice Guy and never fire anyone. Most neophyte business owners tell the same story—how they changed from CEOs who tried to be nice to all their employees to bosses who fired people without compunction. What business owners learn with experience is that allowing nonperformers to slide by hurts everyone else in the company, that being a nice guy toward one person who doesn't deserve it hurts all the other hard-working employees who do deserve your consideration.

Can someone learn this lesson through e-learning? We actually built a program for a client's Human Resources department designed to teach HR how to fire employees. Although the program can't possibly duplicate the emotional impact of firing another human being, it does contribute to the accumulation of experiences that are a part of learning. Good e-learning allows a learner to be his or her own teacher.

6. Memorization Without Corresponding Experience Is Worthless

People waste enormous amounts of time attempting to memorize facts, procedures, and slogans. Such memorization has no impact on behavior; it doesn't translate into learned skills. Yet companies persist in forcing their people to commit to memory the ten principles of quality or to study a list of hiring procedures until they have it down cold. Again, all this goes back to our educational system, where it was assumed that committing something to memory was learning.

Recall Nancy Reagan's "Just Say No" antidrug campaign, and consider why such efforts are futile. As well-intentioned as the campaign may have been, plastering the slogan over the media didn't change anyone's behavior. Having such a slogan imprinted in your consciousness means that you will remember the slogan, not that you will refrain from using drugs.

Memorizing procedures is often a waste of time, as anyone who drives a car or throws a football understands. After driving for a period of time, you don't have to think consciously about procedure one—turning the ignition; procedure two—putting the car in drive; procedure three—stepping on the gas so it's depressed a half an inch; and so on.

Someone once asked me if you should spin the football when you throw it. I used to be a pretty good quarterback and must have thrown millions of passes, yet I had no idea how to answer the question. I had to actually throw the football and observe whether I rotated the ball as I released it. My expertise was unconscious.

Good cooks do not become good cooks by learning the rules of cooking. They learn to cook by cooking. Sure, there's recipes, but they usually don't follow them. They understand what works from their own experience. They innovate, they substitute, they draw their own conclusions. Given the latitude to be different, they can be successful.

Learning procedures at work follow the same unconscious route. Novices need to practice, make mistakes, practice and make more mistakes until at some point they master the procedures and don't have to think about them anymore. All that learners memorize when they study training manuals are words. When learners do something repeatedly, they memorize actions. Telling an employee what the official rules are and then asking him or her to reiterate those rules will produce an employee who is capable of repeating the rules. If you want an employee who can function effectively within the rules, you need to do something more interesting than preach. Your e-learning design should re-create the work environment and the work problems of your learners. Simulation-based e-learning enables (safe) practice, and practice is the *sine qua non* of learning.

7. When You Buy an e-Learning System, It Should Come with All the Options

Do various people learn differently? In other words, does it make sense to design a learning experience one way for John and a different way for Mary? Not really. Contrary to common belief, people don't have different learning styles. They do, however, have different personalities. The distinction is important, since we need to be clear that everyone learns the same way. It is easier to see this watching a dog or a cat than by watching a human learn. Take the dog's bowl and move it into another room. See what happens. The dog may be upset, it may look around, it may try to look up at you for help. It may complain. With help, or simply by exploring, it may find the new bowl. The next time it is hungry it will likely go back to the original location. It will again be confused. After many trials, it will eventually go directly to the new location. This is what learning looks like. The smarter the dog,

*Sounds
behavioristic*

the faster the learning. Learning is the same for everyone—failure causes the rewriting of the rules that failed. To rewrite rules the options are simple—figure it out yourself or get help. In any case, repeated practice is necessary to embed the new rules and replace the ones that have failed. Such procedures are universal.

All people learn through failure and practice, no matter what type of personality they possess. One dog might look to its owner for help, another might complain bitterly, a third might look around frantically, and a fourth might look around calmly. Those are personality differences.

It makes sense to take personality differences into account when designing a system. Our software includes various buttons to push: "Now what?" "Why?" "How?" and others. Simulations must give people options, recognizing that one individual will be confident and willing to try anything while another will be cautious and want to know reasons for taking a step. Some people learn how to swim by being thrown in the lake, and others learn by being gently held. Nevertheless, the learning is the same. It is still involves trying and failing and then trying again. Any good teacher recognizes that some students need to be coaxed while others need to be prodded. A good e-learning system must present the learner with options that allow the learner to learn in his or her own way and own time. A learner who is in control of his or her own experience is likely to learn the most.

Some personality types to consider:

The diver. Some people want no explanations. Many people simply want to dive in. Don't give them long introductions and preparations. Don't give hints. Let them dive in. Always allow a learner to start doing whatever you are asking him to do within seconds of stating the task.

The questioner. Some people are uncomfortable starting to do anything until the entire road that they must travel is laid out before them. Always provide road maps that say what the e-learning system contains as well as provide answers to every conceivable question they might ask.

The explorer. Some people want just enough introduction to let them start looking around on their own. These people want to see what's available without commitment. They want to start but cautiously. Hand holding must be available for them in the form of questions that can be asked at every step.

The little brother. Some people want you to lead them just up to the point where they have to do something and then they are prepared with some coaxing to do it. Your software must hold them by the hand and gently nudge them into action.

8. Open Your e-Learning Course with a Bang

Most employees react to training in one of two ways: They either hate it or look at it as time off from their real jobs. This means that even if you have a good learning system, it might not do much good due to resistance or an uninterested audience.

The best way to break through resistance and apathy is with an opening that's immediately involving and fun. This is not a natural training instinct. Most courses begin with a long and boring introduction about why you'll learn what you'll learn. Before the trainer gets to the good stuff, he or she has lost the audience. Well-designed virtual learning begins with having people *experience* something. Then, they must be called upon to do something as a result of that experience. Training that starts with a speech usually ends with trainees deciding to ignore that speech. Training that starts with an emotionally powerful experience, on the other hand, encourages trainees to think about that experience. Good e-learning entices learners to learn more by making the experience exciting.

We once built a system to teach decision making that started with a helicopter ride that landed you in a town where people were dying of an unknown and obviously spreading disease. Upon your arrival one person after another came up, screaming and crying, asking you to make a decision that would help their particular problem in this crisis. The effect was quite powerful. Learners were ready to start deciding (and to make mistakes).

9. Trainees Should Be Learning from the World's Best

In reality, training participants are probably learning from "experts" with marginal or mediocre skills. An organization is lucky if it has a handful of real experts—men and women who are among the best at what they do. Because of the size of most companies, it's impossible for everyone to apprentice with the best. In addition, these experts retire, quit, or die, robbing the organization of their expertise.

Computers offer companies the chance to preserve expertise. Capturing and integrating experts into a computer simulation or simply creating a database of expertise is something every company can do. If a company lacks experts in a given area, the developers of training software need to find them and videotape them wherever they are to make their expertise part of the collective wisdom of the company, available anytime and anywhere. We once built a program for the army that had all the expertise of the part of the army that did logistics planning during the Gulf War. Forever after this database of stories and advice will be available to help in a current plan. It may not be training per se, but just-in-time performance support is equally important.

Often training is no more than having a question answered when you need to know something. Ease of access to experts is the key to corporate survival in the modern era. The local expert is no longer down the hall, but he or she may be in your office (on your computer) if the training organization has done its job correctly. Capturing corporate memory in an easily navigable system is important in the fast-changing world of the global economy. Companies need to access their expertise on demand, whether their experts are in Kuala Lumpur or no longer with the firm at all.

Unfortunately, most companies don't capitalize on expertise. Instead, managers bring in the world's best experts to lecture. As entertaining as it might be, this lecturing doesn't help novices do their jobs better. Good e-learning enables a company to put its best and brightest within reach of every employee.

10. Simulation-Based e-Learning Is Best Suited to Large Training Populations

In the early days of artificial intelligence (AI), the idea was to capture the knowledge of the lonely expert whose esoteric knowledge would die with him. Expertise in astrophysics, oil drilling in Alaska, and the like, was what AI attempted to preserve. No doubt, there is an organizational equivalent of such esoterica—every company has all sorts of arcane knowledge.

However, rare skills should not be the focus of learning. The most good comes from taking an organization's most common jobs and creating training for them, not for the top positions or the few that are critical. Organizations can gain the competitive edge by improving the jobs performed by lots of people. There's such volatility in organizations these days that the cost of retraining new people becomes prohibitive. E-learning is, of course, the more cost-efficient way to train any new employee.

The other compelling reason to train the many is the fact that more firms are becoming global corporations. An organization's most common jobs can exist in the United States, Japan, France, and Kenya. Although some differences exist in how one job is performed in various parts of the world, global organizations want uniform philosophies, policies, skills, and products. E-learning allows an organization to achieve uniformity in its worldwide training.

The Building Blocks of e-Learning: Scriptlets and the Learner's Personal Goals

What We Learn When We Learn by Doing

The object of learning by doing is the acquisition of scriptlets. A scriptlet is a procedure or a group of actions that we perform so frequently that its completion is almost mindless. The skills we talk about in terms of people's abilities almost always refer to scriptlets that they execute all the time. These are often quite unconscious.

Two good examples of a scriptlet are "setting up a VCR for taping" and "sending e-mail." In the twenty-five years that electronic mail has existed, I have used probably ten different systems. Although I was told how to use each, I rarely remembered what was said long enough to try it out. I could use them when someone watched over my shoulder, but then I would forget by the next try. My actual *learning* of the systems came through repeated practice and repeated trial and error—that is, I learned to e-mail by actually doing it. I am quite adept at the two systems I now use, although I probably don't know all the features of either.

Nevertheless, I clearly have the skill of using the two systems I have. I have no interest in how these systems work, but I am interested in sending and receiving e-mail. This goal caused me to try the systems until I got good at them. These trials were held in the course of use, not as outside practice. This was a case of motivated learning by doing.

Perhaps a more everyday example is using a VCR. I had one of the very first models of VCRs, and over time I have owned many different machines. Each has a different way of setting up a recording, yet I can operate all of them. I find them annoying to use, but I like to record and watch movies, so I have learned to use them. Yet, if I am away from any of them for very long, I tend to forget how they operate. Scriptlets tend to decay in memory if they are not used. Fortunately, I know some generic information about how VCRs work, and this helps me relearn the scriptlet I need. Again, you could say that I have learned the skills of recording on my VCRs by doing.

I mention all this for a simple reason. We want learners to know the exceptional cases from which they can learn and make judgments on their own about new situations. And we want students to know how to do things, to have sets of skills. But when we talk about the *skills* we want students to have, we often get confused by what we mean by the term. We talk about what we want students to know (e.g., math skills), or how we want students to conduct themselves (e.g., personal interaction skills), but not about what we want them to be able to do.

Students will easily acquire scriptlets in the natural course of the pursuit of a goal that is of interest to them. Personal goals play a critical role in how we store and retrieve memories. This is what learning by doing is all about.

What personal goals might your employees have, for example? It is safe to assume that everyone who works for you wants to be liked by others. How do we make use of this in training? Set up situations in which an employee is hated as a result of some action they take in the training. (For obvious reasons, this is best to do in a simulation.) No one wants to feel they have done something bad or made someone feel terrible. Even if they hate their jobs they don't hate the people they meet on their jobs, at least not initially, and they don't want to be hated. Knowing this kind of thing is very helpful in setting up training. Emotional issues are very important. Make the experiences they get in training highly emotional.

How to Do It: Skills as Scriptlets

Skills ought to be taught by the method most appropriate for their acquisition. The hard part is assessing what a skill is and what it isn't.

What we are referring to here is what is commonly meant by skills. The problem with this word is that it has no clear definition. We can say, for example, that someone is skilled at mathematics, is a skilled negotiator, or has mastered basic language skills. When we talk about skills, we are often referring to what we believe a person "knows how to do." Unfortunately, this can mean just about anything at all. Any human action or capability can be referred to as a skill, so the term offers us very little to go on if we want to teach skills.

One problem with the word *skill* is that we can say "John knows how to do mathematics" or "John knows how to manage people" and still feel comfortable that we are talking about skills because we are talking about knowing how to do something. The illusion is that mathematics or management is a kind of thing you can learn to do. We might expect our employees to know how to do systems installation or to sell, for example. But, although these may seem like skills, in each case they are really collections of a large number of scriptlets. This becomes clear when you think about teaching someone to do any of these things.

You can't teach students to do customer service, but you can teach them to handle a complaint, deal with unruly customers, or go out of their way in extraordinary circumstances. In fact, even these scriptlets are likely to be made up of many smaller scriptlets (such as calming down an angry person). Similarly, you can't teach students to do mathematics, but you can teach them addition and eventually how to prove a theorem in plane geometry.

In business, this means we have to stop thinking about teaching management techniques or communication methods. Why? Because these are not scriptlets. If we want students to get good at managing or communicating, we have to understand the difference between a skill that is teachable and a skill set that is not teachable by itself. Whatever managing employees or handling customers might be, these things cannot be only one skill. They are collections of various, possibly quite unrelated scriptlets.

Recognizing the skill set to which a scriptlet naturally belongs is critical to curriculum design. To teach how to handle customers, most traditional training approaches would attempt to teach general communication skills or to teach something about human relations in general. At a high level of abstraction, we lose students' interest. We can preach about the evils of sexual harassment for example, and students will agree that it's a bad idea. But what if they are really attracted to the other person? Reality has a way of making lofty principles you have learned fly out the window if you don't think those principles should apply in this case.

To teach trainees to deal with people, you must teach them to deal with specific situations, not bland generalities. Any time you talk about what one should do in general, you are wasting your time. People learn from repeated experience. Someone who is good at handling a difficult situation is likely to have dealt with that situation many times before. Since this is obvious—we all know it to be true—training must help a student start experiencing whatever it is we think they may experience on the job. Practice, practice, practice. This is how scriptlets are formed. You must figure out the very thing that they will encounter on the job and make sure trainees encounter it, and figure out how to deal with it, in training.

Practice Makes Perfect

The only way to learn a scriptlet is to practice it. The essence of real education is repeated practice—ask any musician. If you wanted to teach "firing someone," you could construct practice scenarios in which trainees gained experience in firing people before trying it out for real. Here again it is the emotion that matters. Start by firing them. See how they felt. Ask them how you could have done it better. Sensitize them to the feelings of others by having them witness and comment upon actual firings. You want vivid emotional reactions to be witnessed or felt and thus stored away in the memories of the trainees. "Avoiding that terrible experience" will stay in the mind of a trainee if the experience is real and frightening.

To motivate a student to learn a scriptlet, one of three things needs to be true: (1) The student must find the result of the scriptlet to be intrinsically rewarding, (2) the scriptlet must be part of a package of scriptlets that is intrinsically rewarding, or (3) the scriptlet must be an example of what we shall term *in order to* learning.

Not every scriptlet is intrinsically rewarding to learn. Sending e-mail and programming VCRs are intrinsically rewarding because you want to achieve the result that comes from doing these things correctly. Other intrinsically rewarding scriptlets might be "making toast," "making a phone call," or "hitting a golf ball." But, on the whole, we learn scriptlets because they are useful in order to do something else.

When you want to teach a scriptlet that is not intrinsically rewarding—filling out a form properly for example—you must link it with the results of the bad performance, or put it in a fun context where the rewards of doing it right are experienced and felt.

Many scriptlets can be grouped together to accomplish a goal; we seek to learn these scriptlets simply because they are part of a larger package. Functioning in a restaurant is, for instance, a collection of scriptlets that includes ordering, paying, and so on. Playing baseball is a collection of scriptlets that includes fielding a ground ball to your left, hitting the curve ball, and sliding into second base. None of these things is ever done for its own sake. Nevertheless, they all take practice, and you can learn to do them well enough that you'll become quite adept at various subtleties that might arise.

In each of these cases, the package itself is worth bragging about, not the component scriptlets. So you can say that you're good at playing baseball or a good Human Resource manager, but no one scriptlet is representative of these so-called abilities.

You need to learn scriptlets by practicing them. When you decide to teach them, however, you must bear in mind their differences. The ones that stand alone, that are intrinsically rewarding, can be taught by themselves. You can learn to make toast or program a VCR in the absence of any other activity or motivational issue A sliding lesson in baseball may be fun for someone who is intrinsically rewarded by getting dirty, but very few people would take lessons on how to sign a credit card slip. Scriptlets that are parts of packages must be taught within the context of those packages.

If, for example, we determine that reading a financial report (really a package of scriptlets) is important to know, we must find a context in which that knowledge matters. Giving the student a decision to make in which the various scriptlets in reading a financial report come into play can make all the difference between a student really acquiring the relevant scriptlets and his or her merely committing them to memory in order to pass the test. It is not simply a question of finding the context in which the scriptlets come into play—they must come into play quite often. This does not mean repetition of the same scriptlet again and again, as is done in drill and practice situations in school. (All too often schools have students practice skills before they actually *do* anything, thereby eliminating both motivation and context.)

How do we know the student knows all he or she needs to in a given situation? We don't. But we shouldn't care too much, either. Good e-learning should have as its goal exposing a student to enough situations that the student will become curious enough to take the learning process into his or own hands. In other words, the role of e-learning is to open up interesting problems and provide tools for solving them. The accomplishment of the goal should be its own reward.

If we abandon the idea of easy measurement of achievement, then we can begin to talk about how to excite learners with open-ended problems and can begin to create educational goals such as learning to think for yourself. Under this view, the problem of how education is delivered becomes far more important than you might initially imagine. Actual content may not be the issue at all, since we are really trying to impart the idea that you can deal with new arenas of knowledge if you know how to learn, how to find out about what is known, and how to abandon old ideas when they are worn out. This means teaching ways of developing good questions rather than good answers. In other words, it means finding and teaching ways to help students learn on their own.

Demo and App of
relevant real-world tasks

The e-Learning Instructional Design Process

This chapter is golden! Very useful stuff, especially the PowerPoint as a prototyping tool. LOVE IT!!

The Problem

The key step in the e-learning design process is the creation of the plan for "interaction design." You cannot design a piece of e-learning without having successfully answered the question, "What will the learner be doing when the learner is using the courseware?" To create a good answer to this question, we have to answer a series of more detailed questions along the way:

- How do we determine what kind of courseware we want to create in the first place?
- How big should it be?
- What kinds of activities should it cover?
- What kinds of coaching and support should we include?

For a design to be effective, it must be true to the task we are trying to teach and to where our audience struggles with that task. This is quite a bit different than, for instance, deciding that we will give some prereading, then allowing the student to ask some questions of the professor, then offering a multiple-choice test. To create an effective learning-by-doing simulation, we have to delve quite deeply into the specifics of what kind of "doing" it is we want.

What this means is that we have to first understand the task in some detail and then model it in the courseware. Take selling for example. We might begin with the goal that "we want our salespeople to sell better." But, to achieve the goal, we would have to dig deeper to understand specifically what it is that's holding our audience back. Ignoring, for the time being, causes that cannot be addressed by courseware (e.g., the compensation system is wrong), here are a few examples of the kinds of gaps we have found. Salespeople can struggle with:

- **The basics of stepping through the sales process** (When do I try to understand the need versus offering a potential solution? How do I bridge between them?)
- **Setting priorities** (choosing between all of the potential sales opportunities they might pursue)
- **Diagnosing problems** in their sales processes
- **Managing the detailed give and take** within a sales conversation with a specific customer

The challenge is that with each of these gaps, the learner is held back by mistakes on what amounts to a conceptually different kind of task. So each calls for a somewhat different style of interaction. This is at the heart of the challenge of successful interaction design. To get it right, you need to (1) understand the need in some detail; (2) determine what kind of mental task is driving the need; (3) model that task in a computer-based program; and (4) do it in a way that efficiently uses both development time and the learner's time in using the courseware. And, since the interaction design is what will drive the rest of the project, you want to be able to do this quickly and reliably.

The Process

It's a good idea to make things concrete at each step of the way for some sample part, then generalize later. It's very easy for people to miscommunicate when they talk in generalizations about something that they are in the process of constructing (and hence probably of which they do not share a concrete vision).

Each step listed below is organized around solving a specific problem (e.g., determining concretely what needs to be taught), with the solution being expressed in a specific work product (the Teaching Points document).

Teaching Points Document

Work Product	Problem Tackled
1. Teaching Points	How do we specify what is to be learned?
2. Design Theme & Risks	What's our assessment of the kind of problem the system is to solve and the kind of interaction it will provide? Also, what are the major risks we will face in developing the design?
3. Review Prior Courseware	How can we leverage our work on prior projects? How might we fall short in the design?
4. Initial Design Timeline	What work products will we produce on this project? What's the timeline and process for getting through the initial design?
5. Sample Content and Task Skeleton	What is the example problem we'll use in thinking through design? How is it structured?
6. Text Walkthrough	How will we break the task down in the courseware? What support will we give the user?
7. Slide Show	How can we test our sense of what the user interaction will be and then convey it to the client?
8. Implementation Review	How can we ensure that we have confidence in the design, that we can efficiently implement it, and that we can identify how much effort implementation will take?
9. Functional Specification	How can we communicate, in some detail, the individual pieces that need to be built and track the issues that remain with them?

Below, I'll illustrate this process by walking through it and showing how it worked in one small part of a course: the ratio analysis activity within the finance course we developed for

Harvard Business School (HBS). This is a course that was developed to teach a tool kit of basic financial activities. The specific learning goal here is to teach how to apply financial ratios in the midst of conducting a financial analysis.

Teaching Points

In most projects, our first activity is to gather data on what the specific need is. What is it that the audience just does not know how to do? What mistakes do they make? Why do they make them? To return to the example of selling, we take the big gaps ("our people need to sell better") and work to break them into the key specific behavioral gaps that cause the big gaps ("many new salespeople believe it is important to describe the benefits of their products early, before letting the customer speak about their needs, because they are afraid of losing control of the conversation"). It is these specific behavioral gaps that the courseware will directly address. Without explicitly trying to understand them, you are destined to only hit on them by happenstance, reducing the concreteness of the development process and, more importantly, diluting the effectiveness of the courseware.

To get teaching points, we interview experts, practitioners, and those who manage or otherwise support practitioners. When possible, we also shadow practitioners as they do the task and try to do the task ourselves. We look for the mistakes and misconceptions they make and then prioritize those, thereby leaving us with a clear set of pedagogical goals for the project.

In order to make an impact on performance when teaching "how to," one needs to:

- Identify high impact behaviors: the behaviors that will have the greatest effect on learners' performance and success on the job
- Figure out how the training can give people an opportunity to practice these behaviors
- Create meaningful opportunities to practice, and offer insightful coaching when the learner stumbles

Teaching points are a distillation of information gathered during weeks of research and interviews. In the first weeks of a project, one must immerse oneself in the details of the job one is going to teach. The client must describe the goals of the training, written documentation must be examined, and if there are existing live courses, one should enroll in them. One must conduct interviews with target audience members and shadow people on the job. Only then can one come back to the office, and say, "So what are we going to teach people about this job?"

The key then is making a list of the behaviors that, based on what one has heard, read, and witnessed, will have the highest impact on people's success on the job. One must think about why these are the important behaviors; why people aren't succeeding at them right now; and what the consequences are when people fail to execute these behaviors correctly. The answers to all these questions comprise the teaching points. A good teaching point will summarize the following information about a specific behavior:

- The mistake that research has shown people are apt to make when conducting an activity
- The situation in which people are likely to be when they make this mistake
- The consequence of the mistake
- The thought process which might lead someone to make this mistake
- Why they believe this to be a correct action
- The correct action
- The reason why this action is correct

In the Harvard Business School Finance project, however, we were initially stymied in getting a covering set of specific teaching points for ratios. This sometimes happens in projects with academic institutions, where the audience is usually students learning about an area, rather than practitioners who do it day in and day out. In such cases, we neither have direct access to people who actually do what we want to teach, nor is it clear that they will be a good proxy for the students we want to teach. In this case, the solution was to have our own people try their hand at ratio analysis and note where they struggled.

Design Theme and Risks

It's really not until we have the first draft of the teaching points in hand that we start seriously conceptualizing the design. The first step is to create a *design theme* for the project. This is simply a few paragraphs that summarize the audience, the core focus and structure of the task, and the expected duration of the activity.

For the ratio analysis activity, we learned from our initial work that knowing the definitions of various kinds of ratios was not a major issue (one can simply look in a textbook for that). Rather, where novices struggled was with the process of starting with a specific question and determining what financial indicators would be useful to investigate it (e.g., bridging from "Is high sales overhead a significant cause of low profitability?" to "I should look at the XXX ratio."). Our focus on this process led to the following design theme:

> **The problem.** Students should be familiar with the four major categories of ratios: Operating ratios, profitability ratios, leverage ratios, and XXX. However, the hard part about using ratios effectively is neither learning these general categories nor memorizing the common ratios that fall within each nor again gathering the data or computing the ratios themselves. Rather, the two hard parts are determining which ratio is the best for investigating a question and how much can one learn from the results.

> **The activity.** The learner is asked to analyze a troubled company, one that may have several problems. He has a boss, who will generate a series of hypotheses about what might be at the root of the problems in the company. And he has an assistant who will calculate ratios for him at will. The learner's job will be to bridge between these, determining which ratios will be useful for investigating a range of hypotheses, as well as interpreting what the results say. As he works the learner will be able to access support about the ratios and be given, as appropriate, comparative ratios across time or across companies to help him interpret his results.

Determining a design theme, while usually a quick process, is also one of the most critical steps in the development of a project. What happens in this step is that the team essentially picks from our library of design architectures and past project experience a style of interaction (or set of interactions) to use. In so doing, the team makes a major commitment (since different styles of interaction imply different levels of invention and can be easier or harder to implement). Here, we chose a general approach we call "hypothesis-driven investigation," which contains a series of activity steps (below). We then chose which of those the student should actually do rather than have modeled for him (these are marked in bold):

> The practitioner first completes an *initial survey* to get the lay of the situation, then digs into iterative cycles in which he searches for useful actions by:
>
> 1. **Generating** a starting set of hypotheses about what might be causing suboptimal performance;
>
> 2. **Selecting** a hypothesis which might lead to substantial real-world improvements;
>
> 3. **Designing** a focused analysis to investigate that hypothesis;
>
> 4. **Implementing** the analysis; and
>
> 5. **Interpreting** the results of their focused analysis to see if it indicates
>   - A deadend
>   - A need for another round of hypotheses and investigation, or
>   - A concrete opportunity for improvement.

Since we had limited experience in building hypothesis-driven interactions, we knew that we were committing ourselves to at least a moderate level of new design.

Initial Design Timeline

This is a straightforward project management step. We will have already boxed out how much overall time we expect to spend on interaction design. However, we won't have split that time up into specific activities. At this point, we simply take the effort to write out our plan for how we are dividing the design into clusters of activities and how much time we expect to spend cycling through each step of the process.

We have found that if we try to be specific before we have the design theme, we will either end up with vague plans or we will misestimate our time required for particular steps. Conversely, we have found that if we wait until later in the process to get specific, we may inadvertently spend too much time in the first few steps without making sure to focus enough attention on getting the work done in a timely way.

Of course, design means invention, so we find that we must be flexible about our timelines. But, as any project manager will tell you, unless you have some set of targets, you may not even recognize when you are off schedule, much less determine what trade-offs or repairs to make to get back on schedule.

Sample Content and Task Skeleton

This next step is the result of perhaps the biggest lessons we have learned in the past few years doing interaction design. What we have found is that in those cases where we struggle as we get into detailed design, it's usually because we did not really understand well enough specifically what the student was supposed to be doing in the first place. This rarely happens in systems that are primarily aimed at teaching interpersonal interactions. Rather, it happens in cases where the learner is creating or interpreting some form of analysis.

The solution is simple. Before we worry about how we model the task to be learned in a piece of courseware, we first worry about how it is structured in the first place. To do this, we pick a sample problem and we work through it. In cases where we see risks and really want to be clear, we will go so far as to create a paper-based workbook that lays out the task. In these cases, we get our first user input into our design process at this point (by having some sample users work the problem using our workbook and having our staff play coach and tutor).

Text Walkthrough

At this point, we are armed with a detailed list of what is to be taught, a general sense of the theme of the design, and a specific sense of how the core task will be structured. What we have not done is lay out how that task will be used as a tool for teaching.

We haven't converted the task into a course. To do that, we need two more pieces of information:

1. What are the additional setup, support, and reflection activities that we will add to the core task?
2. What is our design checklist: the individual pieces we need to design that will then represent a complete design of the course.

Over the years, we have gone from not having this step at all (and simply proceeding into detailed design) to creating detailed text descriptions of the entire design, capturing copious notes on user options and design issues along the way. What we have learned is that a middle ground approach is best at this point, having this step but going rather lightly on it. In particular, we've learned that having a graphical representation of a design is really what is needed to make it concrete. So, in this step, we simply create what amounts to a checklist for what we want to illustrate in that graphical representation. Hence, our text walkthroughs are simply bulleted lists such as this (sometimes elaborated with a brief paragraph about each task):

- **Module introduction:** Boss sets the mission
- **Module background:** User can ask background questions
- **Get to work:** User begins activity

John & I are doing this! It really is useful . . .

(Slide Show)

We now know what we want to teach and, in fair detail, how we plan to teach it. But there are many, many decisions yet to be made as we "detail" the design. Some of these include:

- How will the details of the interaction be staged (e.g., when will the user learn what the scenario is about, when will he be given his overarching role, will he be given his specific mission separately, where will he have access to support materials, . . .)?
- What specific materials will be required to implement the interaction (what background about the scenario that we'll

create will the user need? What coaching materials will he need)?

- How will the specific decisions the user makes be structured? (will he be asked to pick from a list of actions, or pick an action and justify it, or identify a series of goals, then pick an action)?
- How will the user be led to generalize from the specific scenario to the overall task (will coaching along the way be framed in terms of some general model? Will we insert specific moments in the interaction along the way that step back from the scenario and help the learner generalize)?

In most cases, by the time we are at this stage, we are borrowing fairly heavily from work we have done before. So, the job of detailing the design is often picking out from our prior work specific approaches to these questions and pulling them together. And typically, we do this by picking a base case example and then just focusing on where it seems to fall short.

The way we capture this work and make it clear to our clients is essentially to create a storyboard: Let's pick a sample learner, imagine one or two learning gaps he has, and create a walkthrough that illustrates how we help the learner overcome those gaps. On a more mechanical level, how we capture the walkthrough varies from project to project. Over the years, it's often been in PowerPoint; these days we are moving toward capturing it on the Web; and in the future, we are looking toward using a more formal set of templates.

Note that our goals in creating the storyboard are limited. We want it to cover an example of every nonobvious interaction the user might have. But we do not want to get the detailed structure of the story just right, nor do we try to create a great user interface. Instead, we aim to illustrate what functionality the user might have and the concept of how the user will employ the course. By not trying to refine the content or the user interface too soon, we spend less time giving ourselves angst about the details of the interaction until we convince ourselves that its basic structure will accomplish our goals.

Typically, we begin creating these walkthroughs using a simple library of PowerPoint templates (to help us reuse our past designs). We capture in the PowerPoints the specific issues we uncover along the way, so that they go beyond capturing our output at the moment to also record our conceptual struggles, searches for alternatives, and decisions about trade-offs and next steps. Everybody gets to see and work on the walkthrough, from each of our internal team members, to subject matter experts and, in some cases, to representatives of the user group.

Yes!

When we have a simple design, we sometimes skip this step entirely, instead going straight into implementation, directly reusing a prior design. But when we have a tough design, this is the document where we work out our thoughts. We have had projects where we have created up to twenty versions of the walkthrough, as we gather input, test out hypotheses, and work through issues. Clearly, having the walkthrough in a malleable form is important if we are to work through this process efficiently.

Implementation Review

At this point, we have the skeleton of a detailed design. Before we finalize it, though, we want to feel comfortable that it is going to work. We also want to make sure that it will be efficient to implement along several dimensions:

- How much content will it commit us to creating?
- How many extensions will it require in our software libraries?
- How tough will the user interface be to create?

So, we hold a series of reviews with different groups. The core team that has been working on the design up to this time has included interaction designers, content specialists, an interface designer, and a software engineer. Now, each steps back (and perhaps draws in other specialists who can bring fresh eyes) and looks again at the design.

These reviews each tackle two questions: (1) Will this be an effective design? and (2) How much effort will it take to create? More and more frequently, we are asking each of the functional specialists to create some sort of work plan or conceptual map to support the answer to the second question. So, a content specialist might produce a detailed table identifying how many parts of the content of different types the system might create. An interface designer might identify how many different types of screens the system calls for (and how many of those can be "taken off the shelf" from prior designs).

We count on making adjustments to the design at this stage, both to improve it and also to make reasonable cost-benefit trade-offs. For example, when we conducted this review with the ratios activity, we found out that our initial design would call for information to be passed between two different parts of the program in a way that would be quite awkward for the programmer. We then went into a round of redesign that ended up changing very little what the learner saw of the course, but affected how we implemented two widely varying parts of the course at a fundamental software engineering level, thus simplifying the programming without harming the original design.

Functional Specification

The final step of the interaction design process is to convert what has been primarily a walkthrough into an overall specification for the system. This is a job of fleshing out features that might have been paid scant attention up to now and making sure that all of the detailed options have been thought through.

As one example of the kind of thing we specify in the functional specification, we create what we call a "tutoring model." This indicates how we decide when we will proactively give feedback to the learner and how we will decide which specific piece of feedback to give. For instance, in the design of the ratios activity, we at one point confronted learners with a financial hypothesis and asked them to make a series of three choices to test it: (1) Which ratio would they like to use as a test? (2) Does the ratio confirm or deny the hypothesis? and (3) Why? We wanted to be able to coach learners when they make errors. So, to implement this interaction, we needed to specify a particular algorithm that determines what feedback to give. In this case, it was quite simple: Look at the decisions in order, stop at the first one in which there is a mistake, give a piece of tutoring that is indexed to the specific mistake the learner made at that step, and wait for the learner to redo the work. In other cases, the models can be more complex.

Beyond the tutoring models, the functional specification also outlines each of the options that are available at each step, explains how bookmarking and reporting will work, and captures other details of the lower-level functioning of the course. While we have to admit that we have yet to construct a functional specification with which we are fully happy, the idea of the functional specification has been quite useful for us, both in catching errors of omission in the design and in marking a critical juncture in the project. Up until now, an interaction designer has been proactively leading the design effort. But, at this point, other members of the team take the lead and the interaction designer recedes to the background to check on the design as it evolves and address the inevitable questions and issues that arise during implementation.

**PART
III**

e-Learning
in Action

8

Bad e-Learning: Five Examples

Let's face it. Most e-learning isn't really very good. In the rush to put training on the Web, training departments, either out of ignorance or due to cost-cutting measures, or both, have basically adopted the idea that e-learning means putting something on the Web that looks an awful lot like the training manuals that e-learning is intended to replace.

I have spent some time on the Web looking at the e-learning that is heralded as the second coming of education. Most of what I have seen fits into the following categories:

1. Read text; press button for next page
2. Read text; make choice from numbered list; receive score
3. Read question; answer; get feedback; read next question
4. Read lots of text; answer questions at end
5. Take test immediately; learn score; get feedback

If you go to the Cisco site on e-learning, for example, you get a lot of ballyhoo about how wonderful it all is and will be and then are offered one of their free e-learning courses. Unfortunately the course is remarkably consistent in its adherence to the above principles of bad e-learning.

Examples of Bad e-Learning

The following courses may or may not still be available on the Web, but you will recognize many similarities in the e-learning courses with which you are familiar. I should mention that although I'm very critical of these courses, (as I am of most current e-learning), I don't think the designers were necessarily incompetent. They were simply imitating the commonly accepted notion of what education looks like—which does not involve the way people really learn. People really learn by doing a task they care about, failing, and redoing it until they get it right.

A Leadership Training Course

The text accompanying the courses states right up front that *"The leadership decisions you'll make in the exercises may differ somewhat from your real-life circumstances, but most of the principles and ideas can easily be transferred and applied to your job."* This is actually an amazing statement. Research on transfer of learned things clearly indicates exactly the opposite. Principles and ideas learned in one domain are almost never transferred to another arena.

In the exercises, you have a simulated team, with pictures and descriptions for each—that's not bad. The intro says that the exercises focus on two types of leadership styles—task behavior and relationship behavior. It gives a chart showing how these styles fit together.

QUADRANT 1 **HIGH TASK, LOW RELATIONSHIP**	QUADRANT 2 **HIGH TASK, HIGH RELATIONSHIP**
QUADRANT 3 **LOW RELATIONSHIP, LOW TASK**	QUADRANT 4 **HIGH RELATIONSHIP, LOW TASK**

In the exercises, each of the four choices represents the style shown in the appropriate quadrant of the above chart. So the choices aren't all the options that you might have in real life, but rather representations of four different mixes of leadership styles. Not too realistic, it seems, and forced to fit this artificial model. The strategies become very vague and high level (in task sixteen I chose, *"Present the new project to the team and tell them to accept the assignment"*). Figure 8-1 shows what a choice screen looks like.

The system includes sixteen exercises, divided by week. Each exercise is a summary of a situation and choices on how to strategically act. You get points depending on what choices you make—5 points for the best choice, 2 for the second best, none for the other two.

One big problem—you get tutoring for all the choices at once. Though the directions at the beginning encourage you to read all of the tutoring, you don't get a chance to try again and see what happens if you choose something else—it tells you what's right or wrong about all of them right away. The tutoring itself isn't horrible; I've seen worse. Figure 8-2 shows what the tutoring screen looks like.

After each exercise, there's a narrative bridge telling you how the project's progressing and setting up the next choice. The flow is pretty jumpy (e.g., from exercise one to two, I went from deciding how to start the first day with the team to having to deal with an employee who's taking on too dominant a role).

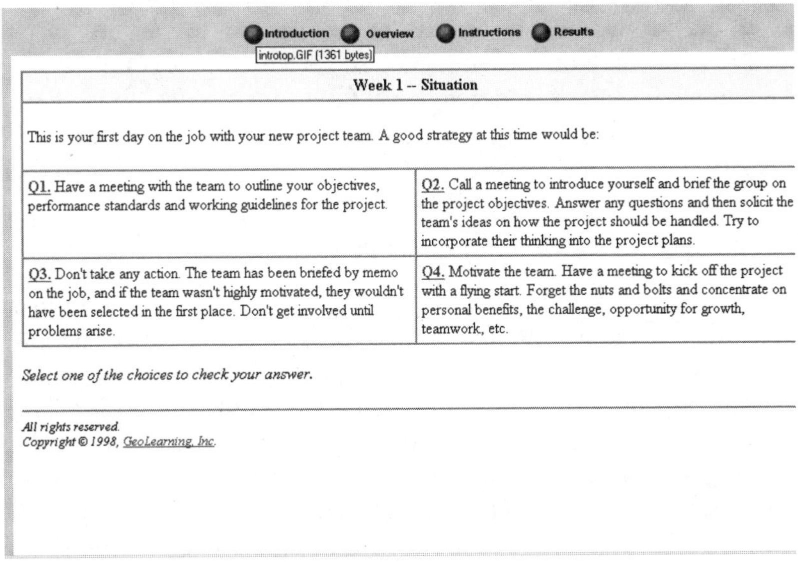

🔘 Introduction 🔘 Overview 🔘 Instructions 🔘 Results

introtop.GIF (1361 bytes)

Week 1 -- Situation

This is your first day on the job with your new project team. A good strategy at this time would be:

Q1. Have a meeting with the team to outline your objectives, performance standards and working guidelines for the project.	Q2. Call a meeting to introduce yourself and brief the group on the project objectives. Answer any questions and then solicit the team's ideas on how the project should be handled. Try to incorporate their thinking into the project plans.
Q3. Don't take any action. The team has been briefed by memo on the job, and if the team wasn't highly motivated, they wouldn't have been selected in the first place. Don't get involved until problems arise.	Q4. Motivate the team. Have a meeting to kick off the project with a flying start. Forget the nuts and bolts and concentrate on personal benefits, the challenge, opportunity for growth, teamwork, etc.

Select one of the choices to check your answer.

Figure 8-1

● Introduction ● Overview ● Instructions ● Results

Week 16 -- Evaluation
The project is reaching completion, and your boss has shared with you that he is very pleased with the overall effort and the results your team has produced. He's further indicated that he has another challenging assignment that he feels the team could handle, independent of your leadership. You feel this is the best compliment you could receive, and very much want the team to take on the project. He emphasized that it would be up to you to present the assignment to the team, and up to the team to decide whether or not to accept the challenge. You should:

Q1. Present the new project to the team and tell them to accept the assignment. This is not your best option. Even though the potential rewards of taking on the project are great, telling the team to accept the assignment is not appropriate.	Q2. Discuss the situation with the team members and "sell" them on the opportunity. Then work with the team to set objectives for the new project. Here you are trying to satisfy the needs of your boss and push for results that could benefit the organization. While your actions are noble, there are other parties involved here. You must first recognize that it is the team's decision and if, for whatever reason, their hearts are not in it, the project could fail.
Q3. Present the opportunity, but do not interfere with the decision to accept or refuse the assignment. The team has proven themselves capable, so their own personal feelings, expectations and plans must be considered the most important element in this decision. This is the strongest option. It is in the best interest of the project	Q4. Let the team decide if they want to take on the new project and then do what you can to be supportive of their decision and solidify their feelings. Let them know how you feel about the project, and if they still don't want to do it, offer to explain this to your boss. While this may sound like you are trying to help the team, your

Figure 8-2

But the main problem here is that there are no consequences for the choices you make—your decisions don't play out. You get general tutoring on why something might be a good or bad idea but no resolution to the conflict you were trying to fix. This is frustrating, doesn't drive any lessons home through results, and takes away one of the main ways people learn. Also there's no way to ask questions to explore a mistake deeper.

You do, on the other hand, get a score which tells you how you did and what kind of leader you are. Good for people who believe that multiple-choice tests are part of the high art in educational design.

A Windows 2000 Course

The courses one finds offered by e-learning companies are mind blowing. It is amazing that someone somewhere thinks people learn this way. NETg offers a course on Windows 2000, for example. In it, an audio lecture tells you about file folders and what to do with them. To advance to the next screen, you hit the fast forward button. On the screen (see Figure 8-3), it tells you, "You learned about the characteristics of files and folders used in Windows 2000" after audio told these things to you and put them in bullets on the screen.

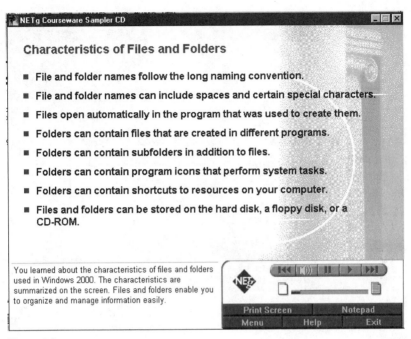

Figure 8-3

It is astonishing to me that anyone has the chutzpah to assert that after seeing a slide or hearing a lecture that the student could have learned anything at all. Learned and heard are not the same word. Bullet points are nice to read. If you think this is learning, read the bullet points above, close the book, and try to repeat them. You won't be able to do it because learning doesn't work that way.

This NETg course does claim to have "doing" and tutoring, however. This is it: In its lesson on opening files of unknown file types, it tells you to click on a particular file (synonym.ctl). If you click anywhere else, a dialog box appears telling you to click on the file. (see Figure 8-4). That is the extent of the tutoring.

After you go through many more Windows functions, all in order, you get to the assessment. Figure 8-5 shows the directions. The assessment asks you to do the tasks the system taught earlier. You do it by clicking on the correct part of the emulated screen. In the first task, I accidentally clicked randomly on the screen before I chose to hit *file*. It immediately told me what the right answer was. I should've clicked this, this, and this. There's no

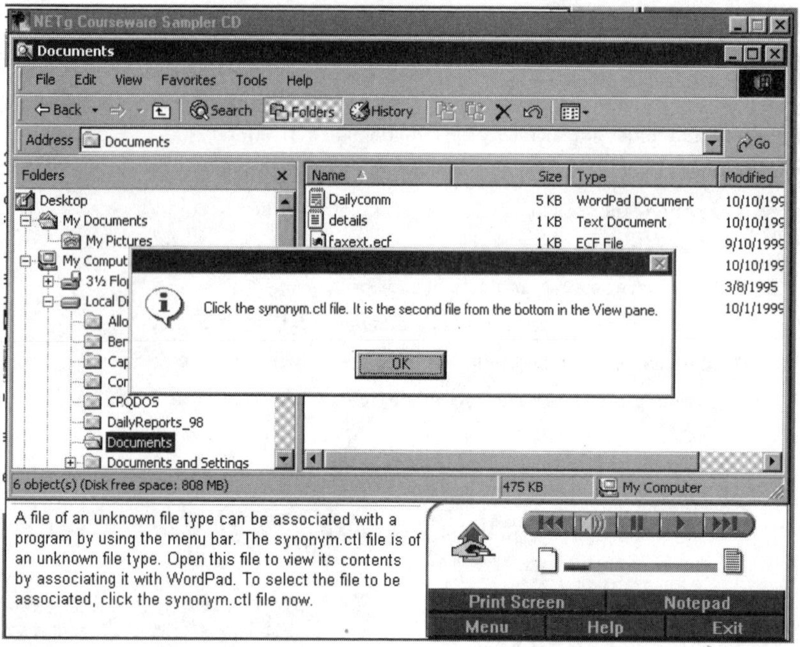

Figure 8-4

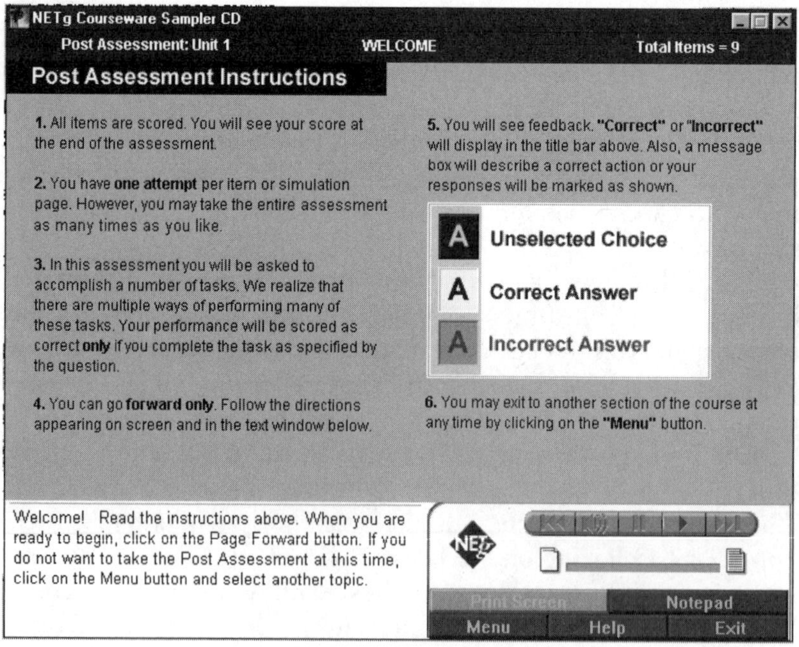

Figure 8-5

chance to go and fix your mistake. At the end you get feedback telling you which steps you got right and which you got wrong. Then you go onto the next task in the assessment. You can advance through the assessment without doing any work by clicking on page forward (the play button).

Is this learning? Not in my book. This is the pretense of learning. Do this, do that, and oh you should have done this is only of value if, when you are done, you have accomplished something you wanted to accomplish, like building a lamp or drying your clothes. Learning involves repeated action in a task, not one-shot action in a task about the task.

Now, what should they have done? If you want to teach Windows 2000, then you need Windows 2000. Then, you need to be trying to do something or be asked to do something—you need to try it, and you need to understand that when you are wrong and things don't work as you expected, why you are wrong. You need to be able to ask questions and then try again. And try again. Until it becomes second nature. Teaching means (1) suggesting a game plan, a set of tasks to try out that build upon each other and then (2) being there with help when things screw up. It's really not that hard to do it right. What the course designers did in this instance just doesn't teach anything at all.

A Proprietary Computer System Training Course

This one has long been a favorite diversion around our office. The system is intended to teach Lufthansa employees about a database called FOCUS. You're guided through the system by a talking bird. You are portrayed on-screen by an attractive woman who is a new employee—you do her work and make her decisions. At the beginning, after a long and pointless introductory montage (quite hilarious), you're brought to the main menu page shown in Figure 8-6.

The areas with writing (and some others) represent a place you can go for "learning." For all learning activities, you gain mileage points (posted near the picture on the wall) by clicking through the sections. In the recreation room, for instance, you can click on a radio to play music, learn how to make a Brazilian drink, or play a ping-pong game on which you wager mileage points (I lost). In the modules, it's so much like binder training that it even looks like it (see Figure 8-7).

Figure 8-6

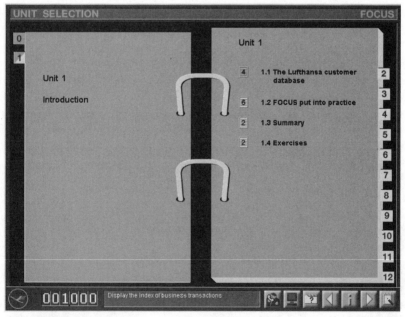

Figure 8-7

For some reason, this section gives long, detailed background about the two *previous* database systems Lufthansa used. After you poke around and read/listen to seemingly endless background stuff, you can do the exercises, which are what you'd expect. One looks like Figure 8-8. No tutoring or anything. Just answer the question and compare it to the right one. In another exercise, you drag note cards to fit with the appropriate term. A later section does have some limited emulation, but no one I know could figure out how to work it.

Now, how could this have been done *right*? My first thought is, there is no way to do this correctly. Here again, learning to use a database involves trying to use it and getting help along the way, not answering questions about it (with or without a bird.) Now, why didn't they do it that way? Because it is difficult to do. Nevertheless, one cannot substitute a lot of graphical cuteness for substance.

An Ethics Course

Mentergy has a demo of a prototype for a Bank One course on avoiding conflict of interest (i.e., when to accept and when to

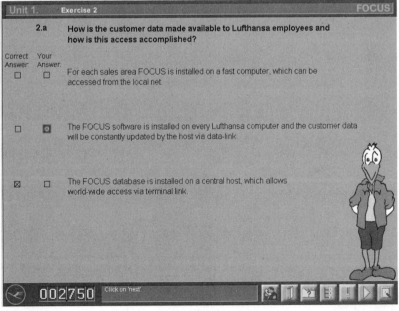

Figure 8-8

refuse stuff from clients). The graphics look good, but the learning doesn't. It starts with a lot of page-turning describing what a conflict of interest is and giving examples. There are two types of "activities" here. The first consists of a page each for "What's OK" and "What's not OK?" You click on something and it tells you why it is or isn't OK (see Figure 8-9).

In the next exercise, you have to decide which of the given scenarios are or aren't acceptable. It looks like the screen shown in Figure 8-10.

Tutoring is generic—after you submit, it says which ones were right with green checks and which were wrong with red Xs. Then there's more page-turning, this time about gifts from customers or suppliers (see Figure 8-11). The activity here is slightly better, but not much. It gives you a text scenario in which a customer named Jake offers you a gift; the system asks what you should do—say yes, say no, or ask your manager. You can get a little more info on the situation by clicking one of the gold eggs at the bottom of the screen. The right answer is, of course, to say no. There is no consequence to your decision, just tutoring.

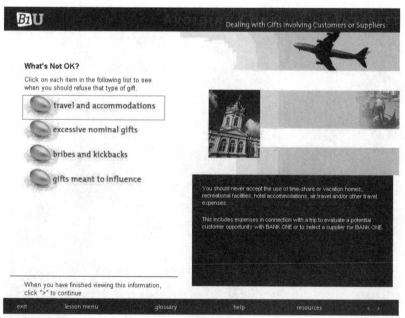

Figure 8-9

You Be the Judge

Which of these gifts is it OK to accept (assuming they are not intended to influence or reward any business decision or transaction)?

Click on each gift that you believe you should accept. If you want to change a choice, clicking again will de-select the gift.

When you have made your final decision, click "submit answers".

submit·■
answers

Click ">" to continue.

exit   lesson menu   glossary   help   resources   < >

Figure 8-10

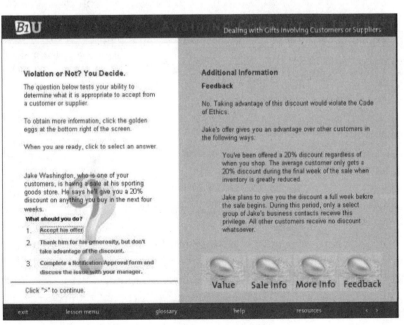

Violation or Not? You Decide.

The question below tests your ability to determine what it is appropriate to accept from a customer or supplier.

To obtain more information, click the golden eggs at the bottom right of the screen.

When you are ready, click to select an answer.

Jake Washington, who is one of your customers, is having a sale at his sporting goods store. He says he'll give you a 20% discount on anything you buy in the next four weeks.

What should you do?

1. Accept his offer
2. Thank him for his generosity, but don't take advantage of the discount.
3. Complete a Notification/Approval form and discuss the issue with your manager.

Click ">" to continue.

Additional Information

Feedback

No. Taking advantage of this discount would violate the Code of Ethics.

Jake's offer gives you an advantage over other customers in the following ways:

You've been offered a 20% discount regardless of when you shop. The average customer only gets a 20% discount during the final week of the sale when inventory is greatly reduced.

Jake plans to give you the discount a full week before the sale begins. During this period, only a select group of Jake's business contacts receive this privilege. All other customers receive no discount whatsoever.

Value   Sale Info   More Info   Feedback

exit   lesson menu   glossary   help   resources   < >

Figure 8-11

Although this course is better than many current e-learning courses and fits our common perception of what education looks like, it is highly unlikely to change employee behavior. To teach ethical rules in a way that translates into changed on-the-job behavior, you have to put the learner in ambiguous situations where there are consequences to their ethical choices.

To use another example, to teach negotiation you have to negotiate. Actually we built a negotiation course with a Harvard professor who is an expert in the subject (Roger Fisher). In this course (available from Harvard Business Publishing), you spend a lot of time negotiating. You also spend a lot of time preparing to negotiate since that is how Roger Fisher thinks you need to do things; but even then you are not listening or reading but trying to identify issues and negotiation stances. You hear from Roger Fisher when you haven't figured it out correctly. You learn by preparing, then doing.

A Legal Training Course

Here you can find a demo that is basically a law conference put online and passed off as a training resource. There are several presentations to listen to. Within each lecture, you can skip to one of many parts or topic areas (nine in the example below). When you're done listening, you can go to a page with questions to ask the speech-giver (see Figure 8-12). Notice how long and involved the questions are, and there's only six of them—probably verbatim from the ones asked at the conference.

The question in most e-learning seems to be, "How can I spend very little effort on putting what I already have on the Web?" If you add a picture or a funny animal, if you animate your response correction, or make funny sounds, it still amounts to the same thing: It is still text on-screen followed by a question and a right answer.

I had been pondering this state of affairs one day when my eyes happened to come across a women's magazine and I realized there would probably be one of those quizzes in there that tell you what kind of person you are. I found one and it reminded me so much of e-learning that I went to Cosmopolitan.com and discovered a whole bunch of them. I selected a quiz called "Do You Fall in Love Too Fast?" and proceeded to fill it out randomly. The questions and multiple-choice answers went something like this:

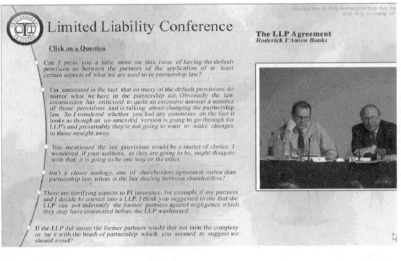

Limited Liability Conference

The LLP Agreement
Roderick I'Anson Banks

Click on a Question

Can I press you a little more on this issue of having the default provision as between the partners of the application of at least certain aspects of what we are used to in partnership law?

I'm interested in the fact that so many of the default provisions do mirror what we have in the partnership act. Obviously the law commission has criticised to quite an extensive amount a number of those provisions and is talking about changing the partnership law. So I wondered whether you had any comments on the fact it looks as though an un-amended version is going to go through for LLP's and presumably they're not going to want to make changes to those straight away.

You mentioned the tax provisions would be a matter of choice. I wondered if your auditors, as they are going to be, might disagree with that, it is going to be one way or the other.

Isn't a closer analogy, one of shareholders agreement rather than partnership law, where is the fair dealing between shareholders?

There are terrifying aspects to PI insurance, for example if my partners and I decide to convert into a LLP, I think you suggested to me that the LLP can not indemnify the former partners against negligence which they may have committed before the LLP was formed.

If the LLP did insure the former partners would that not taint the company or tar it with the brush of partnership which you seemed to suggest we should avoid?

Figure 8-12

1. You get lucky and wind up with back-to-back dates. The first one rocks, so you:

a. Go on the second but mention that your social life is super-busy right now.

b. Feel relieved. Even if the date with the next guy bombs, you'll still have an object of desire.

c. Cancel the second date—you can tell Guy Number One is your one and only.

I answered all the questions in the quiz and, as in many e-learning tests, the Web site automatically calculated my score and generated an explanatory report. According to Cosmopolitan. com, my dating personality type is called "The Sensible Seductress." The test explained, "Congratulations for being able to appreciate the fun of dating without taking every dude too seriously. You let love unfold naturally and gauge each guy by his own unique attributes instead of fooling yourself into believing every stud is your soul mate."

So, am I a sensible seductress? Well, no more or less than I know how to operate Windows 2000 or to make ethical business decisions. I fail to see the difference between most e-learning and what I can only term "M-learning" (magazine learning). The thing is, *Cosmopolitan* probably doesn't think this is learning. It does look a lot like what many e-learning vendors have to offer though. At least *Cosmo* probably thinks it is entertainment and no one will spend thousands getting *Cosmo* to do their learning designs for them.

e-Learning by Doing at Deloitte, Cutler-Hammer, and GE

The learning principles discussed in this book have resulted in training that is far more effective than the classroom-based solutions of the past. My goal in discussing more examples of e-learning by doing in this chapter is to highlight the thinking that went into designing these simulations, the obstacles that had to be overcome, and the reactions to results of e-learning from everyone from top executives to trainees. A key part of designing e-learning is telling stories. Here are some more of mine.

Sculpting Renaissance Men and Women

One organization we worked with (let's call it Company X) had a continuous need for good new supervisors. It often promotes employees from within the company to this position. The company said it wants its supervisors to be like Da Vinci's Renaissance men and women, who can do a bit of everything. This was a tall order, considering that, though these are very skilled employees with loads of technical knowledge, most had no management experience. Coming in, they didn't know how to coach employees on tasks they themselves used to excel at, how to prioritize time and issues, or how to juggle team management with their own work. Suddenly, they had to deal with numerous interruptions each day, and they had no idea how to react to their employees' requests and complaints. Because of this, newly promoted supervisors often experienced considerable job shock. They were surprised by just how challenging their new jobs actually were and overwhelmed by their new responsibilities.

Trying to better prepare its employees for life in management, the company held one- to two-week classroom sessions intended to lay out job expectations. But it was costing a great deal of money to send all the supervisors to the corporate or regional offices for the workshops. Even more disturbing, the company could only hold these sessions when enough people enrolled. Sometimes a supervisor would be on the job for six months before attending the very training that was supposed to let him or her know what life as a supervisor would be like.

Aside from these practical limitations, what was wrong with the company's supervisor training was what's wrong with most classroom training. The organization invited experts to come and give boring lectures on performance reviews, on legal reviews, and on filling out paycheck forms. These speeches were delivered in no coherent order, with no overarching goal or motivation. The new supervisors appreciated the effort, but the training was not working. They still couldn't see the forest from the trees once they got on the job.

Training a Little Bit at a Time

In response to these problems we developed a new curriculum, which included a suite of e-learning programs:

- **Getting Started.** Introduces recently promoted supervisors to their new roles, explains the resources that are available to them, and provides advice on managing transition issues
- **Day in the Life.** Gives new supervisors hands-on experience with key skills they need when they start their jobs, presenting relevant issues as they might typically arise in the course of a simulated day

- **Making Decisions.** A companion to Day in the Life that focuses on the larger skills required to successfully manage a team over an extended period of time
- **Performance Management Training.** Additional on-the-job scenarios that provide focused practice on complex skills required to manage employees' performance (e.g., coaching)

These programs are meant to be used in phases to provide a seamless transition into management, something the previous stand-up training was incapable of doing. The idea is to give supervisors a dollop of training and performance support before they start their new jobs. This first training segment gets supervisors through their first month on the job without making what the company identified as the ten most common mistakes and answers any questions they might have as the questions arise. After they survive their first month, supervisors can tackle slightly meatier training on subjects like coaching, giving performance reviews, and interviewing candidates. Once they've been on the job for, say, six months and are starting to get the hang of it, they can go through training that helps them review their strengths and weaknesses and build a game plan that maps out what they want to accomplish by the end of the year.

Underlying all these systems is a large performance support component composed of expert video clips and other resources. This addresses one key goal of the project, which was to take all the detailed minutia that trainers had lectured about and remove it from active training. The supervisors obviously weren't remembering the material; it's much more useful to them if they can easily access it four months down the road—when they actually need it.

Let's look at one of the components of the suite, a goal-based scenario system, in a little more detail.

Day in the Life

New supervisors need to learn to take charge of meetings, manage schedules, and hold conversations they probably haven't held before. So we built a simulation to give new supervisors practice in holding such conversations, including the ones they're not expecting to have.

Since it was important to make the experience as realistic as possible, we decided to organize the simulation around the framework of a daily calendar, which moves the user from one interaction to another (see Figure 9-1). The user's goal in this simulation jibes with the main real-life goal of overwhelmed new supervisor—simply to get through the day.

The scenarios are designed to cultivate trainees' coaching, interpersonal, time management, and leadership skills over a wide variety of situations. In the six full scenarios and several shorter ones that comprise Day in the Life, the user manages a team through one simulated workday. Along the way, the user tackles situations ranging from the everyday (e.g., a team meeting) to the urgent (e.g., a sexual harassment allegation). The user must make critical time management decisions by balancing scheduled meetings with unexpected situations that arise, altering the course of his or her day.

For example, a team meeting is scheduled for 11:30 a.m. But at 11:25 Peggy, a pregnant team member, drops by (see Figure 9-2). She wants to discuss options for alternative work arrangements after her baby is born.

"There's just a few things I'd like to discuss now that I'm getting closer to my delivery. It might take some time to hash out, but if you could squeeze me in, that'd be great."

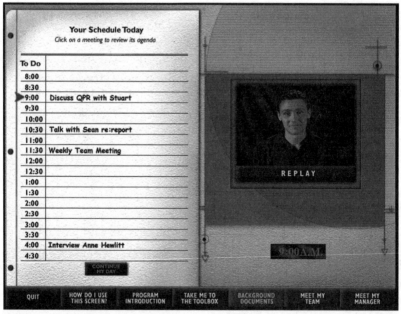

Figure 9-1

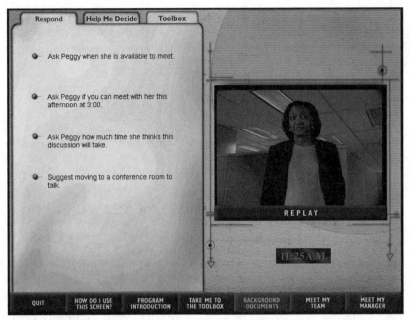

Figure 9-2

The user must decide whether to meet with her right away (and risk being late for another meeting) or somehow find time to squeeze her in later. Whatever the user chooses will impact the rest of his or her day. (In fact, the simulated day can end in any of four different ways.) For example, if the user chooses to meet immediately with the Peggy, he or she ends up twenty-five minutes late to the team meeting. Many trainees make this mistake because they are trying to be sensitive to their employees' needs; but here they do so at the expense of effective team and time management. When the user heads to the conference room to join the meeting, only two team members are still there, gossiping. When they see the user, they are full of smirks and sarcasm:

"We were worried, so we sent Sean to go look for you. Everyone else gave up on you, but *we* knew you'd show up sooner or later."

The user has to reschedule the team meeting for 3:00 p.m. which complicates the rest of the day. Later on, the user must decide whether to meet with an employee who wants to talk about career-development issues or to put the meeting off until the next day. If the user chooses to meet with her immediately, the user has to stay late in order to finish a status report that a manager unexpectedly requests. Since unplanned-for occurrences like these constantly happen in real life, good training must prepare learners to handle them. Some of the other situations the user encounters in the system include:

- An upset employee brings a potential sexual harassment issue to the user's attention.
- An employee is scheduling surgery and asks the user what paperwork he needs to fill out.
- At a meeting the team raises concerns about a new company policy regarding phone use.
- An employee is unhappy with the review the user had given him and wants to discuss it.
- The user must advise an employee who injures herself on the job.

At appropriate points throughout the simulated day, the user receives detailed feedback pointing out what skills he or she performed well and which ones need work. At any time the user can also access on-demand expert coaching to help guide his or her decisions, as well as resources in the Supervisor's Toolbox. Such intricacies are all intended to make the program as realistic and user-friendly as possible. One manager said of the simulation, "It's interesting, exciting, fun, and holds your attention." If a training program can be all these things, people will use it.

And use it they did. The company printed 1000 copies of the CD-ROM, enough, trainers figured, for a year's worth of new supervisors. But they went through seven more printings of 1000 copies each in just the first few months, not because the organization was promoting more supervisors, but because more experienced managers were asking for it, too, as word of mouth spread. "After presenting this series to other members of my department," another manager said, "Their reaction was, 'This is what e-learning is all about.'"

Lessons Learned

- Good e-learning works to decrease job shock by easing newly promoted employees into new roles while simultaneously shortening the amount of time it takes to learn the job.

- Properly built, a suite of several training programs that build upon each other in well-planned stages can give learners the training they need to do their new jobs immediately. These programs can also provide knowledge and resources to assist them as they progress in their roles, become more experienced, and face more complicated issues.
- A good e-learning system can end in a number of different ways depending on the choices the user makes.
- A good e-learning system prepares learners to deal with the unexpected.

e-Learning at Deloitte

Deloitte Consulting is blessed with an outstanding recruiting ability. Deloitte hires bright, ambitious employees who are committed to the organization. They are highly motivated; their bosses are highly motivated; their bosses' bosses are highly motivated. The firm recently underwent rapid growth, and as a result, less experienced managers, who would normally be directing smaller efforts, were now helping project partners oversee gigantic, international projects.

Deloitte's managers were no babes in the woods; they already understood the nuts and bolts of managing. They could create budgets and timelines; they could organize and mobilize team members to work together. But Deloitte felt its less-experienced managers needed more exposure to the art of management. In other words, Deloitte wanted them to gain the subtle soft skills mature managers generally develop over years of practice: aptitudes such as handling disagreements among stakeholders, avoiding scope creep, closing out projects, and using more advanced communication and diplomacy skills. So Deloitte asked us to build a flexible training program to teach managers with all different levels of skill and experience the fine art of project management.

Since the megaprojects Deloitte wanted to teach its people to learn to manage better are cumbersome and sometimes span years, we knew that making up a fictional project authentic enough for savvy managers would be tough. We decided to base the scenarios around a multiyear, global technology reengineering effort for a fictional client called Martin Prince, Inc. (MPI). In creating this fictional project, we took bits and pieces from many real-life cases culled from stories Deloitte managers told.

Mastering Project Management includes six scenarios designed around what Deloitte identified as the six major decision points in the project management process. The scenarios are:

- **Issues Management.** The user must effectively manage the resolution process for a controversial issue.
- **Stakeholder Relationship.** The user must resolve a conflict between two key stakeholders that threatens to derail the project.
- **Scope Creep.** The user must contend with a client's confusion about project scope and subsequent eagerness to increase the scope of the project.
- **Resource Transition.** The user must manage personnel changes at an upcoming phase transition.
- **User Involvement.** The user must balance client concerns and project considerations while attempting to attain user acceptance and testing.
- **Plan Management.** The user must manage a subteam's reported five-day delay.

These were narrowed down from a larger list of the key struggles managers face over the course of any large project. We chose which challenges to highlight in the system by (1) the most common mistakes managers make and (2) the screw-ups that prove most costly to the bottom line. Any of the challenges listed above could occur in any phase of a project; but to give the system a good narrative flow, we decided to place certain roadblocks in certain places.

The Jocelyn Factor

In the User Involvement scenario, the project is entering the testing and delivery phase. But MPI claims that it is understaffed and can't supply the thirty people it had earlier promised for user-acceptance testing (see Figure 9-3). In a meeting, Jocelyn, the MPI project director, says:

> **I believe Dean Wareham (MPI's HR process team leader)
> told you that we're not in a position right now to give you
> thirty people. Everyone here has been working diligently
> trying to complete other projects. If I take them off those**

projects, that work won't get done. Besides, we already gave you some of our top people about three months ago because you claimed our expertise was needed then to identify business requirements. Now you want us to do this again? I thought we hired you for your expertise, not ours! To be blunt, I find it difficult to understand why you need these full-time testers when you had the right people give you information on our business processes! Why can't the current team just do the testing?

The user's project partner notes that this is a high-priority issue that should be handled with caution: It's just as important to make MPI happy as it is to ensure good testing. The user can further research this dilemma by reviewing emails, voice mails, and project documents, or by asking a Deloitte expert questions to get perspective on the situation before making a decision. Since this is a delicate issue, and Jocelyn is testy, many trainees decide to work with her and ask how many resources she thinks she can provide. If the user chooses this option, Jocelyn replies:

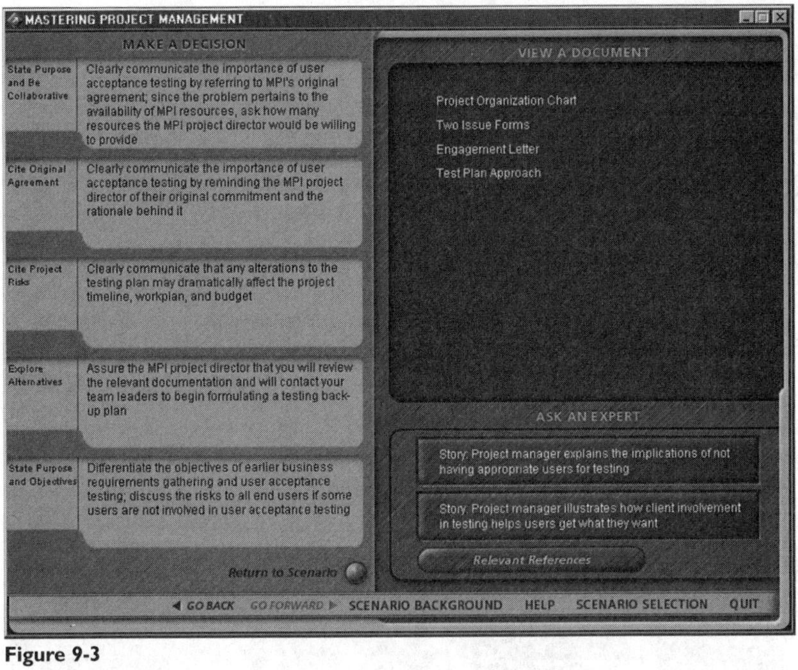

Figure 9-3

Well, I'm happy to see we can work together on this one. Since we've done so much testing already and we're short-staffed right now, I really think it's best to bypass this phase of testing. I assume you have no objection to that?

Mistake tutoring (our just-in-time interventions when someone has failed) warns the user that asking Jocelyn how many testers she is willing to supply might stall negotiations or, worse, keep Deloitte from getting the testers it needs to ensure the success of the project (see Figure 9-4). Tutoring advises that it's important to know when to be flexible and when to put your foot down. So the user tries again. Throughout the course of the scenario, the user must overcome Jocelyn's resistance to providing testing resources by clearly communicating the importance of user involvement in testing. The user also needs to use diplomacy and negotiation skills to discuss problems and potential solutions and help Jocelyn take ownership of the agreed-upon solution. These are tutored with help from experts making suggestions and asking questions every time a user considers what he wants to say next.

One sign that Mastering Project Management has been successful is evidence that the simulations have wormed their way

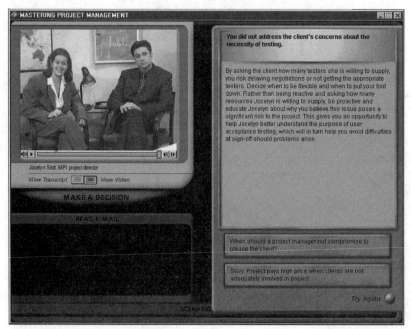

Figure 9-4

into informal corporate lore. The character of Jocelyn, who is a memorable pain throughout the learning system, has so affected Deloitte managers that they have been heard to say, "The client pulled a Jocelyn on me today." This speaks to the importance of strong, memorable characters. But it also makes clear that learning has to be rooted in emotion to have a lasting impact. Jocelyn's unnerving, in-your-face attitude really gets to the users, who are doing their best to make the simulated project go smoothly. People get emotional about this stuff in real life; training that's good enough to prepare them for real life should trigger an emotional response as well.

Keeping It Real

Like many clients, Deloitte worried that having possible choices of what to say that appear on the screen might spoon-feed its sharp-minded users. So they asked us, "Can't the trainees just type in what they want to do next?" The answer, of course, is that we probably could build a system like that, but it would take a lot more time and money than the client was willing to spend. We did the next best thing and made it so that action choices do not immediately pop up when the user reaches a new screen. By having to click on a button to access the action choices, the user must stop and think for a second about how to approach the situation on his or her own. In real life, managers can't always just pick the best from among four options presented to them. They have to be proactive.

Even better, in two of the scenarios, when the user makes a strategic-level choice, a character from within the narrative asks him or her to justify the decision. The user gets a positive or negative video response from this character based on the accuracy of both the original choice and its justification. The idea is to force the user to commit to the choices he or she makes. If learners are invested in their decisions, the expectation failure they undergo when they make the wrong choice is much greater, and lessons learned won't soon be forgotten.

The users loved Mastering Project Management. One of the managers using the system said, "I found the CD extremely helpful and well done. It was great that it was so interactive and that you used so many different mediums to share info. It's the first CBT (computer-based training) from which I have actually learned something." Deloitte told us that during the dean's speech at the new manager's school, the trainees burst into spontaneous applause when he first mentioned the program. That type of behavior rarely happens at Deloitte, and it speaks volumes about the impact the system has had on them.

Lessons Learned

- Quality e-learning can teach complex managerial skills just as easily as it can basic ones.
- Simulated tasks/projects around which e-learning systems are built should feel very much like real projects in order for users to buy into and learn from them. It's often helpful to structure simulations under the umbrella of one overarching project or problem.
- Well-written, memorable characters draw an emotional response from users that ensures they will remember the lessons that interactions with those characters impart.
- It's important to make learners think critically about and justify the decisions they make rather than simply having them choose the best of the options provided them.

e-Learning at Cutler-Hammer

Cutler-Hammer manufactures electrical power management and industrial control equipment and offers advanced engineering systems and services worldwide. Over the past few years, the business has been steeped in the midst of a large-scale transition toward new approaches and methodologies. Instead of just making and supplying products, Eaton wants to be more innovative in its approach to problem solving. Like any organizational change, this has sometimes been difficult, especially since many employees have been with the organization for a long time; the average tenure is about twelve years. Some of these employees tend to resist change, since the company has been successful in the past with the old way of doing things.

Culture Shock

This cultural shift included looking to improve the performance development skills of its 2000 managers in over twenty-five locations. Previously, little attention had been paid to teaching managers how to deal better with direct reports. Many managers are engineers promoted to the position; hence they have tons of technical expertise but often lack the soft skills needed to be really effective managers. In the absence of good training, some managers were having trouble communicating with their employees, especially on difficult, performance-related issues.

Specifically, the performance ratings managers gave were often inflated. Since employees who earned "adequate" ratings sometimes felt they were being looked down on, managers were giving higher ratings so they wouldn't feel bad. As a result, average employees received above-average ratings, thus rendering the performance review process futile. The business wanted to change this practice to a system where an "adequate" rating would once again be the norm, and employees who received such a rating wouldn't think they had done a poor job.

But there were other problems with how managers approached performance reviews. Reviews were done late over 50 percent of the time. When they were given, many managers would read employees' reviews aloud instead of engaging in useful coaching conversations. The organization wanted them to realize that a performance review is more than a listing of an employee's good and bad points. It's not something that should happen once a year, but rather a constant development dialogue with employees that includes listening to their concerns and giving ongoing coaching.

To address these issues, Cutler-Hammer instituted a two-month common review period in which all performance reviews were to be completed. Reflecting the desire to make performance development a continual process, it created the expectation that managers and employees would meet at least one other time over the course of the year to talk about how these employees were doing. It also drew up new review forms with new competencies to help encourage the change. Despite these efforts, the business knew it needed to train managers to grasp the importance of performance development and to start practicing it effectively.

Performance Development Education

A major challenge we faced in attempting to redefine the company's performance management and review training was that its managers are very busy. They don't want to take two weeks out of any business quarter to practice giving reviews. Since they don't need to use these skills every day, mastering them seems of secondary importance to their daily work. Besides, if they take a training course and then wait three months before giving their first review, they'll probably forget everything they learned anyway. This is exactly why we felt it was so important to give managers the opportunity to practice these skills in a safe, simulated environment just before giving employee reviews. With quality computer-based training, managers could use e-learning a week before the review period to begin to brush up on their skills and prepare for the reviews.

In the scenarios we built, the user plays the role of a manager who has just been transferred to a new department. He or she must review and advise three challenging employees (see Figure 9-5):

- **Marie** is a solid performer, but is reluctant to put ideas forward and shies away from taking initiative. She thinks she deserves to be promoted to a position that, it turns out, she's not ready for.
- **Luis** is an experienced employee, having been with the company for twenty years. He is very resistant to change, especially when it comes to integrating new technologies into his work.

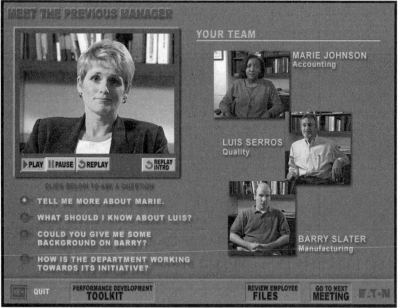

Figure 9-5

- **Barry** is fairly new to the company. He is ambitious and gets the job done right, but not without stepping on some toes. He is overly confrontational and repeatedly loses his temper with other members of the team.

The user works through a series of several meetings with each fictional employee, alternately coaching, motivating, and dealing with problems. The simulation features branching: Users can go down different paths and reach different conclusions, depending on the choices they make. This allows managers to see the downstream consequences of their actions and teaches them how to recover from their mistakes. Not all mistakes are fatal, and the simulations reflect that. In the branches, a user who has made a suboptimal choice has a second chance to either get back on track or screw up worse. The interactions end with simulated performance reviews in which the user must give each employee a rating and carry on a tough conversation. For example, in Barry's review the user must notify him that, because he has not done enough to address his interpersonal problems, he has earned a rating of 4 (on a 1 to 5 scale, with 1 the highest rating and 5 the lowest) (see Figure 9-6). Hearing this, he blows up:

This is pretty cool!

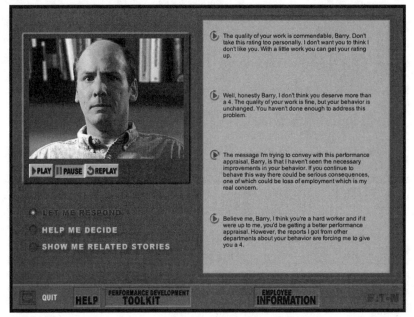

Figure 9-6

What? You know I don't deserve this! I mean, what kind of message are you trying to send here, that you'd rather have some loser around than someone who knows how to get the work done?

The user must decide the best way to communicate with Barry. Over the course of the simulation, the user gains a better understanding of the performance review process as well as valuable experience achieved through practice with coaching and setting goals.

We also developed a performance support system, called Tool Kit, which users can access when they want background information on the performance management process (see Figure 9-7). This performance support system helps managers make the transition from training to doing.

The Tool Kit offers concrete advice and stories from experts for on-the-job support. It also includes a frequently-asked-questions (FAQ) orientation and an introduction to the new performance development initiative, with videotaped leaders driving home the company's commitment to this initiative. One performance support

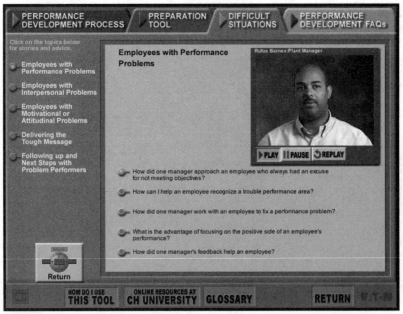

Figure 9-7

component is organized around difficult personalities and problems; users can watch experts tell stories of when they encountered these types of people and how they dealt with them. In order to accumulate good expert stories and advice, we interviewed Eaton leaders who best embody the new approach to performance development—people who have the skills, the right attitude and strategies, and best practices that other managers could benefit from hearing about. There's also a preparation tool to provide continuing support for managers as they prepare for review conversations.

Now, all managers are required to complete the program at least once, and many go back to access the Tool Kit as necessary. It is also being integrated into orientations for professional-level employees. And, in their own performance reviews, managers are now evaluated on how well they give reviews.

In a survey conducted with over a thousand employees immediately after they took the course, 94 percent said it met or exceeded their expectations (almost 75 percent said it exceeded expectations). Even more importantly, 79 percent of the users believed the course would help them do their jobs better. After the review cycle, the business collected more data from a smaller group of those who had taken the training and found that, even five months later, both managers and employees alike still felt that the training exceeded their expectations. As for the reviews themselves, 75 percent were completed on time in 2000, up from 50 percent the year before. The ratings were better distributed, and employees felt their managers were more prepared for their reviews.

Cutler-Hammer Selling

The success of Performance Development Education (PDE) led Cutler-Hammer to ask for our help with another challenge training sales engineers (SEs) in an evolving sales environment. SEs are the front line of the sales force, working with distributors to sell mechanical components to a variety of different customers. In the past, they could just rely on having the best technical product, and people would want it. But no longer could SEs just sell parts; if they wanted to keep up, they had to sell solutions and long-term business relationships. Such a fundamental shift could be difficult to swallow. Salespeople are tough enough to train as it is. But these SEs aren't your regular street peddlers. They have technical degrees and specialized knowledge.

Having already bought into our training approach from the success of the PDE project, Cutler-Hammer asked us to create an e-learning system for its sales force. Since there was no specific training time to be set aside for going through these simulations, SEs had to fit it in their spare time. So it was extremely important to deploy the system in a way that ensured they could use it at home, on an airplane, in a hotel room, or wherever they got the chance. It was also important that the system have video to realistically simulate the complicated sales interactions and meetings that SEs take part in.

We started by having our e-learning designers don overalls and hiking boots and go on a dig with an SE to understand how commercial contractors do their jobs. Then they went to a plastics plant with industrial engineers to understand their perspectives. They had in-person experiences with each business segment to gather stories and get the language down. Because the system was to include challenging technical content, we had to learn how to talk the talk.

The other thing we were trying to do, of course, was to identify mistakes that experienced SEs were making, especially the ones they didn't know they were making. This was important because, if the mistakes were too obvious, the audience would immediately tune out the training. Many of the errors we uncovered had to do with being too eager to close a deal, concentrating on getting the signature on the contract instead of developing solutions and relationships. This is a mistake that had been reinforced over time by the existing sales culture.

The simulations we built centered around three different phases of the selling process:

1. **Conduct Needs Assessment.** The user meets with a customer to gather information in order to put together a successful sales proposal.
2. **Develop Proposal.** The user consults with a variety of internal resources and develops the sales proposal best suited to the customer.
3. **Sell the Proposal.** The user submits the proposal to the customer and must negotiate the sale, dealing with complaints and questions and consulting back-up support he or she has brought along.

Let's take a look at the how we created scenarios for these three phases. In scenario one, the user meets with a representative of Ashland Paper, who is planning an expansion and needs to purchase the distribution equipment to support this upgrade. The user conducts a needs analysis interview with Ashland Project Manager Matt Booth. In this simulated meeting the user determines that (1) space is a major concern, (2) meeting tight time constraints is important, and (3) the mill already uses a lot of equipment from Cube 3 (a competitor) but is unhappy with Cube 3's new designs.

In the second scenario, the user can consult with several people and resources before crafting a proposed solution for Ashland Paper. The user may review needs analysis notes and sales planners, or ask questions of several resources from both the supplier and the customer about the requirements of the job, time and space constraints, and so on. The user works through the plans and specs, and chooses a preliminary design from among four potential proposals. The user must then justify his or her decision by providing reasoning for the recommendation (see Figure 9-8). When the user submits his or her choice and reasoning, the simulation plays a video showing how Ashland Paper might respond

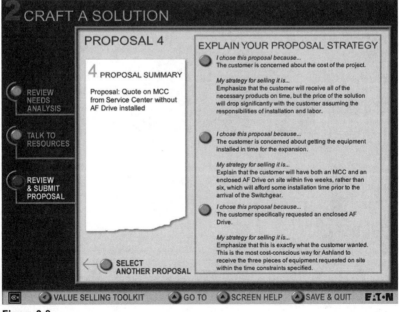

Figure 9-8

to the user's chosen proposal a week later at the sales presentation. The system then gives tutoring on what happened, why it happened, and what the user should have done differently, along with video clips of relevant expert advice.

In the third scenario, the user brings the proposed solution to a meeting at Ashland Paper. The user explains the details and benefits of the proposal. Ashland Paper is impressed with the way the Cutler-Hammer solution manages both the tight space constraints and the tight deadline, but it is not pleased with its cost estimate (see Figure 9-9). At one point, Juan Hidalgo, purchasing agent for Ashland Paper, says:

> **Cube 3 cannot meet the deadline as it were. But the cost discrepancy between your solution and theirs is surprising. You're quite a bit higher than what they quoted us.**

The user can respond in one of three ways: (1) explain that Matt insisted delivery requirements were not negotiable for this project, (2) offer to match Cube 3's price for the project, or (3) offer Ashland an extended warranty for free to make the Cutler-

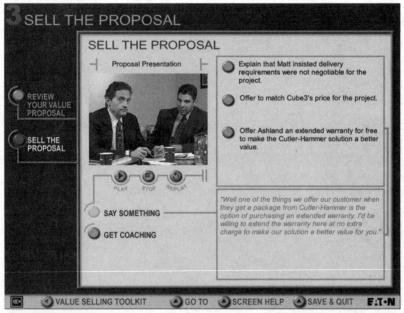

Figure 9-9

Hammer solution a better value. If the user chooses to match Cube 3's price, the system responds with a "what might happen" phone call in which an equipment provider says there's no way she can send the equipment in time for such a low price. If the user offers a free warranty, another such phone call chastises the user for offering a free warranty without proper authorization. This kind of consequence-based tutoring is a big advantage of e-learning—employees can see and learn from the results of their mistakes in a safe environment where they won't actually lose an account or get fired. Instead, they'll remember what not to do so that they can avoid suffering these consequences in real life.

Lessons Learned

- Training is only effective if learners can access and benefit from it exactly when they need it, not months earlier or later.
- As long as the organization has experts in a desired behavior, e-learning can help bring about and reinforce organizational and cultural change by showing learners the consequences of changing or not changing the way they do business.
- To create quality e-learning, it's important to complete in-person research on the training audience's everyday work in order to gather stories, language, common mistakes, and details that can be used to make the simulations realistic.
- Showing learners the downstream consequences of their mistakes helps drive home the lessons behind those mistakes and helps ensure that they don't make the same mistakes in the real world.

e-Learning at GE Capital

GE Capital has twenty-eight diverse and rapidly growing businesses that constantly hire thousands of new employees, from high-level executives to lower-level (a.k.a. nonexempt) employees, at locations scattered across six continents. GEC was looking for a way to standardize its new hire orientation in order to give all new employees similar access to high-quality training that would portray a real sense of what the organization is all about. GEC had previously delivered its new hire orientation through a series of workshops, mostly via dull PowerPoint presentations. Over time it became all too apparent that this was not a good way to deliver compelling training to such a large, extremely diverse global audience.

Showing New Hires What It's All About

What sets the training system we built for GEC apart from other new-hire orientations is that it places emphasis on doing instead of just knowing. Most new-hire programs simply dump a trash heap of information atop the new hire, usually in a deluge of manuals and lectures. We, on the other hand, approached the material GEC wanted to teach by asking questions like, "What does it mean to *do* strategy? To *do* values? To *do* structure?" After extensive interviews with GEC experts, we identified ways to turn GEC's learning goals into doing activities. For instance, in the GE Values module, new hires learn to use these values by advising colleagues about tough decisions and justifying those decisions in terms of values. Instead of some vague lecture on the importance of values, trainees are faced with tough decisions calling those values into play. Trainees don't just learn GEC values in an abstract sense; they *apply* the values in simulated situations that mimic daily life at GEC. The system actually modifies employee behavior by giving the user simulated experience in a real-world context.

Forging learn-by-doing activities out of new hire orientation wasn't as tortuous as you might think. Simply put, if the material is of some inherent real-life use to people, they can learn it by practicing it. The biggest challenge we faced was finding a way to make it a useful tool for so many different levels of employees in so many different divisions of the company. The team had to walk a tightrope to make a mixture of interactions that would be both challenging and relevant for everyone.

For example, in one scenario the user plays the role of a customer service representative trying to figure out if he or she should speak to management about an automated call response system. In another scenario the user acts as a high-level executive faced with a decision on whether or not to move quickly into an emerging market.

A Closer Look

The new hire orientation system we created for GEC consists of five separate modules. What follows are two of them.

The GE Values

The user learns about nine GE values and their relevance to decision making by applying these values to day-to-day experiences. In one scenario, for instance, the user runs into Jane O'Conner, a new GEC administrative assistant overwhelmed by her workload (see Figure 9-10). A video shows Jane lugging a cart of boxes into an elevator. Exhausted, she turns to the camera and says:

> I've got so much work to do, and this is only the first load of boxes. Oh, I'm sorry; I didn't introduce myself. I'm Jane. I was just hired as an administrative assistant here at GE Capital. Well, maybe you can give me some advice about what to do. My boss manages construction projects. We are so busy! We've got projects in places I haven't even heard of. As if I already didn't have enough work, now I've got executives coming to me with work that has nothing to do with the projects I'm already on. I've been thinking of ways we could maybe better cope with the workload. But I'm afraid if I suggest something, it'll look like I'm complaining, not willing to work hard. What do you think I should do?

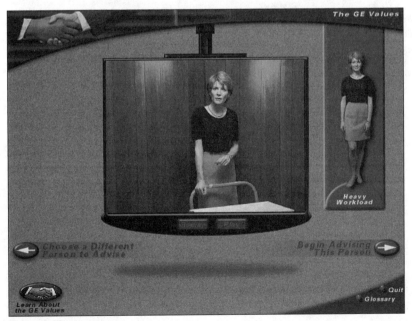

Figure 9-10

The user must advise Jane by approaching the problem in terms of GE Values. To arrive at a decision, the user first listens to four "Value Advocates," each of whom gives a short speech on the importance of a particular GE value (see Figure 9-11).

For additional help, the user can also learn more about GE values from expert video clips, or view notes that have been compiled from resources he or she has previously accessed. The user then chooses to tell Jane whether she should (1) prioritize all of the tasks in order of importance and tackle the workload one task at a time, (2) recommend outsourcing some of the work to another company so that everything gets done and gets done right, or (3) recommend that the administrative staff finish individual work before the deadline and then divvy up the remaining work.

Once the user chooses which advice to give Jane, he or she selects the GE Values that he or she thought about when making the decision, and indicates whether each value supports, conflicts with, both supports and conflicts with, or isn't relevant to the advice. The user then types in a brief explanation of how the value justifies the advice. Just like in real life, values sometimes conflict, and the user must make trade-offs or compromises. The user gets

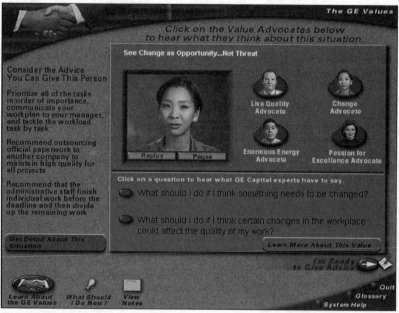

Figure 9-11

feedback on the values and justifications before submitting the advice to Jane.

There are no wrong answers in these scenarios. The system simply shows the results of the user's advice three months down the road via video clips of Jane explaining what happened as a result of the advice the user gave. Each choice carries with it certain positive and negative results. For example, if the user recommends she prioritize the work and tackle it task by task, Jane doesn't get all the work done on time but finishes the most important work, which pleases both the client and her boss. If, on the other hand, the user tells Jane to recommend that the administrative staff do individual work first, she finishes her work and her manager is impressed with its quality; she feels bad, however, that another administrative aid couldn't get a crucial year-end status report to the client on time because she had so much work to do. The user can also compare the advice and reasoning he or she provided to the advice a GEC employee who is experienced with GE values would give Jane.

Integrity and Compliance Awareness

Compliance is a particularly challenging issue to teach through simulations because, if not done right, people can fake their way through. If he knows the e-learning course covers sexual harassment, even the biggest pig in the world will be on guard and know not to pat the simulated secretary on the behind. To leapfrog this pitfall, we created a new design architecture called Observe and Critique. In these simulations, the user encounters three people who are potentially violating GE's integrity and compliance policies. The user watches a video of these people behaving in a certain way and must assess their actions. The user has to identify if those people made mistakes, which policies (if any) they violated, and why. The system provides access to experts, feedback, and coaching for mistakes. The characters in these scenarios don't do things that are explicitly right or wrong; they wander through the gray areas of tough issues. We purposely scripted situations that seem wrong but aren't or vice versa. This increases expectation failure, and the memories it drives home, when the user makes a wrong choice.

Satisfying Results

The system has been a stunning success at GEC—new hires feel better prepared and have increased job satisfaction. This in turn allows the organization to better attract, retain, and develop talented employees. "I'm really impressed with how successfully new hires are making the transition from 'recruits with potential' to 'talented employees,'" said Mike Markovits, manager of the Center for Learning and Organizational Excellence at GEC. The businesses within GE have been clamoring for the system, and we have since translated it into several languages.

Lessons Learned

- Employees learn about their organization's values by applying those values (in real or simulated situations), not by reading about them.
- New-hire orientation can and should be presented through learning-by-doing activities.
- Students can learn valuable and complex lessons from simulations in which there are no clear-cut right and wrong answers, but rather detailed and realistic long-term consequences that play out based on the decisions they make.

Conclusion

These are just some of the simulations we have built for companies. Each of these companies has begun to take e-learning very seriously. Typically after working with us they begin to understand what can be done, and they get excited about doing more. Often they try to do this on their own. The push to faster, cheaper e-learning often sacrifices quality for quantity. Can big companies do this on their own? Sure, if they understand what they are doing. The learning theory that drives all this work allows a designer to conceptualize the world through the eyes of the learner. A learner-centered design can be done by anyone who really appreciates what learning looks like in actual people. One needs to resist the natural desire to tell and replace telling by *enabling to do*. That kind of transformation is nontrivial. It requires one to take a fresh look at each training situation and figure out how to turn passive into active.

Designing e-Learning for Frontline Hourly Employees: Stories from First Union and GE Card Services

The last chapter described a few projects that worked for organizations wanting to teach relatively sophisticated skills to bright, college-educated employees eager to do well in their chosen careers. Other organizations, however, are more concerned about another group of workers and skills. These firms want to teach "people" skills to the employee who may never have gone to college. They want to train the customer service technician, waitress, store clerk, and anyone else who interacts with the public; the companies want to train this employee to deal with people empathically, knowledgeably, and innovatively.

Recall some recent interactions with customer service representatives—a hotel reservations clerk, a rental car clerk, your doctor's receptionist, a retail person, or a credit card or bank-by-phone rep. The odds are that you've had some frustrating, unpleasant interactions. Perhaps you wanted to get some information but were treated like you were asking for the combination to the corporate safe. Or you came away from an interaction feeling like the other person had about as much warmth and personality as a piece of lint.

First Union and GE Employees Are Naturally Smart (and So Are Yours)

First Union and GE don't hire Harvard MBAs (we'll get to them later) to staff their call centers. But the people these organizations hire are by no means dumb. Some of these employees, however, didn't do well in school. The problem may have been that they grew up in environments that made it difficult for them to concentrate in class; they were distracted by poverty, hunger, gangs, or the general boredom and irrelevance of the high school curriculum. Whatever the reason for their poor or average academic achievement, the vast majority of these people are intelligent.

By *intelligent*, I mean that such holders of "low-level" jobs do know how to perform complex tasks. These people have mastered an astonishing variety of skills, from driving a car to ordering food in a restaurant, to speaking English (and if you think learning English is easy, try teaching it to a computer). Such adults, then, are perfectly capable of acquiring and using the people skills necessary to establish good relationships with customers. They won't learn these skills, however, if the training *tells* them how to establish these relationships. Many of these people aren't good at doing what they're told; that's why they may have had problems in school. If, however, training puts them in scenarios where they can *do* without being told, they'll be much more likely to learn. Put them in simulated situations where they can fail in private and where they're motivated to acquire skills, and they'll pick things up fast.

But what if the people are dumb? Say that a certain percentage of people who are hired for customer service jobs are slow to learn, easily distracted, or burdened with some type of learning disability. Even then, these employees can acquire key customer service skills if they're allowed to practice them—because of the script-based nature of thinking. Why does almost everyone know how to get served quickly in a restaurant? Because they've been through that script time and again—they've practiced it to the point that they've mastered the skills involved. If training puts people through a script repeatedly (in ways that foster learning) instead of simply telling them how things are done, such hands-on practice will lead to mastery instead of misery.

Most training does the opposite, especially when the trainees aren't college graduates or the jobs are entry-level customer service positions. The training programs attempt to teach trainees to memorize and follow specific principles and rules: "Here are the ten steps to follow when a customer complains. . . ." Is it any wonder that so many customer service representatives act like robots? Certainly it's important for these employees to understand what the company's principles are and what policies they should follow. Rules are fine; following them with mindless obedience is what is so shortsighted.

Before describing First Union's and GE's call center customer service training, I can't resist making one more point related to the smart people/dumb people issue. Some smart people may be able to understand an abstract explanation and translate it into appropriate behavior some of the time. In other words, you could tell Albert Einstein how to program a VCR, and he might be able to do it right the first time without the benefit of repeated attempts. Or maybe he couldn't. A dumb person probably couldn't do it. On the other hand, many smart people can't do this trick of translating abstract explanations into corresponding behavior. Try giving a straight A high school student a list of twenty rules about how to drive a car and see how long it takes before he crashes into a tree. If the written instruction approach doesn't work well with smart people, why use it with dumb people? It makes more sense to use an approach that works no matter what the learner's level of schooling or intelligence.

Call Center Training

Working in a call center is no easy job. The pay isn't great; the work can be difficult, stressful, and thankless. Depending on what type of call center they work in, customer service reps have to know all about the products their organization offers, how to enroll customers in different services, specific customer service protocols, general courtesy and people skills, computer systems, troubleshooting, and often much more. Call centers are strict environments that require their employees to say and do things in specific, precise ways; they have to in order to ensure a standard of quality service. So, if employees don't greet customers in exactly the way they have been told to, their supervisors will reprimand them. Call centers extensively track their employees' activity—they calculate calls taken per hour and minutes spent on each call, all in the name of efficiency. Employees are encouraged to talk and type simultaneously to eliminate wasted time so that they can get to the next incoming call quickly. The goal is to eliminate the customer's wait time, because, as the cliché goes, time is money.

Most call center employees have little or no college education. Many are women going back to work after raising kids or college students or high-school grads working their first "real" jobs. With this kind of audience, it's more important than ever to avoid the pitfalls of overly conceptual training. This, of course, is a trap most call centers (and, to be fair, most other organizations as well) fall into. In these training environments, no one really learns anything. How could they? Having never practiced what they actually have to do on the job, service reps struggle mightily once they are forced to start thinking for themselves while taking live calls.

This vague, ambiguous approach to training is especially galling when you consider the differences between call center training and the training we looked at in the previous chapter. Call center content is much more rigid and procedure-based than the purely soft-skills content of managing or selling. In call centers, there are well-defined skills and protocols to be taught. There is a process. And there's nothing learning by doing teaches better than the real-world application of a process. So the very nature of call center work—with its multiple job components that must be performed at the same time—cries out for a learning-by-doing approach to training. Preparing employees for the whole job at once—by putting learning into the context of solving a customer's problem instead of memorizing computer screens—can vastly improve the quality of call center employees' work, not to mention the quality of their working lives.

Why Curriculum Redesign?

As I've mentioned, there's a huge amount of things call center employees must do and know, including computer systems, customer service, compliance, products, and procedures. Because of the complexity of the job, call center trainees sometimes need more than just simulations to be trained properly. Sure, e-learning is the best way to teach the most important skills trainees need to learn. But many trainees need to practice actually talking on the phone, and current simulation technology doesn't prepare them for that. Also, it would be prohibitively expensive to create e-learning solutions for every single skill that call center employees need to learn. Sometimes the right thing to do is to overhaul the call centers' existing training programs and create learn-by-doing curriculums that combine e-learning with other, non–e-learning activities. A few such activities are:

- **Classroom call monitoring.** As a group, students listen to live calls in the classroom and discuss issues with the trainer.
- **Shadowing.** Students observe experienced employees taking live calls and record or discuss their experiences.
- **System screen slide show.** Students watch an animation of different system screens and processes as a way to introduce system functionality at the start of the simulation modules. They can include a voice-over guide and/or text-based frequently asked questions (FAQs).
- **Screen shots with questions.** These exercises are designed to teach students how to interpret different screens on various computer systems.
- **Facilitated role play.** The trainer and students simulate calls, with the trainer playing the role of customer. Students have the opportunity to verbalize responses in a training environment.
- **Staged calls.** These are calls made by the quality assurance team and/or facilitators to introduce students to live call-taking in a safe environment.
- **Buddy banking.** Students take live calls, paired with an experienced employee.
- **Discussion/debrief.** The trainer leads discussions and answers questions. Debriefs are held after sessions of live call taking or call observation.
- **Call taking.** And finally, students tackle solo live-call taking.

We often do curriculum redesigns for call centers because (1) the complicated, integrated style of these jobs requires learn-by-doing training that goes beyond simulations, and we can help with that; and (2) we can save organizations money by cutting time out of their existing training curriculums in ways that we might not be able to with, say, a selling or coaching curriculum. So let's take a look at a couple of call center curriculum redesigns we have completed, with an eye on results.

Curriculum at First Union

First Union Direct created the "Future Banking Initiative" to provide its customers with more banking options and to encourage them to start doing more banking by phone. As a result, the volume of calls received by customer service call centers, not to mention the complexity of customer questions and requests, increased dramatically. To deal with this sudden influx of new calls, First Union had to hire and/or retrain 3000 professional service representatives (PSRs). Faced with a massive training effort, First Union needed to find a way to make it faster, cheaper, and more effective than previous training.

The classroom training that had been in place was long, boring, and provided little opportunity for PSRs to develop skills in the context of the real-world working environment they were thrown into after training. Training was presented mostly through teach-through-telling lectures organized around 80 of a possible 150 different call procedures. Some of these procedures are used as rarely as my good china. First Union was trying to cram too much nonvital information and procedure into training.

The main problem, though, was that new hires were learning in separate curriculum segments about activities they would have to do simultaneously once they started taking live calls. For instance, they might hear some lectures on customer service, then on computer systems, then on compliance and legal issues. But when they started on the floor, they had to summon up their knowledge and skills on all these issues at once, while still focusing on the customers' requests. As a result, even after six weeks of training, new hires starting their jobs felt overwhelmed and underprepared. With no real-world context for the information they had been told, they were experiencing significant job shock. Worse, customer service was suffering and in turn hurting business.

So First Union came to us with the hope that we could help them develop more self-reliant PSRs, employees who would feel comfortable and confident from the minute they started taking live calls. Specifically, First Union wanted its PSRs to learn how to do the following things well:

- Effectively use First Union's computer system (called Einstein)
- Demonstrate general customer service skills
- Perform the appropriate procedure for the call type
- Expedite a call

To save money and ensure good customer service, First Union also wanted to reduce training time if possible and provide consistent training across all locations. There is a major obstacle, though, implicit in shortening any call center training: In banking (also with credit card centers, as you'll see when I discuss GE Capital) there's lots of things that trainees are legally required to hear, regardless of their educational value. It's sometimes hard to significantly cut training time because of all the things trainers have to say and trainees have to hear. So it's not always as easy as cutting loose the previous training's dead weight. Curriculum designers have to find clever, innovative ways to reduce training time.

Making Job Training More Like the Job

We first looked for a central approach or theme on which to base the training curriculum. The old way First Union trained PSRs was by walking through Einstein screen by screen and giving, "Here's what you can do on this screen" lectures. We thought it would be better to teach customer service, the computer system, procedures, and compliance all together. This makes sense because, as I've mentioned, PSRs have to fuse these skills once they start taking live calls. In real life, they do all of these things at once, whether they're conscious of it or not.

One of the goals of training should be to give new hires a wide but accurate view of what their working world is going to be like. That way, they might quit if they can't handle it or don't like it. This is fine. If they do quit, they'll quit right away because they've been exposed to the true characteristics of the job. They won't wait it out and quit after you've paid for four weeks of training for them. And those who do stick around won't quit once they get to the floor because they'll know what to expect from the job and will most likely perform well.

So we started looking into ways to train around the different types of calls that reps get, because similar call types require similar processes and activities. That way, after going through simulations and stand-up training, trainees would associate the different computer screens (and when and how to access them) with call types and customer requests instead of trying to memorize the function of each screen.

The team discovered it could logically break all customer service calls into five critical call types: handling general inquiries, handling product inquiries, changing accounting information, moving money, and addressing perceived problems. This categorization could then be applied to teach PSRs how to execute the procedures they needed to do their jobs well. The curriculum we created, called Service Interactive, converted much of the content previously covered in tedious, ineffective lectures to computer-based simulation, role-play, and hands-on experiences.

By breaking the types of calls received into different groups, and training around those groups, trainees can start taking a significant amount of live calls by the end of the first week. If the first call group constitutes a large volume of calls, trainees can be taking about 40 percent of all live calls after the first week. And aren't these organizations hiring new people because they need help on the floor? They might as well use them as soon as possible. And when trainees learn the next call group, they can begin taking even more calls.

The idea at work here is to start with the easiest call types (ideally, these will also comprise a high percentage of total calls) and then move onto more difficult calls. The first group of calls, for instance, general inquiries, is relatively manageable for new trainees to handle. Since trainees are learning this content in a larger context that includes other things like customer service, procedures, and the computer system, even the most basic call group is hard enough for starters. But, when trainees see that they can in fact handle these calls, they gain confidence and, with that confidence, motivation to learn more.

How e-Learning Fits In

The e-learning portion of the training curriculum allows trainees to practice skills they learn in the classroom portion of training. The system centers around the five call groups, with two to three scenarios dealing with each call type (see Figure 10-1). In each scenario, the learner plays the role of a PSR, the goal being to handle all simulated callers' requests quickly, accurately, and professionally.

Figure 10-1

The simulations closely mimic the actual Einstein screens the PSR will use on the job. As the user listens to a simulated call from a customer, he or she can type in the customer's account number, which brings up a screen with the customer's name, address, social security number, and so on—just like in Einstein (see Figure 10-2). This emulation makes training realistic and helps reduce job shock once the learners start taking live calls and actively use the system.

In the scenario entitled "Blame Game," for example, the user services a customer with a refund request, which falls under the addressing perceived problems call type. The user must first appropriately greet the customer, Granville Wennington, and verify his information. Mr. Wennington is angry because a check he wrote posted incorrectly. He says:

> Well, finally, someone offers me service. Look, I wrote a
> check last week for $5.25 to my barber, OK? But,
> according to the statement I just got in the mail, the
> check wound up posting for $15.25. Now, I've been going
> to Harry's House of Hair for twenty years; and in those
> twenty years the price of a haircut has never changed, not

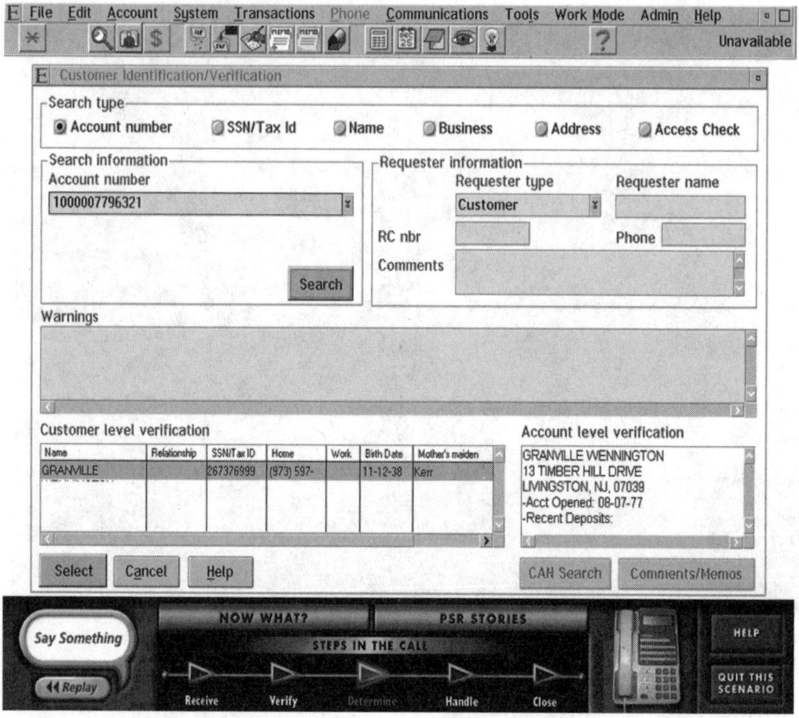

Figure 10-2

once. If there's one thing I know it's that Harry charges
$5.25 per cut. So I know that you took some of my money
from me. I've had just about enough of this bank. You
know, I'm a longtime customer, and I'm disappointed with
the service I've received, and I want my refund right now.

Mr. Wennington wants a refund, and justifiably so. Dealing
with difficult customers like this one is important, because, yes,
people do get this mad at call center reps in real life (ever found
yourself in Mr. Wennington's shoes?). If training does not prepare
them for such abuse, PSRs will be shocked and frightened when
such abuse is directed at them, and they won't know how to react.

To effectively complete this scenario, the user must

- Demonstrate the ability to use Einstein
- Follow appropriate First Union procedures
- Handle the call in a confident, positive manner

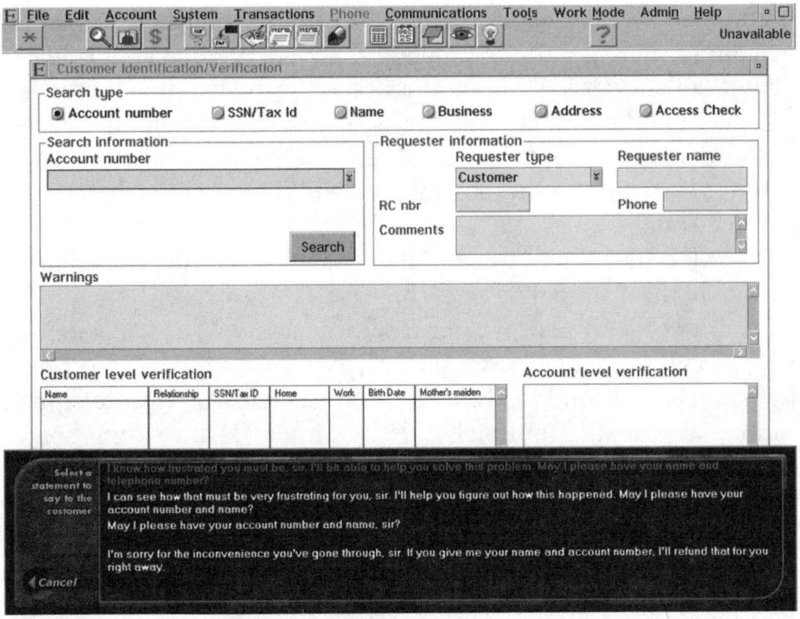

Figure 10-3

- Demonstrate the ability to solve Mr. Wennington's problem quickly and effectively
- Empathize with Mr. Wennington's negative complaints and demeanor

At any time during the scenario, the user can take advantage of several important features. The Say Something button leads to choices about how to respond verbally to the customer (see Figure 10-3). By hitting PSR Stories, the user can access relevant video stories from expert PSRs. The user can click on Now What if he or she is not sure what to do next. When the user makes a mistake, an animated menu pops up from the bottom of the screen to offer coaching and advice. The system also offers help, a progress bar, and a picture of a phone the user can click to access phone options, such as hold or conferencing with a supervisor.

How It All Fits Together

Getting the e-learning and stand-up training to work together wasn't hard, because even the stand-up training we created was interactive. It included activities like the ones I listed earlier—including listening to sample calls and then debriefing about them, talking collaboratively about the best ways to handle situations, role-plays, and more. In fact, this is one of the reasons that every last bit of content doesn't have to be included in the training documents. If it's important and relevant, it'll come up in discussion with the trainer.

In order for trainees to get the most out of such discussions, it's preferable that internal people who have experience with the products and company culture run training sessions, as opposed to professional trainers who might only be experts at reading training manuals out loud. If, however, the facilitator *is* a professional trainer, we usually approach this by either (1) providing some "train the trainer" material to familiarize the trainer with the activities to be performed, as well as the basics of learning theory; or (2) creating more-detailed training documents that can support trainers who lack true content knowledge. Such documents, though, wind up being more time consuming and expensive for the client.

Results

The simulations and the new curriculum we created for First Union Direct, used with over 3000 new hires annually, have been wildly successful, with immediate and measurable results. Training time was cut from six weeks to five, a 15 percent reduction that translates to savings of $1.25 million a year. Giving trainees the opportunity to practice taking calls early often accelerated the learning process and improved their on-the-job performance when they started. Incredibly, trainees using the new course made 40 percent fewer errors than other new hires and 20 percent fewer errors than even experienced PSRs. This reduction in errors saved First Union an additional $3.4 million a year. Just as impressive, Service Interactive PSRs transferred 20 percent more calls to sales. This increase in PSR revenue credits added up to an additional $1.4 million in sales, not to mention the significant savings resulting from increased customer retention and decreased employee turnover. So this curriculum design saved and earned First Union money in a big way.

Qualitative feedback from First Union has been equally glowing. Since instating the new curriculum, First Union Direct managers report less job shock and lower attrition rates. In the pilot test, not one trainee dropped out after hitting the floor. Even the trainers have reported feeling energized and reinvigorated since the training has become more engaging. One training director noted, "The new curriculum provides more hands-on training and is better at getting new PSRs prepared for actually answering the phones [which is their primary job function]. The old curriculum was better at getting PSRs prepared for the [multiple-choice] tests."

Lessons Learned

Complex tasks

- Learning by doing is especially useful in situations where employees need to complete multiple tasks at once.
- Stand-up training within a curriculum should be interactive, too.
- All good training should give learners a wide, accurate view of what the job will actually be like—both the good and the bad.
- E-learning that seeks to train learners on computer systems should emulate those systems as closely as possible.

Curriculum Design at GE Card Services

Customer service representatives (CSRs) at GE Card Services (GECS) handle inquiries from customers who use private label credit cards (such as those issued by large retailers like Home Depot, QVC, and Disney). New hires are placed into one of two divisions: Reps in the Customer Service division deal with inbound calls from credit card users with questions and requests while reps in the Collections division place outbound calls to customers about their accounts.

GECS's existing new hire training consisted of a four- to six-week long, instructor-led course focusing mainly on GECS's computer system. Trainees also learned about the four main skills GECS feels are needed to make a call successful: welcoming, understanding, helping, and keeping. CSRs are rated on their ability to perform these skills. GECS managers were unhappy because new hires were not reaching minimum performance standards quickly enough. So they asked us to redesign one-third of the stand-up curriculum and to develop a multimedia training system. The hope was that we could make the training both faster and more effective.

How We Made GECS's Training Work

Borrowing from experience gained in redesigning First Union Direct's curriculum, our approach was to once again align the training experience more closely with the actual job experience by using more real-life activities in training. We also designed the curriculum to better teach GECS's computer system in conjunction with customer service instead of in a void. Like the First Union training, GECS's curriculum is organized around learning how to identify and handle five major call types. We came up with these call types by researching and grouping together the most common caller inquiries and situations. The stand-up portion of the training incorporates role playing and hands-on learning.

We also developed e-learning systems that provide both soft and technical skills training and address the needs of both Collections and Customer Service trainees. The Collections Training system consists of thirty-two scenarios in which new hires work as collections associates holding phone conversations with fictional clients. The simulations actively emulate the computer system GECS associates use to record payment arrangements, account comments, and the like. The Customer Service Training system includes thirty-five scenarios grouped into the five call types. Acting as a CSR, the user interacts with customers who have requests dealing with credit line increases, fund transfers, payment extensions, and other issues.

She Looks Like Her License

In She Looks Like Her License, for example, the user acts as a CSR fielding a call from Stan Zenardi, a merchant. Stan has a customer who wants to use her credit card but doesn't have it on her. Stan tells the user:

> **. . . I have a customer here who wants to buy a couple cans of paint from us, but she doesn't have her credit card with her. Is there anything we can do about that?**

The user must navigate the emulated computer system to find the appropriate search screen, then respond to the caller (see Figure 10-4).

If the user chooses an incorrect response, tutoring pops up that informs the user what he or she said, what went wrong, and what to do next (see Figure 10-5).

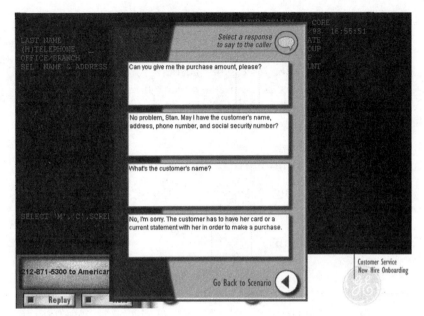

Figure 10-4

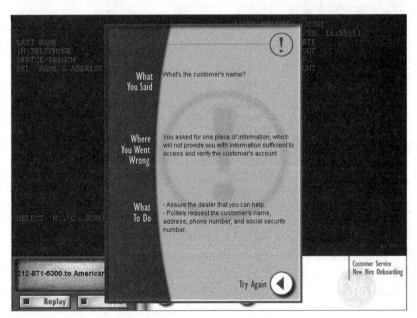

Figure 10-5

Using the customer's phone number, the user can access her account information (see Figure 10-6).

The user must then ask Stan for the customer's identity using her driver's license then access her account information to check her remaining balance. If the user isn't sure how to proceed, he or she can click on the Now What button at any time to get a hint as to what action needs to be taken next.

Getting Trainees Up to Speed, and Fast

The classroom training and the simulations were designed to fit seamlessly together to provide complete, thoughtful instruction and timely practice sessions. Overall, training for each call type looks something like this:

1. Trainees attend instructor-led classes, where a specific call type is introduced and discussed.
2. During the classroom session, trainees listen to one to three taped calls that illustrate a specific call type; then they discuss it collaboratively.

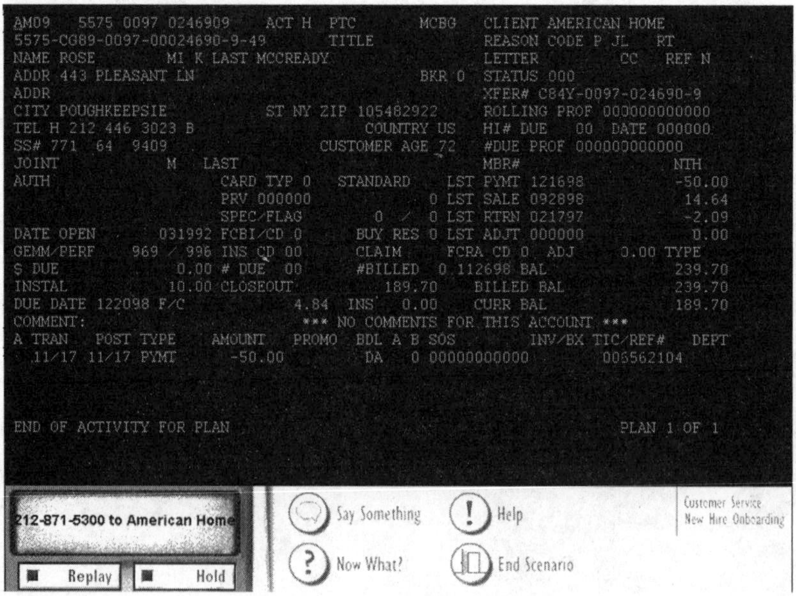

Figure 10-6

3. The trainees perform a classroom activity, such as role playing, around the skill.
4. The trainees work through the simulations.
5. Trainees shadow experienced CSRs on the job as they take live calls.
6. By the end of the course, the trainees are taking more and more live calls on their own. (Trainees take their first live calls on day 5 and gradually increase the volume of live calls as the course progresses.)

Each year this new curriculum is used by over 2000 new hires across twenty-two operating centers, and GECS is ecstatic with the results. It has cut training time up to 50 percent, to three weeks from the previous four to six. There has also been a significant drop in the time needed to prepare CSRs to handle real customer calls. Under the old training, CSRs waited four weeks to start handling live calls, while under the CA-designed training, they begin with live customer calls after only five days of training. And CSRs now reach quality goals 30 percent faster than before. Dennis Moloney, learning technology manager of the Performance and Learning Systems Group at GE Capital, said, "After training using this software new hires started performing at higher levels than experienced employees."

Lessons Learned

- It's vital that training teach individual skills within the context of a larger goal (e.g., helping a customer) rather than in a vacuum.
- Curriculums effectively using learning by doing can significantly decrease training time and expenses while vastly improving performance.
- By properly divvying up job tasks into groups, you can get trainees to master the most common practices first and build on that success with the other groups.

Other Call Center Projects We've Done

After the success of the GECS curriculum redesign, the organization came back to us wanting more. Having just purchased a company that serviced the Wal-Mart credit card, it wanted to train new hires in the same way the original GECS training had, but on the Wal-Mart computer system. But this wasn't as easy as dropping in new screens. We changed the emulation, added extra tasks, and more. The team also created a paper-based version of this system, which reads like a children's *Choose Your Own Adventure* book —learners are instructed to turn to different pages depending on the choices they make.

First Union, too, came back with more work for us, centered around the Future Banking Initiative. The training managers wanted us to complete a curriculum redesign to train reps to provide greater customer service to customers banking online with First Union. To reduce costs for First Union, we only created sample training documents, letting First Union put together the rest. In general, there is a danger implicit in this approach: If the people creating the documents are the same people who created the old "everything and the kitchen sink" approach to training, they might be tempted to include more information than is necessary, bloating the training with things that would be of little help to trainees even if they did remember it, which of course they wouldn't.

In another money-saving move, the simulations we built do not offer full emulation of First Union's computer system for online banking. Instead, appropriate screen shots are provided coinciding with each task, but learners cannot type into the screen or move to a different screen within First Union's computer system. True emulation is preferable because it allows the simulations to simultaneously train learners on the computer system, customer service techniques, and the content. But these screen shots are still helpful in making the interactions look and feel real enough so that lessons learned there can be applied later on the job. This tactic also prevents the technology from dating itself should the client update its computer system—the simulations can be built so that new screen shots may be easily inserted to replace old ones.

The biggest difference between the First Union Online Interactive simulations and the original First Union Direct simulations is not a money-saving scheme, but rather a design advance. In previous call center simulations, the action choices and the words associated with those choices (remember, the exact words call center employees say are very important) went together. But when our designers discovered what types of things PSRs in an online call center have to do—like know the customers' computer hardware and software and troubleshoot connectivity and usability issues—they decided that their jobs were more diagnostic in nature than other call centers.

So, for the Online Interactive system, we redesigned the interactions so that learners must first choose the high-level action they want to complete and then pick the words to convey that action. This, of course, was much more complicated to write and program, if only because of the potential combinations of choices involved. The tutoring, then, had to focus on the most egregious mistake the user makes, even if he or she makes more than one. Since it's harder to get through the interactions with this design, we wrote the tutoring to be softer and to hint more closely at the correct path. The last thing we want is for users to get hopelessly stuck, then get frustrated and give up.

We have completed several other projects for First Union call centers—including work for the Collections, Wholesale, Sales, and Commercial divisions. For almost all of these simulations, we came up with a new way to construct the choices the learners had to make. Each design is based on the most difficult and most important thing the reps in a particular call center must do—say the right words or make the right strategic action choice.

The success of these and other call center curriculum redesigns and simulations for First Union and GE has led to other such projects for clients like Hewitt, Grainger, and Merrill Lynch. And, in the course of completing all these curriculum redesigns, we learned a thing or two ourselves.

Learning from Our Own Mistakes—What We Know About Designing Curricula

With each curriculum design we take on, we learn new and valuable lessons—about client expectations, teaching styles, and content—that we apply to subsequent projects. The main challenge with curriculum design is to create experiences that help trainees learn just in time and set a foundation for future learning. And we have to do all this without overwhelming the learners or their organization's coffers, while still integrating technology when that makes sense.

To accomplish this, we try to keep in mind both what makes sense for each topic considered in isolation as well as what makes sense as part of an integrated training solution. From a learning standpoint, we stress problems and examples (especially common situations learners will face on the job) over solutions and principles as the context in which to teach the content. Learners should practice early and often, through doing activities (such as practice, simulations, role-plays, etc.) instead of passive activities (lectures, reading, audiovisuals, etc.). With all this in mind, we have developed the following four basic principles of curriculum design from our experience consulting with companies over the years.

Don't Teach What You Don't Have To

Many a training effort becomes bogged down because it tries to teach workers every last bit of knowledge they might possibly need at some point. Having seen this too many times, we developed the 80/20 rule of thumb: If in a task analysis of a call center we find that there are 100 tasks that employees need to complete, 20 of those tasks will most likely account for 80 percent of the call volume. So we try to focus the crux of the training on those 20 tasks rather than on the full 100. For the other 80 tasks, we can provide on-the-job support to help out if and when those situations arise.

In other words, don't waste everyone's time with things that aren't going to come up much. Chances are they'll forget it anyway. There's no way that trainees will learn everything they will ever need to know in a six-week training course, especially if those six weeks are packed full of rarely used information they won't remember. Usually, it's much more effective to focus on teaching workers how-to skills and then to provide them with resources that they can use to get detailed knowledge as it becomes relevant. Trainees are better served by using that time to get more practice on the information and types of calls they're going to encounter frequently. Just get them to really know and extensively practice the important aspects of the job, and let them fill in the gaps on the floor.

Now, it's often very hard to convince training managers to take any information out of training, especially if they're the ones who created the previous, unwieldy instruction in the first place. Just tell them that by pulling detailed knowledge out of training and putting it into performance support resources, you can often both reduce training cost and improve performance. Try to make them understand that, no matter how excellent their training was, if employees only deal with something once every six months, they'll forget how to do it, guaranteed. Another approach is to ask, "Would you rather spend time on that skill, which employees only use once every six months and which doesn't really affect business, or on this one, which they use every day and has a clear monetary impact on business and profits?"

Organize What You Teach in a Way That Makes Sense to Learners

When organizations try to teach a large body of knowledge, they often fall into the trap of providing a "checklist" curriculum; they march trainees through a large number of topics without considering whether or not they can understand how those topics relate either to each other or, more importantly, to the job. This approach generally leaves trainees unable to remember much of what they are supposed to be learning or to apply what they do remember on the job. Instead, strive to organize training around a model of how the job really works, a model that makes sense to the learner.

As I've discussed in this chapter, for call center curriculum redesigns we perform a detailed task analysis, then categorize those tasks into a set of call groups—each group consisting of types of calls requiring similar skills and procedures. In deciding which calls go in which group, we ask ourselves, "What's the caller calling about?" and "What does the rep have to do?" Through doing activities, trainees can apply their knowledge in all areas by practicing dealing with a particular type of call. Then, if they eventually get a call they haven't practiced, they can hopefully relate that call to others that they do know how to handle, and they'll deal with it successfully.

Only Teach at the Appropriate Moment

People really only learn when they are ready, not when it happens to be convenient to provide them with training. When creating an approach to delivering a substantial body of content, be careful not to give too much too soon. You can't force-feed training.

E-Learning Is Not the Answer to Every Training Problem: Use the Most Appropriate Delivery Mechanism for Each Lesson to Be Taught

Each instructional medium has its strengths and weaknesses:

- E-learning can provide cheap, safe, learn-by-doing opportunities; give users a consistent message; and provide individualized feedback.
- Live training can provide social networking opportunities, cover skills like intonation that are difficult to coach using current technologies, and give learners a chance to talk about specific issues they face on the job.
- Performance support systems can provide learners with just-in-time help while they work. These systems can also be used to support the more uncommon and auxiliary information that trainers want learners to have access to.
- Mentoring can enable learners and coaches to build a human bond and enhance career development.
- The point is, e-learning solutions have to be just one weapon in the learning specialist's arsenal.

CHAPTER

e-Learning at
Harvard Business School

Kill Anthony

As the country's premier MBA program, Harvard Business School (HBS) figured its incoming students would probably already have some background in basic accounting from previous experiences in school or in life. So course work at HBS begins with a required first-semester class called financial reporting control. This class focuses on more complex issues like using financial accounting systems and structuring financial reporting systems. To help incoming students brush up on accounting over the summer before classes began, HBS recommended they complete a workbook called *Essentials of Accounting* (a.k.a. "The Anthony Workbook"). *Essentials of Accounting* was written in the 1960s by Robert N. Anthony, a behaviorist disciple of B.F. Skinner.

But Skinnerian learning theories are more concerned with stimulus responses in experiments with, say, pigeons, than with thought processes or how people actually learn. Much like a high school Spanish workbook, "Anthony" is chock-full of fill-in-the-blank exercises. For example, when learning about accounts, students are asked to write the word *accounts*. The problem with this is that, even if students know enough about what an account is to correctly write the word in the blank, they aren't faced with a realistic problem to which they must apply it. So, how are they supposed to put this knowledge to use? Hands-off, mind-numbing exercises like this don't make for good learning. HBS professors do claim that "Anthony" might actually be effective in drilling home certain basics of accounting ideas and terminology—if anybody used it. (I doubt this. Professors just like to say that this kind of stuff works, when they know in their hearts it doesn't.) Of course, since it's deadly boring, very few incoming HBS students get through the workbook. So, when Cognitive Arts began to work with HBS to build prematriculation courses (to be taken over the summer prior to start of the first year of graduate school) our mantra became "Kill Anthony."

Aside from *Essentials of Accounting*, if incoming students felt underprepared, they could head to school three weeks before the semester began to take a brief review course that touched on some accounting, finance, and quantitative methods. But, since most students don't realize they need to learn something until they screw up trying to do that thing, only a small percentage of the incoming class even signed up for it.

There was nothing to prepare incoming MBA students for the basic finance they would need in business school. Under HBS's old course path, students didn't take finance until their second semester, *after* completing the first-semester accounting course. So forcing them to study finance the summer before classes started didn't make much sense. But, beginning in 2000, the department decided to stretch the second-semester finance course into a two-semester sequence starting in the fall. This curriculum change spawned an immediate need to get incoming students ready for finance as well as accounting.

HBS professors were already complaining that they were spending too much time in class reviewing T-accounts, bond ratings, and other things you don't necessarily need sixty of the brightest business minds on the planet to teach. They wanted to level the playing field by raising the bottom tier of incoming students to a minimum skill level in both accounting and finance. This would allow professors to focus class time on more advanced (and more interesting) material.

Harvard saw e-learning as a chance to, eventually, completely remove from the classroom certain skills that could be better taught in other ways. Since professors were sick of wasting their time and that of their students by getting everyone up to speed with basic accounting and finance in class, creating online prematriculation courses for these two subjects seemed like a good place to start. Such courses could help make sure that, in the future, incoming students would all have the opportunity to prepare for business school in the same way; such courses could ease students' fear of not knowing what HBS wants them to know coming in.

The Learning Triumvirate

Universities traditionally serve as centers for research and knowledge creation as well as education; but avenues to share that knowledge with the rest of the world are often limited. Harvard is fortunate in this regard to have Harvard Business School Publishing (HBSP). In addition to making and selling its own products and publications, HBSP also functions as an arm of the university to disseminate knowledge from HBS's world-renowned faculty to a broader population. So HBS, HBSP, and Cognitive Arts all teamed up to create online accounting and finance courses to fulfill two distinct objectives:

- Satisfy the professors' prematriculation needs
- Create a product that HBSP could sell later to other business schools and corporations

So, our mission was not only to build a system suitable for a software-only prematriculation course. We also had to make sure that the look and feel, topics covered, and language of content were all suitable for a broader population that included other business schools, consulting firms, and corporations. In order to make the courses marketable, HBSP wanted the approach to be more managerial than academic (in other words, less high-level concepts and more doing). This, of course, made us happy, and HBS in turn came to agree that this was probably the best way to teach the material.

It's Academic

Harvard Business School has a long-standing tradition of teaching business through case studies. Since good case study instruction references real-world examples and requires students to actively think about solving problems, the theory behind it, while not quite learning by doing, is compatible with learning by doing. While a case study gives you information and asks you what you think about it, with no real answers, learn-by-doing simulations constantly force you to make active choices. The similarities between these two proven teaching methods made HBS professors feel good about the way we wanted to structure the courses.

When working with an academic institution, the normal development process goes out the window. As I have noted elsewhere, the normal process looks like this:

- First, we talk to people out in the field, people who practice those skills regularly, to find out what mistakes they make. The idea here is to identify learning goals that, if you change the behaviors associated with them, will have a measurable business impact.
- Then we write teaching points to crystallize these behaviors into actions, things that you *do*.
- We then ask companies to prioritize these teaching points depending on what results are most important to them.
- We then develop learn-by-doing simulations around the teaching points to bring about this desired impact. When the new training systems are put in place, companies can track actual progress made against learning goals.

But in the abstract realm of academia, it's often more difficult to determine where and how people actually screw up in the real world. And if it's harder to find concrete mistakes, it's intrinsically harder to connect mistakes directly to desired changes in behavior. For example, who in the world actually does basic accounting? Well, nobody, because accounting software takes care of that now. Without real-world consequences, it's tougher to link performance to results in the same way that a sales simulation could say, "The firm lost this multimillion dollar deal because you didn't seek the client's input."

In the absence of such real-life data, how could we learn what types of mistakes students would make? Luckily, we had the luxury of a content team that, though quite sharp, didn't have any experience with accounting or finance—so the team members were bound to make typical beginner mistakes. We also had a great resource in the Harvard professors who'd taught this stuff for years and knew where their students struggled. So, since no one could really point to how students actually use and make mistakes with basic accounting and finance after graduation, we did the next best thing. We asked professors where their students had trouble and what questions they frequently asked in class. We also spent several weeks with the professors uncovering precisely what they wanted to teach and why. In doing so, they identified high and low-level priorities regarding:

- What subjects should be covered
- How much time they wanted students to devote to each topic
- What things they wanted students to be able to do when they finished
- What things they wanted students to know but not necessarily know how to do
- The relative importance of each of these things

Let's look briefly at one specific example of how we gathered content for these systems. In order to get a feel for how the financial analysis simulations might flow, we role-played with the finance subject matter expert (SME). We asked him to play the part of a client seeking investment advice from a team member who was acting as a financial advisor. The SME coached the role-playing team member as she responded, and someone else scribbled it all down. Once we were confident with our grasp of the interactions and content, we discussed how to shift what they had learned from the role-play into a realistic online activity.

Can Accounting Be Fun?

Because most Harvard MBA grads are more likely to become senior managers than bookkeepers, we initially wanted to build simulations that taught them to be intelligent consumers of financial accounting work products. By that I mean that the learner would review accounting reports and make executive decisions based on them. But the professors made it clear that they wanted to teach the plumbing of the financial accounting system: that is, bookkeeping. Now, bookkeeping is castor oil content—it doesn't taste good, but it's good for you, so close your eyes and swallow. Our challenge was to make accounting interesting.

So we came up with simulations requiring the student to actually do nuts-and-bolts financial accounting. In each of the goal-based scenarios that make up the heart of the system, the student plays the role of an accounting consultant at CJ&M, a fictional accounting consulting company. Throughout the course, the student consults with three different businesses—a service firm, a merchandising firm, and a manufacturing firm—each facing a critical business challenge. In order to help, the student must do analyses of financial statements, translate a series of business events into accounting transactions, build new financial statements, and analyze those new statements using financial ratios.

The first simulated project is at Click n Pick, an Internet Web design company. The student must help Click n Pick prepare for a quarterly shareholders' meeting by explaining the company's financial happenings to Click n Pick executives so that they can explain them to their shareholders (see Figure 11-1). Raj Nanda, cofounder and head of design, explains:

It's a pleasure to meet you; I'm thrilled that CJ&M could send someone over so quickly. Tats, Catherine, and I may be

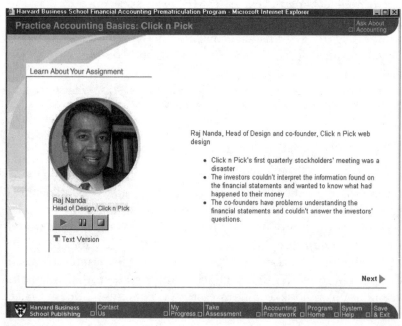

Figure 11-1

the best techies in this city, but when it comes to reading and understanding financial statements, forget about it. We tried to hold our first quarterly stockholders' meeting under the guise of a Fourth of July picnic. Sparks were flying all right, but they weren't coming from any fireworks. Our investors looked over our financial statements and couldn't figure out what they meant. One of our chief investors, my Uncle Bob, was particularly livid. He demanded to know what happened to his $30,000. Why was our cash balance so low? We couldn't answer him. All I could do was offer him some potato salad. And that's why you're here. It's a tough job, but our assistant Marilyn will get you up to speed. Once again, welcome to Click n Pick.

Click n Pick wants to show its shareholders that, despite its declining cash balance, the company is still very profitable. The student can help with this by tracking how the cash position and net income change over the quarter. To do this, the student needs to record transactions in the journal—first deciding whether or not each individual transaction should be recorded, then how to express it in the journal (see Figure 11-2).

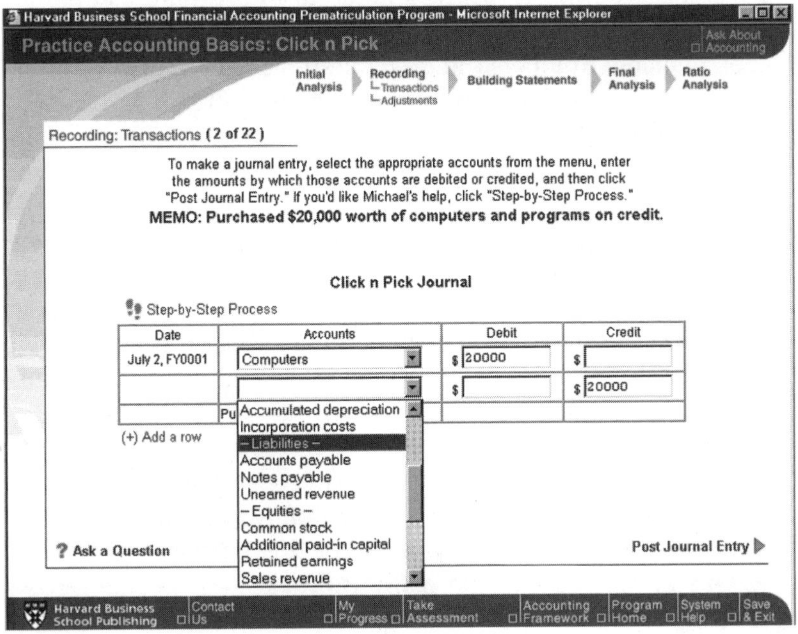

Figure 11-2

Pop-up tutoring informs the student what he or she did wrong, suggests a better approach, and points toward system resources and refreshers that might help as the student tries again. After the student records and makes adjustments on all twenty-two transactions, he or she moves on to build the statements, then performs final and ratio analyses. Individualized feedback summarizes where the student performed well and where he or she struggled, detailing specific problem areas and offering the chance to ask follow-up questions of accounting experts.

If at any point the student wants to go back and review accounting basics, he or she can head to Pierce Agency, an advertising firm. There the student is able to follow along step-by-step with employees and stakeholders as they explain how they use accounting on the job. At each step, the student can ask questions about the accounting he or she sees.

You Don't Even Have to Raise Your Hand

If simulations are the heart of the accounting and finance courses, this timely access to experts is the lungs. We built a large system of interrelated text descriptions and explanations, graphical animations, and audio expert stories gathered from HBS professors—all to let users reference finance or accounting experts and information on demand. Students can pose questions whenever they want, and explore issues to the depth they desire (see Figure 11-3).

Many e-learning solutions use simulations, of course. (Although many I have seen are really forcing users to make right or wrong choices that are thinly veiled multiple-choice exams. Without the ability to actively ask questions when they arise, not much true learning goes on.) In a sense, simulations themselves merely set the table for learning—if students have a goal and a vested interest in succeeding, all of a sudden they'll begin to care about the subject. Eighty percent of the work is getting them to this point. Then, when learners make a mistake and see the consequences of that mistake, specific goal-directed questions are bound to pop up in their minds. This expectation failure is the only way for students to learn if they don't think they need any help. To put this another way, if a user doesn't have a bunch of questions in his head, he probably isn't learning much. A good e-learning solution causes those questions to come to mind and then provides the answers.

Figure 11-3

On-demand expert questions are also useful if learners have little or no idea where to start and need some help making a decision. In this sense, you can look at expert advice as proactive tutoring that informs and supports learners' actions. As one student wrote in a course evaluation for the accounting system, "Being able to pull up the 'Ask the Accountant' while working on a section was great. If I answered a question wrong, it was easy to immediately learn why and correct my mistake." Asking questions in a simulated environment also provides the opportunity to learn from many different experts instead of just one (which would be the case in a regular classroom). To this end we have compiled a list of issues that are likely to come up while a student is engaged in the simulation. As the student moves around the simulation the questions change so that the appropriate question is always readily accessible. We interviewed a large number of Harvard faculty for the answers on these key questions. They are exactly the kinds of questions that professors hate to answer and students hate to ask, like "what is a debit," as well as questions asking for stories to illustrate complex points.

Tool Time

Karl Kester—head of the Harvard MBA program and lead subject matter expert on the finance project—said he wanted the finance course to teach students how to use a set of tools in a financial tool kit. This made the designers' eyes light up, because it's much easier to teach the application of a set process than to ask learners to understand in a general sense what something *is*. Since the content was packaged in a way that could translate well to learn by doing, we just needed to find a mission to call these tools into play. So the team created simulations where clients come to the user—who acts as a junior financial advisor—with different investment needs. The user must recommend the right financial instruments and investments for each situation.

In Looking Ahead, for instance, client Sonja Stone is looking for a smart way to invest her excess cash. When the student meets with her, she says:

> **Hi. Just so you know where I'm coming from, I'm kind of set when it comes to finances. I've got money saved up—a 401K, an IRA, and all that. But I have this extra cash that's sitting around—I need to put it to good use for all those retirement expenditures I plan to make. I'm a little confused about this. I mean, it's funny, you know. You mention that you're looking into investing for retirement, and suddenly everyone's an expert. The taxi driver's been giving me stock advice. My grandma swears by bonds. And my brother is suddenly a number 1 derivative guru. But what's the best investment for me? I don't need any additional income at this point, though I would like to fix up my home in a few years. I'm not much of a gambler, but I do like some surprises—I guess new and risky investments are good. Look, I've worked hard. Being chief engineer isn't easy. I'm single, and I want to make sure I can live comfortably when retirement rolls around.**

The boss tells the student to narrow down the choices by recommending stocks, bonds, or derivatives. Before deciding, the student can investigate all three options by asking questions about the basics and vocabulary of each instrument. He or she can also review Sonja's priorities. Then, the student must choose which investment instrument is best for Sonja and justify the decision, as well as provide reasoning for why the other two options are not the best idea. The system provides What Happened Here? tutoring for wrong choices and justifications.

If the student correctly chooses to recommend stocks to Sonja, she mentions three specific stocks she's considering and asks the student to help her choose from among them. In order to make a recommendation, the student can ask questions of James Oshuo, an equity analyst who can provide specific information on each stock (see Figure 11-4).

Again, when making a decision about which stock to recommend, the student must justify why he or she chose one particular stock and not the others (see Figure 11-5).

Once the student selects the best stock for the right reasons, the boss congratulates the student, who then moves to a reflection page summarizing lessons learned in the scenario.

HBS also wanted to give a general overview of the financial system to get people to know *that* there are convertible bonds, *that* there are different kinds of derivatives, *that* there are people who provide capital, et cetera. These concepts are harder to teach well through simulations, since they are not things you do but

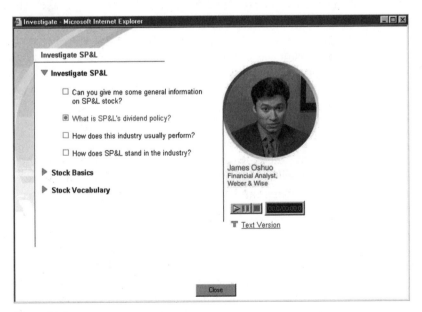

Figure 11-4

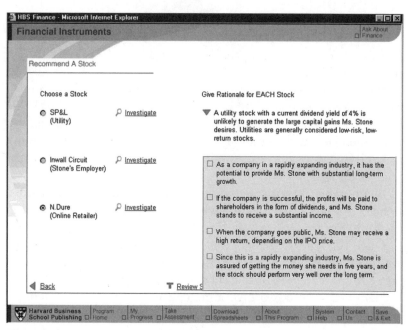

Figure 11-5

rather things you know. Though this material made up only a small portion of what needed to be taught, HBS professors stressed its importance. Since we didn't want to make the system any more complicated than it already was, we took some of this very general information and made up a story about a fictional company. The story functions as sort of a living case study, complete with Flash animation that the user can follow to see the roles of different players on the financial stage. Each character in the story introduces a different element of the financial system; at each step the user can pause and ask follow-up questions to more deeply explore a particular issue. This is not exactly learning by doing, but it is a cheap, simple way to fit this small yet vital bit of content into the courseware.

The professors also wanted to teach more complicated valuation techniques. In the second set of scenarios, the student plays the role of a financial analyst for North Brew, a leading distributor of canned beer. In order to stay competitive, North Brew is looking to purchase a microbrewer named Castle Island. North Brew wants the student to see if the acquisition makes sense by analyzing the company's financial health using ratio analysis, performing financial forecasts, and calculating projected values.

The student begins by using the Dupont formula to do a breakdown of return on equity for a ratio analysis on Castle Island (see Figure 11-6). The student then answers questions based on the Dupont analysis to create a memo assessing the opportunities in purchasing Castle Island.

After the student successfully pieces together the memo, North Brew's CFO asks him or her to forecast Castle Island's income for the next three periods, making decisions about each line item in the income statement and balance sheet (see Figure 11-7).

Once the student has completed the forecasts, he or she must determine if the acquisition is a good deal by calculating the net present value.

HBS wanted its students to be able to apply the skills they picked up in each of these scenarios down the road in real life. As such, HBS's hope was that its students could develop the skills and confidence necessary to open up a case study at 10:00 at night, sit down at their computers, fire up Microsoft Excel, and start running forecasts or calculating net present value. In other words, they didn't want to teach just content, but also how to use these tools in Excel. Now this is hard to do. After a lot of effort and a

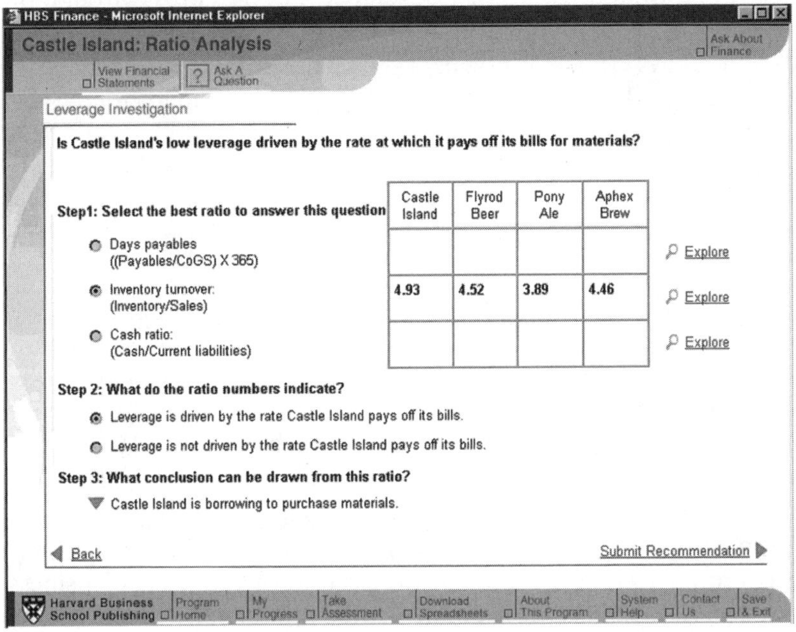

Figure 11-6

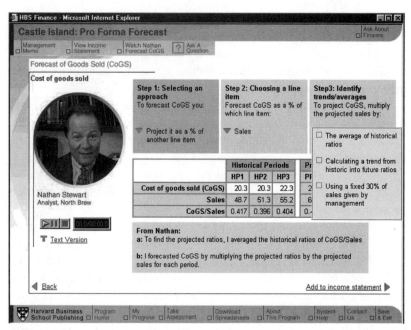

Figure 11-7

healthy amount of failure, we developed a design breakthrough by actually incorporating Excel spread sheets into the course. This design allows students to learn how to use the tools they need in the real world and connect those tools with the finance content. Though it functions independently of the system, the spreadsheet component offers mistake tutoring that fits seamlessly within the framework of the rest of the simulation—never interrupting the learning experience (see Figure 11-8).

Suiting the Class to Each Student's Needs

With any teaching or training effort, some learners will know the material already, some will catch on quickly, and others will struggle mightily. The challenge, then, is to build simulations that make good use of each learner's time while still keeping all activities under the umbrella of a realistic, overarching problem. In a given scenario in the accounting course, there are upwards of sixty accounting transactions, all in the service of one larger business event. We designed the system so that if students already know

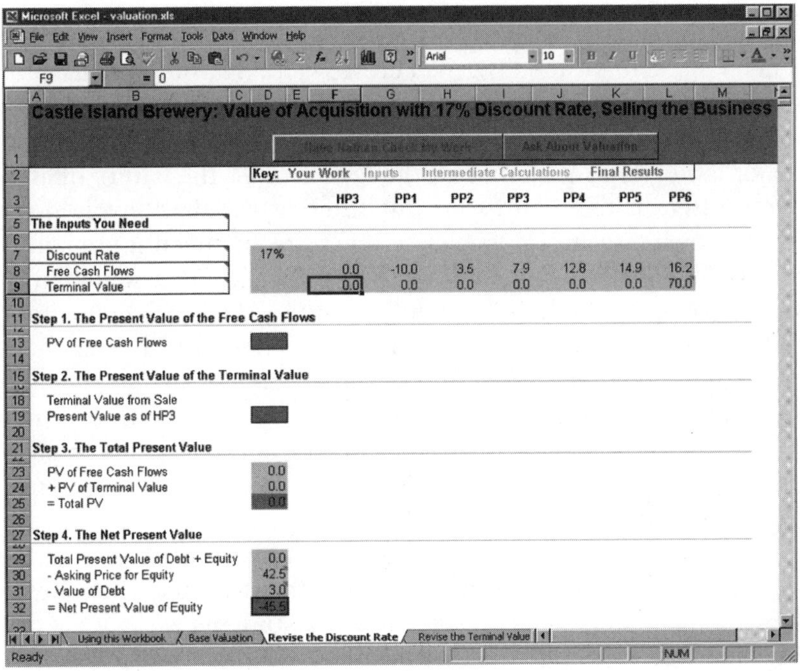

Figure 11-8

the stuff or catch on quickly, it won't take long at all. If, on the other hand, students don't know what they're doing, they can go through a longer process, working through smaller steps and getting their hands held until they feel comfortable. This method works because the system touches upon so much of the essential content of basic accounting through the simple repeated activity of actually doing bookkeeping again and again. If students know the stuff already, they breeze through; if they don't, they learn it in a more methodical, in-depth manner.

We included a similar component in the net present value section of the finance system: If students get stuck, they can go away and build up their skills before retackling the problem. This is a flexible and efficient use of the student's time—they get help if they need it, and they're not bored if they don't. It is also a distinct advantage of quality e-learning over the traditional classroom. Instructors don't have to slow the whole class down to accommodate a few people, and they don't have to worry that they're going too fast and leaving someone behind.

Integration

This was the first time HBS had created an e-learning prematriculation course; so just as important as making the system was making the system work. In other words, implementation was a major issue. As I mentioned in the last chapter, the nature of any Web system is that, with so many different variables involved in using the site, technical issues are bound to be much more complicated than with a system designed for CD-ROM. If something goes wrong, testers have to figure out if it's the user's computer, the server, or a bug in the system itself. When asked what they didn't like about the program in course surveys, many students responded that the program was too slow, particularly when using a modem. Because the survey did not include questions on students' machine specs, it is unclear how many of the problems were related to connection speed.

But there were other, nontechnical issues as well. HBS had to decide when to implement it, how to tell the students, what to tell the students, and how to make sure the students actually do it. Beyond that, HBS officials had to figure out what to do if a student doesn't complete the program—not sign him or her up for classes. At HBSP, other questions arose as they prepared to launch the system to the public: questions about how to market it, how to track it, how it might work within other computer systems, hosting issues, and more. As of this writing, both organizations are still ironing out the wrinkles, learning as they go.

Success

In the summer of 2000, HBS began requiring all incoming MBA students to complete the online accounting prematriculation course before arriving at Harvard. The finance course requirement followed in the winter of 2000–2001. Overall, students now feel better prepared for the more advanced accounting and finance material they are faced with when they arrive at school. As one immediate measure of success, students who took both a preassessment before going through the accounting course and a postassessment after finishing it improved their scores by an average of 24 percent.

Professors note that, when students go through both prematriculation programs prior to starting classes at HBS, they are able to quickly jump into interesting and difficult content in class without spending much review time on the basics. This has made the professors very happy (and us, too, since this was one of the major goals of the project).

Students are also going back to reuse parts of both courses as refreshers when they struggle with a particular concept. Students discuss the programs during their course work and even recommend sections of it to one another for additional help.

In course evaluations and focus groups, students have commented that the content is excellent and presented in a compelling way and that the system is well designed and easy to use.

- One wrote, "I found the course to be extremely helpful, providing an introduction to accounting and enabling the student to assess specific weaknesses for further independent study. The feedback provided at the conclusion of assignments and the assessment [was] particularly valuable with respect to determining areas for further study. As a candidate with limited accounting experience, the program has been of substantial benefit to me. I would highly recommend [it] for future students."
- One student hit on one of the best things about a good online course—that, unlike a class lecture, it's always there when you need it: "I think this is a great resource and one that I hope will be available to us in the future to use as a resource. I really liked being able to drill down to the specifics of how a certain transaction should be recorded."
- A different student stressed the importance of making the learning environment realistic and entertaining: "I've never actually found accounting to be fun—this program really made it fun and brought it alive (i.e., showed how the concepts and practices applied in realistic situations)."
- Another liked the course for more practical reasons: "This module is a fantastic learning environment. I'll admit that I was not psyched about taking an accounting class at a local college (as many of my friends who have attended HBS in previous years did), and the self-paced, totally comprehensive module that you put together really gave me the confidence and background I needed to feel very good about tackling accounting both at HBS and afterward."

- The Excel portion of the program was a fan favorite in the finance course: "The Excel piece was so valuable—not only in learning forecasting, but also how to use Excel itself. I was really intimidated by it, and now I'm not."
- Another student specifically "... liked the step-by-step approach and the fact that I could ask questions/get help throughout the program."

Lessons Learned

- E-learning is perfect for prerequisites because it can help create a level playing field for all students coming into a class so that the professor doesn't have to waste valuable time and resources reviewing basic concepts.
- The development process is more complicated when you're teaching abstract concepts that no one actually *does* in the real world.
- Getting students to ask the right questions should be one of the main goals of any courseware.
- Good e-learning speeds up or slows down to accommodate the pace of each student. Learners should be able to whisk through sections they find easy, and they should be able to slow down and spend more time on the details of concepts and practices they don't immediately grasp.

12

Web-Mentored Courses: How Columbia University Uses Live Experts to Enhance e-Learning by Doing

We have looked at Web courses and we have looked at training systems that use simulations more complex than the Web can reasonably handle at this time. But there is a third, very appealing option that we have explored in our partnership with Columbia University.

Cognitive Arts and Columbia University have come together to build high quality e-learning courses as a way of offering the educational advantages of Columbia to a wider audience. Why should a quality education be available only to the few and the elite? There is much that a great university like Columbia can do to improve education throughout the world using this new medium. E-learning should radically alter the very nature of education. E-learning is about change, about the ability to implement new ideas. It's a way of beating the traditionalists in education.

Other universities have attempted to "put their courses online." Typically this means taking a lecture course and tossing out the lecture. Many times these courses are just lecture notes, pointers to resources, and quizzes. The problem, as most professors realize, is that lecture courses aren't very effective in the first place. Professors have to give constant tests just to make sure the students show up. The students try to figure out what they have to be "responsible for" and "what will be on the test." The rest of the time, professors drone on and students snooze away. Professors try to figure out how to keep the students awake, but have a hard time of it because the lecture format simply isn't conducive to learning.

Students need to think actively about what is being said in order to understand it. They need to express their own ideas, try something out, or ask questions. But even if their minds *are* working, even if they *are* really trying to listen, the professor just keeps talking, sometimes even speeding up so he or she can "cover the material." The whole idea that material is "covered" by simply mentioning it for a short time flies in the face of everything we know about learning. To learn, you must practice, you must fail, you must explain, you must wonder. None of this can happen in a lecture course. Lectures exist because of the economics of the university environment: The more students per teacher, the better the numbers work out for the university. Trust me, no one was considering the needs of the learner when they decided to stick one hundred students in a lecture class. So copying the lecture format for an e-learning course might work in the sense that students looking for credit online may well decide that they can endure yet another bad learning experience presented in a new medium. But no real learning is likely to take place.

How can we make better online university courses, then? First we must turn traditional courses into learn-by-doing courses. Second, we can offer these courses in the way we have been describing so far in this book, via simulation, or we can make them into Web-mentored courses.

Why Web-Mentored?

When you do something in a simulation, the experience of immersing yourself in it and the emotional impact of your failures there serve as a strong impetus for learning. But not every subject works like that. Sometimes only a real live person can provide meaningful help, because the required comprehension of the work a student has produced is beyond the power of a computer. This is a job for Web-mentoring.

The first courses we produced for Columbia Interactive use Web-mentoring. The idea is simple enough: If you are writing something, for example, you need the feedback from an expert—a writing teacher. No present-day computer could possibly evaluate your work. Luckily, there are many people in this world qualified to teach. Unfortunately, these people are not always where the students are. So, if we want to create one-on-one learning environments, Web-mentoring makes lots of sense. We can create goal-based scenarios that allow the student to navigate a site and learn on his or her own to a given point. Then, when work has to be produced, the student can submit his work to an actual person who can evaluate it and provide feedback. This idea has been used in a number of Columbia courses, in subjects as varied as writing, computer programming, economics, and psychology.

The American Language Program Online

First, let's talk about writing. Cognitive Arts and Columbia University's American Language Program have teamed up to create a series of online courses in business communications for nonnative speakers of English. The audience for these courses is working professionals who have intermediate to advanced fluency in English and whose jobs require them to communicate clearly with American businesspeople. Most of these students have previously taken courses in English as a second language; but instruction there typically focuses on general language use. These courses, on the other hand, concentrate on reading, listening to, and writing effective American business English.

Like other goal-based scenarios, the business communications courses place the student in an authentic role—in this case working for an American company. Depending on the course, the student might play an advertising account executive, a corporate special events coordinator, a sales executive, or a member of the management team of a start-up company. In each of these roles, the student must understand substantial written and spoken communications from simulated colleagues and clients. The student must then respond by writing a variety of typical business documents, from simple business emails to proposals and business plans.

For example, in the high-intermediate course, the student plays the role of an e-solutions executive who works for a Web design and e-commerce consulting firm in New York City. As the scenario unfolds, the student interacts with a potential client—a very traditional department store chain being forced to move online by competitive pressure. The goal is to sell the client on hiring the student's firm in order to create an online store that maintains the company's high-quality image. In the process, he or she receives a swarm of voice mails and written messages and, in turn, writes fourteen documents, including requests, reports, niceties, and several sections of a proposal.

Since the student is engaged in a relatively unconstrained, creative endeavor, his or her work can't be evaluated solely by software. So these courses employ a skilled human tutor who answers the student's questions and evaluates his or her work. All tutors are adjunct faculty of the American Language Program and are certified ESL teachers with advanced degrees and significant teaching experience.

The Write Way to Learn

The high-intermediate course is designed for students with considerable previous instruction in English in their home countries. Such students typically communicate in English with some accuracy; they try to use complex structures but still make mistakes in grammar and phrasing that affect their ability to communicate effectively.

The course begins not with an English lesson but with an email from the student's boss:

From: Anna Russo@heliant.com
Date: Monday, October 11, 2000, 1:12 PM
To: You@heliant.com
Subject: Report summarizing clients similar to Isabella's

Hi:

Welcome to your first day! I'd like you to gather some information in order to write a report. I just got off the

phone with Elizabeth Page, the tech strategies director from Isabella's. She seems **VERY** interested in upgrading Isabella's current informational Web site to a full-scale e-commerce store.

I'd like you to collect some information on any of our clients, past or present, who have needs similar to Isabella's. Then, I'd like you to communicate it back to the team. As our CEO likes to say, "Communication and teamwork make our dream work!"

Get started by writing an e-mail to the other four e-solutions executives in your division (Samantha, Jack, Thomas, and Terry). You can send one e-mail to all of them at the team@heliant.com. Ask them to send you any information about clients with needs similar to Isabella's. Tell them to include the following information:

- Client's company profile—revenue, industry, location(s)
- Their e-commerce needs
- The solution Heliant designed to meet those needs
- Quantifiable results of the e-commerce solution

Then, summarize the information you receive in a report of no more than a page or two. If you notice any similarities among the e-solutions we've delivered, please include them at the end. They might help us develop our solution for Isabella's.

Please send me the report a.s.a.p. and copy the team as well. I want us all up to speed on this within three days, at the latest.

Thanks, Anna

P.S. This should be a nice way for you to meet your fellow ESEs.

Receiving such an email can be a daunting introduction to the course, especially given that the student is expected not only to comprehend it, but also to respond. The student must produce two complex written communications: a request to coworkers and then a report summarizing the information gathered.

But help is on the way. Extensive performance support materials aid the student in understanding particular types of communication. These materials include help with vocabulary and grammar, as well as comprehension and inference questions. Comprehension questions, for instance, help a student make sure that he or she has understood all the important aspects of a communication. For example, the following comprehension questions are associated with the above e-mail:

- Who is Elizabeth Page?
- What is Isabella's relationship to Heliant?
- What information is Anna asking you for?
- How will this information be used?
- How long should your report be?
- What is the deadline for finishing your report?
- How should you get the information you need to write your report?

These questions are provided only as a self-check on the student's comprehension. Answers are not submitted to the tutor, nor are answers provided (other than in the message itself).

Writing a Business Document

Once the student has understood the communication, he or she must respond by writing appropriate documents. In the screen shown in Figure 12-1, the student is asked to write a request for information to coworkers, followed by a summary report. The student composes these using his or her own word-processing program. To help with the writing process, the student has constant access to extensive, task-specific performance support. For each type of business communication, this support includes:

- A strategy for writing this type of document effectively for various audiences
- A prototypical organization for this type of document, listing what's typically included in its introduction, body, and closing

Figure 12-1

- How to format this type of document in a variety of media, such as e-mails, memos, letters, and so on
- How writing style supports effective communication in documents of this type

In addition to offering specific, indexed support, the program also encourages a principled writing process that begins with high-level considerations before moving step-by-step to the increasingly specific concerns of how to effectively carry out the communicative strategy.

The student can also take advantage of a concise grammar reference that gives examples of grammatical elements related to different types of communication (such as making requests, softening requests, and justifying requests). Students who want to know are pointed to a standard grammar book used by nonnative speakers. Given that many students learn better from examples than from general advice, the program provides a range of examples of each type of document. These examples are purposely short and use simple language to minimize comprehension effort, since the student is actively focused on the writing task at hand, not a complicated grammar lesson.

Before submitting a document, the student is encouraged to check his or her work. The system provides a checklist that focuses on key aspects of:

- The document's organization: "Do I state my request directly in the introduction?"
- Style: "Is my style polite yet confident?"
- American business writing: "Is my document reader-centered (focused on meeting the reader's needs)?"
- General language use: "Do I use appropriate and varied vocabulary and sentence structures to make my document interesting and easy to read?"

If the student can answer yes to all these questions, he or she has probably produced a good draft that is ready for detailed examination by the student's tutor. The finished document is uploaded to the course Web site, where the tutor can access it.

Tutoring

A student works with a single tutor for the duration of the course. This one-to-one relationship allows the tutor to deeply understand the student's needs. Knowing these needs helps the tutor provide personalized coaching that will dramatically improve the student's writing ability over time.

The business writing courses employ a mastery approach to learning. In other words, the student writes and then revises each document until he or she gets it right (though a student will typically write three drafts). The tutor's feedback on the first draft focuses on high-level issues: the document's strategy, organization, format, and style. The tutor doesn't yet address specific language usage unless the conceptual aspects of the document are essentially right (see Figure 12-2).

Feedback on the second draft typically centers on specific language usage, from word choice to grammatical errors. By the third draft, the student has usually produced a document that puts it all together. However, if additional work is needed, the tutor will request a fourth draft. Tutors rarely request more than four drafts because after that student frustration often sets in, greatly

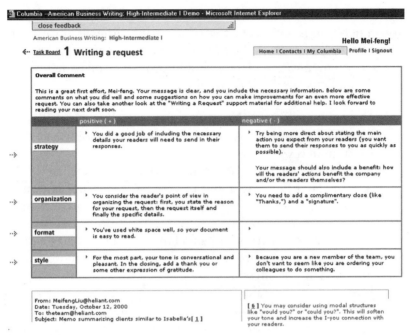

Figure 12-2

reducing the educational benefit of the additional work. The tutor corrects any remaining problems in the final draft so that the student can see the best possible version of his or her document.

Results

We have piloted both the intermediate and high-intermediate courses with business people from around the world. All students improved significantly. As expected, they learned to produce the organization and format of common genres of business writing and also improved the accuracy of their language use. Students, regardless of their cultural backgrounds, adopted the informal and direct style of American writers.

The pilot students were extensively surveyed task-by-task as they worked through the courses. All students found the courses to be directly relevant to their work, challenging, and even fun. All reported that the courses met or exceeded their expectations. In fact, over 80 percent said the courses were as good or better than working with a classroom teacher (interestingly, 30 percent commented that they missed having classmates). All students reported that the online support materials were "just right" or "too much"; most reported that they made little or no use of offline materials, such as dictionaries and grammar books. Since this is a communication class, I should probably conclude by letting the students speak for themselves:

- Martha Ortiz said, "The course was so realistic, I felt like it was created just for me. I could take advantage of what I was learning in my real job."
- Yu-Shiou Flora Sun said, "The scenario is an excellent idea. It is my favorite thing about the course. It teaches not only the writing but also lets me observe American business in a role-playing situation."
- Elena Getmanschcuk said, "I feel my writing skills are better than they were before taking the course. I feel more comfortable with business writing. . . ."
- Hector Carreon said, "When reading the support for my first task, when I began the course, I thought it was great to have all this information to consult during the course, and it met my expectations. However, after my coach feedback, I was convinced the course was exceeding my expectations, which was absolutely confirmed with the further feedback and the level of communication I could keep with my coach."

Lessons Learned

- For complicated, unconstrained, creative tasks such as writing, a live tutor is often needed to provide the detailed feedback and special attention learners require.
- Good e-learning throws the user headfirst into the task or problem to be addressed right away.
- It's important to give learners sufficient and appropriate resources to help them do their work (without doing it for them).

Programming in Context

Programming courses have traditionally been strong on doing. But, while students do write programs to solve homework exercises, they do not learn how programs are really written—that is, from specifications based on a client's needs, developed in several iterations, and maintained by more than one programmer. Programming is a complex task full of pitfalls—there are many ways to write a program that functions but is buggy, inefficient, hard to modify, or impossible to read.

In the programming courses Cognitive Arts and Columbia have built, the student is immersed in real-world situations in which he or she faces the same challenges as professional programmers. Playing the role of an entry-level programmer at a software company, the student learns how to write modern, Web-deliverable applets and applications with graphical user interfaces. Every program the student writes is typical of real programming projects. These assignments are not unrelated tasks, but parts in a series of steps building a complete, complex program.

As in a real job, the student's primary responsibility is to implement a design laid out in project notes. Because the courses are designed for first-time programmers, the projects introduce the student to basic concepts first. Later tasks allow them to build on previously learned skills.

The safety net is that the student has a mentor who reviews the code the student writes. It is important to note that the code is critiqued, not graded. Wherever there is a problem in the code—from subtle bugs to needless complexities to poorly named variables—the mentor inserts a critique pointing out the problem and why it matters in real code. The student then redoes this code and resubmits it. This "do/review/redo" cycle continues until the student has learned not only how to code, but to code well.

What the Student Sees

In the introductory C++ programming course, the student plays the role of an entry-level C++ programmer at a software development company called Pathfinder. Pathfinder has a contract with another company, Frank's Landscapers, Inc., to develop a software tool that can be used to create quick layouts of customer designs and estimate costs. The student receives direction from virtual coworkers, who communicate through email messages. There are six steps to completing a particular task:

1. **Read the task.** Students receive task assignments through e-mails and documents from coworkers. In the introductory C++ course, the team leader, Steve, describes a graphical

interface the student needs to build, and a coworker gives detailed design suggestions and a design sketch. Pop-up help in the right hand column defines terms used in the e-mails, gives hints, recommends text material to read, and so on.

2. **Create the work.** Now the coaching begins. The student expresses his or her level of confidence about doing the task (see Figure 12-3). The less confident the student is, the more help the coach offers.

   The student can access reference and help material in the form of FAQs, online tutorials, interactive demos, and other material.

3. **Check the work.** The student writes and debugs the program using a standard compiler, going back to the course as needed to get help generating the code, resolving errors, and so on. Once the student has developed working code, the next step is to check it. An e-mail message from a third coworker instructs the student on how to test the code. The message lists what the application for this task should do, as well as common bugs and logic errors to watch out for.

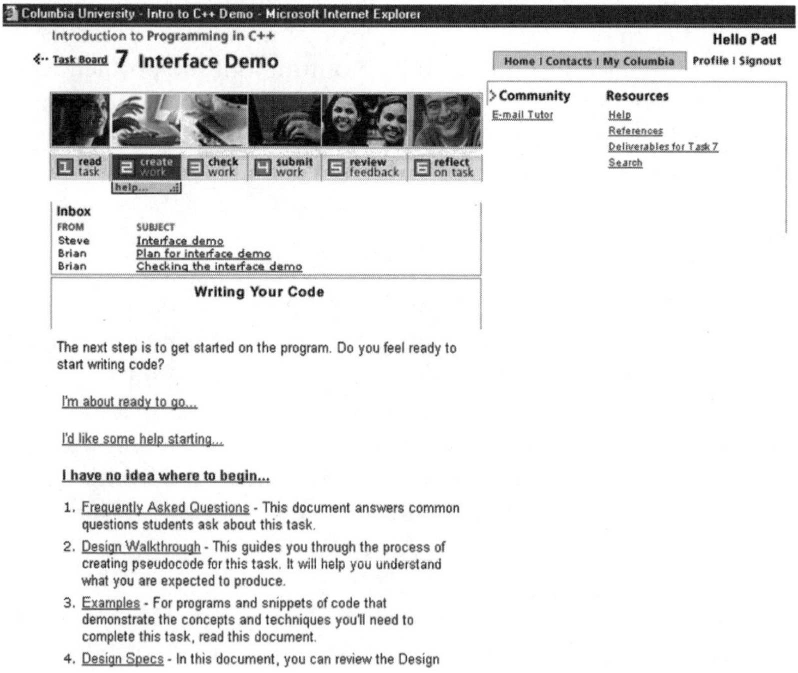

Figure 12-3

4. **Submit the work.** Once the code has been checked, the student copies and pastes portions of it into this window to send it to the mentor (see Figure 12-4). In general, though the student has had to write and debug a complete program, only a few key items are sent in for review. Typically 80 percent of most programs are straightforward; it's the other 20 percent that we ask them to send in for review. In this way, coaching and critiquing can focus on the most problematic aspects of programming.

5. **Review feedback.** The mentor reviews the code, then sends back comments about whether the code could be improved, and how to do so. The emphasis is not just on code that works, but also on code that is well written. Feedback and review continues until the mentor feels the student is ready to move on to the next task (see Figure 12-5).

6. **Reflect on the task.** After the code is complete, the student reviews the skills he or she has acquired during the task as well as the kinds of applications he or she should now be more capable of writing independently.

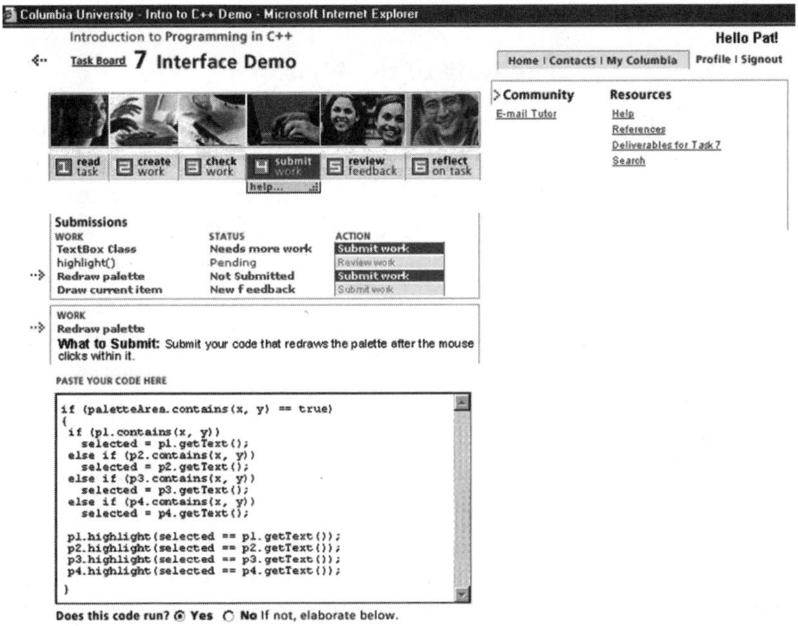

Figure 12-4

Figure 12-5

The Role of the Mentor

Mentoring is a critical process in these courses. Each student needs advice, encouragement, and criticism in order to move from novice to expert. The most important activity the mentors perform is reading student code and giving detailed, informative critiques. These critiques emphasize not just programming language details, but also general principles of good coding widely accepted by software engineers as important to programming in any language.

The student receives detailed comments on every mistake and dubious design choice, as well as suggestions for alternative approaches. The student can then fix the code and resubmit, until both his or her code and understanding are solid. There is no "this is your grade, now move on." Rather, the student applies advice given in the review and resubmits. The mentor critiques the new code and points out any problems introduced by the changes. The cycle repeats—usually only one or two more times—until both student and mentor are happy with the results.

Mentoring Tools

To ensure that all students receive consistent, high-quality feedback, we provide mentors with a large database of carefully written critiques covering 90 percent of the most common mistakes. These critiques include both general principles and task-specific issues. Mentors also have software tools that make it easy to insert critiques into their messages with just a few clicks of the mouse button. This combination of project structure and critique database tools allows a mentor to provide high-quality, detailed comments to most code submissions rapidly and consistently. This makes it possible for one mentor to handle as many students as a typical university teaching assistant, while giving each student the kind of individual attention and feedback normally available only in one-on-one apprenticeship situations.

Lessons Learned

- Making learners' projects or tasks realistic not only puts the content in the appropriate real-world context, it also motivates learners to try hard, since that context is probably why they're taking the course in the first place.
- By focusing on the 20 percent or so of a subject that's most challenging and mistake-prone, you can more quickly get learners up to speed on how to handle the most important issues they'll face in the real world.
- Web mentors should focus their energies on providing detailed and constructive feedback instead of on grades or credit.

Introducing Economics

Cognitive Arts and Columbia have built a Web-mentored Introduction to Economics. The course consists of eight learn-by-doing scenarios designed to teach the student the basics of micro- and macroeconomics. The student plays an economic consultant hired to advise a wide array of decision makers, from a young couple to the president of the United States.

Each scenario consists of two distinct phases—one self-contained and one Web-mentored. In the first phase, the student does an assortment of procedural economic analyses with the help of an online coach. For instance, the student can create and manipulate a series of graphs to analyze the overall effect of different variables on key economic estimates. The program offers just-in-time advice when the student wants help and detailed feedback when he or she makes a mistake. In the second phase, the student pieces together a policy recommendation, supported by expert video and outside reading he or she has done. The student submits this report to the tutor, who reviews both quantitative and qualitative aspects of the work and provides feedback.

Building a Foundation in Economics with Plywood

Let's look a little closer at a couple of the proposed scenarios. In one microeconomics scenario, the student advises the governor of Florida, who is concerned about the availability and price of plywood in the wake of a major hurricane. The governor is considering a number of policy options to deal with the effects of increased demand for plywood. These options include imposing price ceilings, issuing vouchers, banning high-cost suppliers, and having the government buy the plywood to sell at a subsidized price. The governor wants the student to investigate each of these policies, using market demand and supply curves to analyze market restrictions, surplus, and subsidies.

For each potential policy, the student will need to determine:

- What will the price of plywood be?
- How much plywood will be available on the open market?
- What will the policy cost the government?
- Could there be problems with plywood availability or plywood distribution?
- Will there be any problems involving the resale of plywood?
- Who will gain from this policy, and who will lose?
- What kind of trouble might this lead to?
- What are the selling points of the policy?

To answer each of the qualitative questions, the student draws from expert material in the system as well as readings from articles and the textbook. For the quantitative answers, the student uses a graphing tool and other online resources. The student puts together a recommended course of action, based in part on the governor's economic and political preferences. All the while the

Order ID: 002-0988802-6129012

Thank you for buying from prof_books on Amazon Marketplace.

Shipping Address:
Joel Gardner
747 East 200 North
Logan, UT 84321

Order Date: Sep 4, 2009
Shipping Service: Expedited
Buyer Name: Joel Lee Gardner
Seller Name: prof_books

Quantity	Product Details
1	**Designing World-Class E-Learning : How IBM, GE, Harvard Business School, And...** **Merchant SKU:** DI-6RAA-2CTE **ASIN:** 0071377727 **Listing ID:** 0603ELZCN4F **Order-Item ID:** 36944608565362 **Condition:** Used - Like New **Comments:** No writing, no marks, dust jacket excellent

Thanks for buying on Amazon Marketplace. To provide feedback for the seller please visit www.amazon.com/feedback. To contact the seller, please visit Amazon.com and click on "Your Account" and click on "Your Account" at the top of any page. In Your Account, go to the "Orders" section and click on the link "Leave seller feedback". Select the order or click on the "View Order" button. Click on the "seller profile" under the appropriate product. On the lower right side of the page under "Seller Help", click on "Contact this seller".

student is learning about economic issues like supply and demand, consumer and producer surplus, and a range of policy choices and trade-offs, all in a real-world context.

The President Wants Your Economic Advice

In another scenario—this one focusing on managing short-run economic fluctuations—the President of the United States calls on the user to analyze the economic effects of a sharp decrease in oil supply. By manipulating relevant graphs, the student evaluates the effect of the crisis on GDP, prices, unemployment, and interest rates. The student can also hear expert testimonial to compare the current oil shortage to similar economic events in the past. Once the student has determined the overall effect of the cutback, the president asks for an evaluation of several policy options: a tax cut, an increase in money supply, and an "unmanaged outcome" solution. The student analyzes the effects of each plan, then submits a report to the president that includes his or her recommendation as well as supporting evidence from experts and outside reading.

Such expert advice serves as a key element in making decisions and formulating recommendations in each of these scenarios. The student has access to hundreds of video clips of world-class economists, including faculty members from a variety of schools including Columbia, Harvard, Princeton, and the University of Michigan. So, in a sense, the student has not one professor but many. Students also have assigned textbook and article readings associated with each task. There is motivation to do the reading, since it will actually help the student complete the tasks more effectively; they can actually apply what they read instead of just regurgitating it.

Lessons Learned

- Teaching complicated abstract principles such as economics by having students apply those principles in real-life situations helps them remember not only how to do those things, but also when and why they're important.
- By letting users ask questions of multiple subject matter experts, you can provide them with many teachers instead of just one.

- The idea of one teacher, one course is an idea from another medium and another century.
- Academic courses need the kind of artificial goal-based scenarios that allow the student to play a role he will probably never play in real life. This provides motivation and excitement with respect to what otherwise might be rather dry material.

Getting the Scoop on Developmental Psychology

We have also built a Web-mentored Columbia University course in developmental psychology. In this course, the student learns about:

- Prenatal development
- Brain and cognitive development over the first three years
- Social and emotional development in the first three years
- Language development
- Cognitive development and intelligence
- Peer relations and aggression
- Achievement and motivation
- Moral development

To gain and apply knowledge of these concepts, the student acts as a journalist writing for a fictional developmental psychology newsletter whose main audience is parents and professionals.

For each task (one per week for a total of fifteen) a simulated editor gives the student a story assignment based on letters from subscribers. The stories the student writes not only respond to readers' questions or concerns, but also include a generalized discussion of the issues for a larger audience. For example, one proposed scenario involves a toy maker who writes asking for an evaluation of the marketing claims his company is making about some of its toys. The letter begins:

> **My company has been developing several prototypes for toys. We are finished with our design phase and are ready to market our products. We wanted to make sure that the claims we make for our toys are accurate. Our advertising department wants us to make very broad claims, and I do not want to mislead our customers. I am enclosing pictures of our prototypes and the descriptions of each.**

Can you tell me if the descriptions are in line with what developmental research has shown?

The student's editor agrees that the toy maker's claims are too broad and asks the student to write an article responding to the issues the toy maker brings up. The student draws upon available research to evaluate advertising claims about the toys in terms of cognitive development. In other words, he or she will look at the descriptions of the toys (such as "this toy will enhance your baby's memory" or "your baby will lift the flaps to find engaging patterns and colors") and explain which ones make sense for the age range and which ones don't, and why. For instance, maybe the toy does enhance memory, but only for children at least two years old. Or maybe a three month-old baby doesn't have the motor skills needed to lift the flaps or the visual perception to perceive the patterns they've designed.

For another assignment, a reader could send in a video of her son's aggressive behavior. The student's editor, then, asks the student to write an article addressing such issues as peer rejection, parenting practices, and effective intervention strategies.

Along with each assignment (generally beginning on Monday), the editor also suggests related textbook passages and research articles to be read offline. Again, the student is encouraged to do the reading because it actively informs the task to be completed. In response to each story assignment, the student completes research and then writes a draft that he or she will submit on Wednesday. The student will receive feedback from the mentor on Thursday, then make appropriate changes to resubmit before the next task begins the following Monday.

Get By with a Little Help from Experts in the Field

The course offers a myriad of resources to help the student learn the material and to craft his or her responses effectively. These components include:

- Hundreds of video clips of developmental psychology experts from Columbia, Stanford, Cornell, and elsewhere
- Video of important developmental psychology experiments
- Video clips of the course authors (two from Columbia and one from the University of Virginia), who speak directly to the students to answer task-specific questions

- Online summaries of relevant developmental psychology studies and articles
- Online reading guides that help the student understand the reading's relevance to the assignment and highlight its main points.

These tools and others are all intended to make learning the material an active, "doing" experience. And if students can learn by doing developmental psychology, economics, computer programming, and business writing through computer-assisted courses where they apply their knowledge in real-world situations, they can learn by doing almost anything.

Lessons Learned

- Outside assignments and reading can work within the framework of an e-learning class, as long as what students learn from those assignments can actually help them complete their main tasks.
- For subject matter that doesn't naturally call into play some basic mission or activity, you can create one that's realistic and provides a means to apply the material in a useful way.

Conclusion

These courses are the first building blocks of the Virtual University. No one school has a monopoly on the best teachers or the best ideas. Each professor brings his or her own perspective on similar material in an introductory course. In the Virtual University you can have the best and the brightest as your teachers, representing potentially divergent points of view. E-learning allows for anytime, anywhere education that will change the very nature of what it means to go to college. And since these courses can be taken in high school as well, high school, too, will change. The shift from lecture courses to learning-by-doing courses will excite students and free faculty to pursue more interesting teaching and research issues. In a few years we will see a new world.

PART IV

Assessing and Measuring e-Learning

13

Let FREEDOM Ring:
Seven Criteria for Assessing the Effectiveness of an e-Learning Course

I have been describing some e-learning solutions that I believe were done well and constitute the beginning of the e-learning revolution. But how do we know if a course is any good? In this chapter I offer a set of criteria that any course designer must consider. I will explain the learning theory behind these criteria in this chapter, but the original research that supports the theory is referenced in the learning theory bibliography on pages 259–261.

Time

Implicit in a traditional course is the notion of time. A course at a university has a definite length, a certain number of sessions or seat hours. It usually has a defined amount of homework and readings. And it frequently has an exam that students are granted an allotted amount of time to complete. All this is totaled so that a college degree is awarded after a certain number of credit hours have been accumulated. Or, to put this another way, after you put enough time into school with adequate performance, you will earn a degree.

The notion of time is taken seriously by universities. Universities aren't happy if you find a way to finish school too quickly. I finished all the requirements at the University of Texas for a Ph.D. in two years, but still had to register (and pay tuition) for a third year even though I wasn't in the state at the time because the university did not grant Ph.D.s in two years. Most universities have rules like this.

Corporations have issues with time as well. When we are asked to redesign training for a business by taking its existing training method and putting it into software, a curious question emerges: How long should the course take? Businesses have answers to this question that are based entirely on economics. This should not be surprising. Perhaps more surprising is that universities' answers to this question are also based on economics. The answer to this question ought to be, "The course should take as long as it takes to learn the stuff we are trying to teach." This is obvious. It is also obvious why schools never take this answer seriously. Different students learn at different rates. Somehow having one student take twice as long in a course as another is never considered reasonable, even though this is the obvious course of action. We can't just let students go home early, or keep others a few months longer, can we?

Economics come into play in curious ways. Businesses will ask for a course that provides forty hours of instruction. Why? Because trainees are being flown into training centers to which they travel on weekends, the work week is forty hours long, and airfare is the same if you stay for five days or three. Universities can only get professors and students to put up with classes that meet three hours a week for ten or twelve weeks. Anything else is heresy and will not be tolerated by anybody—students, professors, graduate schools, or employers. Just try suggesting that a course meet sixteen hours a week or only one hour and university administrators throw up their hands trying to figure credits, distribution requirements, and the like.

In any other aspect of society where learning is considered to be an issue, time is of no consequence. For instance, the state licensing bureaus need not ask how many hours of courses you have taken. They simply administer the exam. Classes and seat hours are not relevant. On the other hand, insurance companies insist on drivers' education courses that do have seat hour requirements. What is the difference? The difference is whether you buy the idea that performance is what matters or symbolism is what matters. Universities are much less interested in performance than in symbols. One would think, with corporations, it would be the other way around.

Obviously all this changes with e-learning. A course should last as long as it takes the learner to complete it. This means that a course must offer a task for the learner to accomplish. When that task is accomplished, when a student can demonstrate that he or she has learned to do what the course set out to teach him or her to do, then the course has been completed. Completion of a course means mastery in an e-learning environment. Anything else makes no sense.

Measurement

The issue of measurement must be fundamentally reexamined in an e-learning environment. Education is governed by measurement today. Not only does every student and parent want to know how the student is doing; so do employers, graduate schools, and myriad other institutions, even automobile insurance companies (good grades will actually get you lower rates if you are a student!). Because everyone cares so much about grades, schools are far more concerned with grading and testing than with teaching and learning. Now, this may seem like an extreme statement, but any teacher knows that the most frequently asked student question is: *Will this be on the test?*

The problem in a world of virtual, goal-based scenarios is that doing is not as easily measured as knowing. We really don't know what we know about how we do things. We can conduct an interview, manage employees, deal with personal problems, drive a car, hit a golf ball, and so on, without explicitly knowing how much pressure is exerted when we swing or how we decide to challenge an employee or support him or her when he or she is screwing up. We learn these things by doing them, and we cannot necessarily articulate what we know about them.

So how can success in a course be determined in e-learning? In a learn-by-doing course, the ability to do should be the ultimate determinant of success. My favorite analogy here is always the driver's license. If you can drive, you get one. The silly multiple-choice test associated with the driver's exam is just that—silly. The real question is: *Can you drive?* Once it has been determined that you can, you get a license. Not a license that says you got 92 percent. No grade is attached. It's a yes or no affair. And so it would be in any doing course. The question is: Can the student do what we asked him or her to do? If not, the student keeps trying until he or she can.

We can certify those who have performed well in the simulation. Our job is to build simulations well enough so that they include a variety of situations that we feel are important enough to have been the kinds of things we would have tested for in the multiple-choice test. If we want to know if a student understands the meaning of a certain sign, for example, we need only have that sign appear on the simulated roadway.

I do not believe that we are measuring the right things. We shouldn't be measuring the students in e-learning. Well-designed e-learning courses will entail an implicit measurement: the ability to do something offered by the course will have been mastered by the student. So, in the place of measuring the student, I offer the idea of measuring the courses themselves. Designers of e-learning need to know if their course is any good. That, I believe, is worth measuring.

Measurement of Courses

Typically we don't think about measuring courses. Traditionally, courses were never measured at all. Students in college could exhort fellow students to "stay away from Jones" or "not to allow yourself to graduate without taking Smith's *Introduction to Widget Making*." But that was as far as it went. In recent years there have been course evaluation forms for students to fill out in most universities; in business, trainees often get to rate the perceived value of the courses they have been made to take.

As an example of the former, I offer some of the comments students made about my own course at Northwestern last year:

> The professor was incredible.

> Without doing too much work, you'll learn a lot about what you think and why you think it.

> Interesting class, but don't get fooled into believing you're learning.

Wow. I never knew such a great class could exist. I'm afraid that now, I will be disappointed by all of my other classes at Northwestern.

Easy A, but the most boring, pointless lectures.

Take this class—Schank is great—it'll be the highlight of your semester.

Don't take this class if you have any expectations to learn. My tuition was wasted by taking this class.

This is the most interesting and provocative course I have ever taken.

As we can see, while they make interesting reading, the evaluations are not wildly valuable to the professor or even to a prospective student. How do students evaluate courses? The means they employ may or may not be useful to us as we seriously consider what makes a course good. It is important to note that students' own conceptions of whether they have learned may not be the real issue. The problem is that students have a variety of expectations for what a course should contain and accomplish. An entertaining professor may get high praise, but he or she may be imparting very little. A professor who imparts a great deal of information in a dry way may be formally fulfilling the criteria of the course, but may leave the student knowing a lot less than the professor was trying to impart.

In fact, the general model of university courses, where professors have a given amount of material to cover and can vary the ways they cover this material, sets the baseline with which any course designer begins. Since we have all been through many courses of this type, we expect that courses will look like this. As connoisseurs of courses, we can decide for ourselves which ones meet our tastes best. The problem is that what we like and what we remember may not be the same thing. The issue, after all, is memory. What a student takes away from the course in the long-term is the only issue that matters. Students, naturally, cannot comment on what they will remember five years later. Mostly, they comment on what they are feeling about the professor. Five years later they may not remember a thing. Or they may remember one or two poignant moments. Or, if it was a very good course, they may not be able to recall the course itself at all, but they will have used the material in the course in some way in their daily lives. It is this latter state of affairs to which the course designer aspires. Our question is whether we can determine the possibility of this outcome by examining the course itself.

To advance the field of assessment in education, we must seriously consider establishing realistic, memory-related evaluations of the courses themselves. We must know how good a course is, in principle, according to certain metrics that we can agree upon that have some psychological validity. Ideas like "the professor was incredible" are somewhat informative, but the needs of business make it clear that the professor cannot be the central focus of the evaluation. Businesses usually don't employ professors, and while one professional trainer may vary in quality from the next, the idea is to limit that variation. In universities as well, it is unfortunate to rely upon such measures. Professors can be very entertaining (or not), but entertainment is not the primary issue in education, after all. We need to find measures of a different sort, ones that will inform a student's decisions about what courses to take, will inform a professor about what kind of courses to teach, and, more importantly, will inform courses designers of what should and what should not be in a course.

Because there will be many e-learning offerings, and these will become available to both corporations and individuals, it is important to evaluate these courses so that potential students can make reasonable decisions about where to spend their time and money. Harvard is a good place to go to school, presumably because the courses are better at Harvard than at most other places. Of course, this presumption is quite uncertain. What is more sure is that a Harvard degree and connections with students and faculty made during time spent at Harvard can be quite valuable in life. We don't really know if the courses there are better. We have no real way to tell. Students can nevertheless choose Harvard and feel that they have made a safe bet. Virtual Harvard courses will entail more tenuous connections with students and faculty, and there may be no degree. All that will be left are the courses, and there is no reason to believe that Harvard's virtual offerings will be any better than anyone else's. Students will need help deciding. Corporations will build courses as well. Will they be better than Harvard's? How would we know? To provide that help, we must find a good way to evaluate courses.

Things Not to Measure

We must start with what not to measure. It is important to realize that the only measurements that we've had, apart from student's subjective evaluations, have been the amount of time a course takes (seat time) and the amount of material covered by the course (coverage). Both of these measures are not only silly, but detrimental to our understanding of how courses should work.

As I mentioned earlier, seat time is used by most universities and by many businesses. It isn't discussed very much—courses are usually forty hours long—because the structure of schools and business training is built around these fixed notions of seat time, and it is very difficult to change them. The obvious alternative to seat time—students should be in a course for as long as it takes for them to learn what the course teaches—is a radical attack at the system. The reason that this idea is so radical is that it causes us to assess a course and ask just what it teaches students to do.

In the following section I introduce the seven ways to measure a course, the first letters of which combine to form the acronym FREEDOM. In the next chapter I will discuss more about how to measure using these criteria.

Things to Measure

1—Failure

A good course must enable failures that surprise the student. Failure is the key to learning. We have to work hard to recover when things don't work out the way we expected. That work is what learning is all about. For this reason a course must be surprising. We learn when what we expected to happen fails to happen. When things occur in life just the way we imagined they would, then we can say we already knew what would happen, and there is little to learn from the experience. Knowledge is, to a large extent, about predicting events. The rising of the sun in the east in the morning is a predictable event if you know about that subject. To those who have no rules about such matters, each sunrise could be a surprise. Knowledge is the opposite of surprise. If the sun failed to rise, we would want to know what was going on. Failure of predictions based upon knowledge causes us to attempt to revise our knowledge base. We seek explanations from ourselves or from others to help in our quest to make accurate predictions.

For this natural learning process to work in a course, the course must surprise its students. But, more than that, it must put students in a situation where they are entertaining predictions in the first place. We won't fail to predict properly if we weren't already trying to understand and predict the events that are unfolding in front of us.

Lectures are rarely surprising, although they can be. If a good speaker sets up a situation that the listeners are following closely, then they may be surprised if events don't turn out the way they expected. Careful listening requires prediction. Comedians take advantage of this aspect of human understanding all the time:

Last year we went on safari in Africa. We took pictures of the native girls, but they weren't developed. We are going back next year.

Groucho Marx

Jokes like the one above count on the fact that a listener will have decided a particular sense of the word *developed* because of the context of *pictures*. This is the kind of prediction we are talking about. Violating it, in this instance, simply makes us laugh. In more serious venues, when we are trying to understand something more complex than a one-liner, a failure in comprehension of this sort makes us think about what happened.

In order to create an active listener, one who is paying attention to what is being taught, you need to make sure than there are many surprises that force many explanations. This is another way of saying that a student can't simply be listening or reading. He or she must be predicting as well, and the teacher must make sure that the predictions the student makes are sometimes wrong so that thinking will begin. The student who learns the most is the student who encounters a difficulty, takes the wrong path, wonders what to do to fix things next time, and then eventually succeeds. Good educational software enables that kind of experience.

No person who enters a course of study and remains unchanged by it has learned anything at all. A student must change his or her beliefs, point of view, and emotional stance toward a subject as well as acquire new knowledge. Knowledge is not acquired in a vacuum. Learning does not mean simply adding a set of facts to your repertoire of knowledge. This inert view of knowledge underlies the current structure of courses in school.

The idea is that people have a bank of knowledge, and what a course does is simply add to it. Unfortunately, it's not that easy.

In reality, people have attitudes, beliefs, procedures, and a range of other kinds of knowledge besides factual data. Learning means altering this less-static type of knowledge as well. We need not only to inform in a course but also to create a structural change in memory

People have complex memory structures that they use to help them understand the outside world and to function in that world. As I have said before, they know how airplane trips work and use that knowledge to help them understand stories about such trips or use that knowledge to help them take a trip themselves. They understand how human interaction works, and, here again, they use their knowledge to guide their comprehension and their functioning. The knowledge that they have changes daily. Each time there is another trip or another human interaction, there is the potential for change.

This kind of change happens through the use of memory structures that contain expectations about what will happen next. As these expectations prove to be wrong in some way, people change them, sometimes consciously and sometimes without realizing what they are doing. When a restaurant's food that was good is no longer good, we change our view of the restaurant. This is how natural everyday learning takes place.

For some reason, learning in school has always had a different set of underlying assumptions. We act as if being told about the restaurant's food will change our point of view, when, in fact, only eating will really cause a mental change to take effect. We learn very little by listening in the sense that what we learn can be repeated but does not become part of our processing apparatus. Memory changes when something causes it to change, when we experience something that makes us look at things a new way. A course must do this to be effective. No course that simply tells about the world will serve to change memory in any profound way. Memory change comes from failure. A good course must provide such failures.

2—Reasoning

A good course encourages practice in reasoning. Education is about teaching people to reason. If reasoning were a subject per se, you could teach people to do it, and they would be forever capable of reasoning. Unfortunately, reasoning in physics isn't exactly the same as reasoning in political science, although they do have some things in common. To learn how to reason in our daily lives, we must practice reasoning in task-specific situations. Reasoning on the job is the most important part of learning a job. It's easy to learn procedures; it's much harder to learn what to do when those procedures fail or when there are no rules that fit the situation. Being able to handle new issues that come up is the hallmark of intelligence.

Thus, it is the job of every course to teach students in that course to figure things out for themselves. Yes, there are rules; yes, there are ways of doing things; yes, there are facts and cases and examples to be followed; but most of all there is figuring out what to do on one's own. Learning in a course really means preparing yourself to go out into the world and practice what you've learned to do, and this means doing it without help.

Courses put out by businesses, on the Web, or otherwise, frequently fail on this important dimension. They want to tell students what to do instead of allowing them to figure it out for themselves. A good course must put students in complex situations, in the intellectual equivalent of a maze, and have them figure their way out. If a course doesn't allow students to reason on their own about real issues that may or may not have clearly right answers, then it fails on this dimension.

3—Emotionality

A good course must incite an emotional response in the student. In many ways, emotions are one of the fundamental bases of memory. We remember what we care about. We dwell on what we are upset about. We recall happy days and sad days. We get excited and we get depressed and we remember why. We remember being angry or hopeful. In short, we remember that which has caused us to feel something. Conversely, if we feel nothing, we remember little. A good course must evoke emotional reactions in its students.

Now this is easier said than done. How can mathematics be emotional? Well, of course, it is for many students, usually negatively so. Students remember the stress induced by the course, but not the course itself. The issue for a course designer is to find a way to evoke emotional responses naturally. One such natural emotion can be found in the sense of accomplishment felt by someone who has worked hard to achieve a goal and gotten there. Students do feel this emotion in many courses that currently exist, but usually that emotion is tied to a grade earned or an exam that has been studied for and completed with success. The problem here is that students are likely to recall the process of studying or the emotional reaction of getting the good grade, and neither of these relate to recalling the content of the course itself.

The issue for course designers and teachers is to get the emotionality to be tied to the content in some way. What this can mean in practice actually boils down to one of two things: either a powerful demonstration or a powerful reaction to doing—the frustrations associated with doing and the sense of accomplishment associated with achieving a goal.

Put into practice, this means that in the telling model of education, memory alteration can be achieved, and thus learning will take place, to the extent that the story being told or images being shown are emotionally powerful. One might expect that one could learn about the Holocaust, for example, by seeing vivid pictures or hearing firsthand stories. Even without doing, we could learn if the emotional impact were high.

But in a doing environment this means we have to control emotions associated with the doing. Thus, we can expect that if students were treated badly in some way (in a simulation), they would recall what happened to them and what they learned with no trouble at all. Similarly, if it were possible, we could easily teach about the Holocaust by making students experience some of the same experiences. This would probably best be done in simulation, given the rules of education under which we live; but from a memory point of view, if you want students to remember, the more real it is, the easier it is to remember.

But what about less-emotional subjects? It is very difficult to make dry subjects emotionally impacting in a lecture setting. This is quite a bit easier in a doing setting, but it does require some creativity to make good doing situations. As long as there are people involved (simulated characters in a simulation, for example) it is possible to have them act badly, be upsetting, be threatening, be exciting, and so on. People remember interactions with others. Good courses provide those interactions and make them memorable.

4—Exploration

A good course promotes exploration and enables inquiry.
When a child asks a question it is a wonderful thing. If a child asks, it is usually because he or she wants to know or at least because he or she wants to engage an adult in conversation. Conversation is, at its base, the root of learning. We learn in conversation because we have to play our role in the conversation. We have to keep up our end of the dialogue. This means that we must think of something to say in response to what we have heard. The process for doing that thinking requires that we analyze what we have heard sufficiently so that we can extract an index from it and match that index to something we already have stored in our memories. In other words, listening means matching what was said to what we know. If what was said is mundane and already well known by us, then we match to an identity and say something like "right" or "I already knew that" or "that's what I thought." When the match is partial, when we knew some of what we heard or found some accord with what we thought and some discord, or found something similar but not identical, then we have something to say back. We can say what we were reminded of, or we can argue with a part with which we disagree.

This is the basis of dialogue, and dialogue eventually leads to the third possibility—that something someone says has no match at all in our memories. In such a case, we work hard at finding a place to put the new information. We need to store it someplace that relates to what we already know. So we become curious; we attempt to understand better so that we can fill in the holes in our knowledge and effectively relate what we heard to what we had known. This means we must inquire. Our part of the dialogue turns into questions at this point. We ask if what we heard really happened; we ask for explanations of what happened; we ask for facts that would make clear what we didn't know that confused us. To put it another way, when we are confused, we can learn because we suddenly want to know. Without inquiry there is no learning.

To inquire we must have something to inquire about. If there are no people to interact with in a simulation, then there must be a world with which to interact. Exploration means examining the world around us in sufficient detail to become curious about it. A good course promotes curiosity. Exploration is the starting point for curiosity.

It must be the goal of every course to cause students to begin to wonder about issues within the framework of the course. This means they must be able to look around, to go where they need to go and do what they need to do, in order to satisfy their curiosity. This is not simply an issue of having students ask questions. The real question is whether students are curious about the subject matter. While this might be expressed as a question in class, it could also be expressed as navigation with an automated video database, independent work in the library, or discussions with fellow students. A successful course enables exploration such that students can become interested in knowing more and can begin to find ways to get the information they seek.

5—Doing

A good course encourages practice in doing. Doing is what learning is all about. We learn so that we can do. Everything in education tends to point the other way: The idea behind most schooling is that we learn so that we can know. But knowing without doing is a rather meaningless state of affairs. Not all doing is physical, of course. Mental doing or social doing are also kinds of doing. Learning to do means learning procedures and practicing those procedures.

Most courses leave doing out. Most courses are a kind of preparation for a doing that never takes place. Sometimes arguing about ideas, a kind of doing, does occur in a course. Sometimes laboratory work in a course allows some practice in doing. But in a standard lecture course there is usually no doing at all.

A good course must not only include doing but also be centered around it. The course should be about preparing students to do something, having them do it, and then having them reflect upon how well they did it and prepare to try again.

Measuring how much doing there is in a course is not trivial except at the extremes. A straight lecture course has no doing. It totally fails on this criterion. A course where all you ever do is practice what you're learning to do will score very high on the doing scale, but may fail in the other important aspects we have discussed here. Doing is the central element in assessing the quality of a course, but it is not the only element. In attempting to understand how to assess a course, we must bear in mind that, while doing is the key element, there can be bad doing courses as well. A course that entailed doing without good teaching, for example, would not be a very good course.

6—Observation

A good course allows students to see things for themselves.
When we look to measure most existing courses, we find that they are often lacking in the doing criterion. But, curiously, observation is an element that current courses do often use. The idea of *visual aids* has been with teachers and course designers for a long time. Teachers often show students pictures of what they are talking about; lecturers frequently show interesting slides; parents, when reading to children, know to let the child look at the picture at frequent intervals. We all know intuitively how important mental images are. When we try to recall something, we often find ourselves picturing a scene or a face. We think about past events in terms of mental images, and our memory is aided by them.

The pictures we recall best are, of course, those that satisfy the other criteria listed here. They relate to things we care about and are curious about—things that we find surprising, that cause us to view the world in a new way. Images can be pleasing because they are pretty or interesting or even repulsive.

When we examine courses for their use of observation, we need to bear in mind that the primary criterion we care about is memorability. If we are likely to remember the image, then it is potentially of some educational value. Of course, there are other criteria, like relevance to what we are trying to teach, for example. A course that consisted of only memorable pictures might be interesting on some level, but there needs to be more. We can remember interesting sights, but what we remember about them must be germane.

Allowing students to observe things has another purpose beyond memorability. Observations, as any scientist can tell you, are the beginning of the data gathering from which conclusions can be drawn. And, although human resource management may not seem like science, for example, observing the behavior of employees is certainly the right way to start in learning to make decisions about them. Courses that provide observations that need to be dealt with and analyzed are courses that will cause students to think about what they have seen. And analyzing what you have seen is the beginning of learning.

7—Motivation

A good course supplies motivation. The first thing that we need to measure in a course is the extent to which it motivates students to care about learning what is going to be taught in the course. Students won't learn anything in even the best course if they can't figure out how what they will learn applies to them. To put it another way, every student in every course has the expectation that what the teacher is trying to teach will somehow be relevant to his or her present or future life. It is obvious, if one takes this idea seriously, why so many courses in school fail to really work (and why, for the most part, training courses that businesses offer have a better track record).

A student who is learning about long division, or reading Dickens, or studying ancient Greece, has questions in his or her mind about the real-life relevance of what he or she is learning. Some students simply grant the school system the wisdom to know what is relevant and dive in. Others suspend disbelief long enough to pass the tests that will get them to wherever it is they think school will get them in life. For them, the relevance to their own lives is in the grades, and they do what they are asked. For others, the belief in the system and the quest for grades do not supply the necessary motivation, and they lose interest and fail to learn what they are being taught.

In corporations the story is actually quite similar. Trainees may believe that a course is relevant because management said so, or they may believe that they need to do well to secure their job, or they may just try to fake it and get by.

It's more than worrying about whether students are paying attention or have a good attitude. The problem is deeper than that. Motivation is an integral part of memory. Even if you accept that you will not fight the system and will try to learn whatever it is you were asked to learn, you may have a great deal of trouble remembering in the long term what you were not inherently motivated to learn in the first place. You can't fool your memory into being motivated.

Memory is the name of the game here. The desire of any teacher, and of any course, is to have the students come away with their memories permanently altered. Most courses cause a temporary memory alteration. In other words, students can pass the test and then have no ability to pass the same test years, months, or even days later. College students report overwhelmingly that they could not pass the same tests that they passed a year earlier.

Now, compare this to exams that test whether someone can do a job that they already do. If that test is a good test, no studying should be required. Every employee who does his or her job well should know most of the answers to any reasonable question about the job. If he or she does not, then the test is bad. The reason for this is easy enough—practice makes perfect. Memory for new information requires motivation to pay attention in the first place and practice in the use of that information in the second place.

Even if a student plays along and does well in a course that is not intrinsically motivating, it will be very difficult for that student to remember the course's content. To remember something, you must know where to put that thing in memory. If I tell you a random number, you can keep it in mind for a short while; but after some time, you can't recall it because it was meaningless—it didn't fit with any other information you had or any goals you were trying to achieve. If I tell you how to do something—an operation on the computer, for example—you will remember it as long as it takes you to do it. Then, if you don't do that operation for a while, you are likely to have to ask me for the same information again.

To really acquire new information, you must recognize the need for that information. This is another way of saying that you need to know where that new information will go in memory. Now, we don't know that sort of thing consciously, but we can know unconsciously what it is that we need to know. We know we don't need to know the date of the Battle of Waterloo; we know that we might need to be able to convince somebody of something in an argument. It is thus far easier to teach the latter than the former. If we should, for some reason, want to teach something that it is not inherently motivating to know, then it is important to embed it within something that is motivating to know. (The date might be the key to winning the argument, for example, although this begs the question of why anyone would want to teach the date in the first place.)

A good course supplies motivation or builds upon motivation that is there in the first place. If the material to be taught has no inherently motivating reason to learn it built in, then the course must supply the motivation. We don't have to explain to students why they need to learn to drive or why they would want to know about sex, but we do have to explain why they need to know history. Since that explanation itself is still unlikely to supply the necessary motivation, it is incumbent upon the structure of the course itself to supply the motivation. That is, we cannot simply tell students why they should be motivated, as this will not motivate them. We must build upon the motivation that students naturally have and weave what we want to teach around it.

A successful course has the students in it clamoring for more. They should be sorry the course is finished because they were so motivate to learn more.

In summary, let FREEDOM ring.

CHAPTER

14

How to Apply
the **FREEDOM** Criteria

The set of criteria we decided upon in the last chapter is intended for use in judging any course. Our problem now is to figure out exactly how to use it. We must determine a set of rules to measure a course. This is of increasing importance, since every day more courses (of dubious quality) are appearing on the Web. With large numbers of virtual offerings by universities and corporations, it is imperative that we find a way to evaluate these courses in a consistent way.

The real question is: *Will a student learn anything from this course?* Curiously, this is not the typical question that college students ask at a university. They ask about grading policy, workload, and the entertainment value of the professor. In the virtual world, these questions are all moot. Like students in adult continuing education courses, virtual course students will care if, after having taken the course, they can do something they could not have done before.

Two Categories of Measurement

With this in mind, let's attempt to use the seven criteria for course evaluation. The seven criteria are actually quite different from one another. They fall roughly into two categories. These categories reflect a central issue in measuring courses, namely, that on some dimensions, courses can be measured on an absolute basis, independent of the students in them, while with others, the measurement depends entirely upon the students in the course. This is actually an interesting issue. No matter how good a course is, it could be inappropriate for a given student. And, no matter how bad a course is, it could be quite exciting for a student who loves the subject. The seven criteria reflect this division in the following way:

Student Independent

Doing

Reasoning

Exploration

Observation

Student Dependent

Motivation

Emotion

Failure

No course can be absolutely good. What I mean by this is that even the best course could be simply wrong for some students who were not ready, too advanced, uninterested, or emotionally unprepared for it. Simply put, it's harder to assess the student-dependent aspects of a course. The student-independent measures are much more straightforward, so let's start with them.

Measuring Courses (Absolutely)

The four relevant student-independent measures are:

Doing

Reasoning

Exploration

Observation

When we say that a criterion is student independent, we mean that a course can be judged on this criterion without concern for who is in the course. In the strictest sense, this can never be entirely true. For example, we can measure how much doing there is in a course independent of the students in it. Nevertheless, it could be the case that some students are incapable or unprepared for the doing even though it exists in the course. But it is a student-independent measure because we can assess by focusing on general issues of appropriateness rather than asking how an individual student dealt with the problems.

Student-Independent Measures

Measuring Doing

A course either has doing in it or it doesn't. The amount of doing it contains can be measured as a percentage of the time used by the overall course. Thus, for example, a course in how to drive might be 100 percent doing, it might be 50 percent driving and 50 percent listening (I include observing within listening here), or it might be 100 percent listening. The issue is what overall percentage is doing. There is a right answer to this question: A course should have as much doing in it as is necessary to ensure that its participants have mastered the doing by the end of the course, and it should have as much listening in it as is needed to aid in successful doing. The problem with this answer is twofold. First, under current educational conditions, courses do not stop when the student has mastered the doing. Rather, courses stop when they are over, even if the student hasn't mastered the doing. This state of affairs is quite unfortunate and is reflective of the quality of a course. Secondly, the ideal amount of listening in comparison to doing is certainly arguable and is something quite complex to measure.

In any case, these issues can be discovered empirically. My argument here is that it's easy enough to differentiate doing from listening. So the right answer is that a course should be mostly doing and that listening should be in support of doing. However, the amount of listening needed would be predictably higher the more theoretical the skill being taught. In any case, listening should come *after* difficulties in doing rather than in preparation for doing. All of these issues can, and I hope will, be empirically determined. The way to do this is to test courses that are focused around doing to see if students feel they had too much or too little help in doing and to see how easily students mastered the doing under a variety of circumstances. In this way, the actual numbers can be determined. We are looking for the ideal percentage of doing versus listening and the proper placement of the listening in relation to the doing.

To make this more specific, let's consider three examples: a course in driving, a course in chemistry, and a course in leadership. The driving course is as close to a 100 percent doing course as we can imagine. There could be some preparation, but it really isn't necessary for anyone who has been around for sixteen years in a modern society. This again brings up the issue of readiness for doing. We will assume here that students are ready and that the courses we imagine are taught at the right time to the right person.

(Now, bear in mind that this is a mighty big assumption. Quite often courses are problematic for just this reason. Typically, calculus is taught simply because it is the next math in the sequence, regardless of whether the student has any need for calculus in anything he or she will ever do. In business, courses on corporate values are often taught to new employees who have no sense of the situations they might find themselves in their new job and cannot relate at all to what they are being told. The proper timing of a course is an important issue, but not one I intend to tackle here.)

So a driving course is inherently a doing course, and all listening or observing needs to be in support of the doing. The course is finished (ideally) when the driver can drive well. This is what we call a *doing-driven* course. For doing-driven courses there should be little or no listening, so we would expect the measures developed for such courses to reveal a very high percentage of doing.

A chemistry course is another issue entirely. To talk about this kind of course at all, we must ask why students should learn chemistry. This is not a simple question, but the answers to this question will help determine the correct doing measurement. One reason to learn chemistry is because you want to become a chemist. Another might be because you want to become a doctor, and chemistry is required. Another might be to learn about the world in which you live. A fourth might be to help you do scientific reasoning.

Now, each of these reasons has a different impact on determining the right doing/listening ratio. The first (becoming a chemist) should be a doing-driven course. If you are trying to learn to do something, the right way to learn it is to do it. The second (becoming a doctor) should be a doing-driven course, but of a different sort because it would involve learning a different set of skills. The third (learning about the world) would not be doing-driven, but would still involve learning to do various things in life for which a knowledge of chemistry would be useful. This kind of course we call *doing-centered*. By this I mean that while doing is at the center of the course, it is not exactly the real intent of the course. The fourth (scientific reasoning) would be a *doing-enhanced* course. The intent would be to learn to reason, so chemistry would be learned in that context. What that means is that a set of problems might be presented, knowledge taught to help you solve those problems, and then the problems would be tackled. In such a course, doing helps teach reasoning, but reasoning (which is, of course, a kind of doing) dominates the course. This might mean that argumentation and discussion are more at the center of the course.

There are many issues here. Current university structures typically create one chemistry course to attempt to deal with all four of the reasons we have discussed for taking the course. Typically, these courses satisfy no one; but they work from the university's point of view because the school can cram many students into them. The resources don't exist to attempt to satisfy all these different needs. Ideally, the goals of the student should drive the structure of the course. So we cannot give hard and fast measures for how much doing should be in a course without knowing what the student is trying to learn. What we can say is that doing-driven courses ought to be almost entirely doing, doing-centered courses ought to primarily doing, and doing-enhanced courses should have great deal of doing in them. Determining which of these types of courses is ideal depends upon the goals of the students in the course.

I mention a leadership course to point out that it is all too easy to imagine that telling people about something will help them do it. Leadership courses are quite often mostly listening. When they involve doing, they usually use odd situations like roughing it in the woods, which is OK if that's the kind of leadership skills you are trying to teach. Office leadership or thought leadership might not be the same, of course. To turn such a leadership course that quotes Alexander the Great and Machiavelli into a doing-driven course isn't that simple. But we can prepare future leaders by having them make decisions and attempt to understand the consequences of those decisions, enticing them to learn about leadership by confronting the failures of others and enticing them to make bad decisions of their own. Until you have failed painfully while trying to lead, you know nothing about leadership.

The key issue in measuring the doing in a course is determining which of the three types of doing courses is most appropriate to the situation at hand.

Measuring Reasoning

How often does a student in a course need to reason something out for him or herself? This is the key issue in measuring the reasoning inherent in a course. Many existing courses ask students to reason. They do so through homework and tests if those assignments are well designed. They also do so through class discussion if there is any and if it is of the proper type. We can measure the reasoning in a course, therefore, by asking the following questions:

1. Are assignments given for which there are no obvious right answers?
2. Are the problems presented to students to work out on their own fundamentally different from ones they may have worked on in class?
3. Are students asked hard questions in class and given the opportunity to come up with original answers to those questions and the chance to defend those answers?

A course will score high on reasoning if a large percentage of the course is devoted to these issues. Any course with resounding yesses to the above questions is doing well on the reasoning dimension.

Measuring Exploration

This is actually very simple to measure. It is a function of the opportunity to explore a situation by either asking or experiencing, as well as of the possibility for answers. A course would measure well on this dimension if it provided the opportunity for students to seek the answer to any question they had. Sometimes traditional courses do provide that opportunity. What they cannot do, however, is provide that opportunity to everyone, partially because there isn't enough time and also because, no matter how much time is provided, it is invariably the case that some students are too shy to ask. Some courses allow exploration, but most enforce sitting in a classroom rather then going out into the real world.

Further, what many courses do not do is present situations in which inquiry is necessary. Telling the student more than the student wants to know, for example, tends to kill off inquiry. What is needed is to create situations in which questions naturally come to mind and where there is available help. This often means putting students in doing situations, which are likely to promote inquiry, because a student may have difficulties in doing. Inquiry tied to difficulties in doing is what we are aiming at.

On the answering side of the issue, one answerer is really not sufficient. The idea that only the teacher knows the right answer is an idea from previous conceptions of education and needs not apply in virtual courses that can have many possible (electronic) experts available. The variety of responses available to an inquiry is a very important measure of a course.

One question to ask at this point is about the extremes. What if a course were entirely questions and answers? Would that be a good course? Obviously not, if there were no doing involved as well, but it really isn't a bad goal to aim for. The problem is that this implies a one-on-one structure and thus would mean that it might work well for virtual courses but would be hard to implement in a live course.

Exploration is vital for education. The key issues are:

1. When a student has a question, can he or she ask it?
2. How many varieties of answers are possible?
3. Is dialogue encouraged?
4. Are the issues covered interesting enough to warrant inquiry and dialogue?

Measuring Observation

It might seem that the more images there are, the easier it would be to remember the content. Images can come from pictures shown in a course or from situations witnessed and experienced within the course. The latter are always preferable because they relate to doing. The former, which are a lot like listening, can still be memorable, depending on how vivid they are and on the emotional impact they convey. Obviously, a course that is entirely pictures could be memorable, but it could also be deadly dull. The real issue is how well the images relate to the content at hand. Another way of putting this is that images should have emotional impact that relates to the doing in a course. For example, images of car crashes in a driving course are probably of some value, but they would be of real value if they related to particular maneuvers that a given student had just attempted.

So we cannot simply count images. We can, however, ask if every doing is accompanied by images and if every telling is accompanied by images and if those images were emotionally powerful and relevant.

Student-Dependent Measures

Measuring Motivation

A good course provides motivation. But different students come into a course with different levels of motivation. The question is: How do we assess a course with respect to motivation if each student is different?

The truth is that all students are similarly motivated; the differences lie in the details. For example, we can assume that any student would be motivated to learn something if he or she knew it would help in achieving a goal that he or she had. Students are motivated to learn to drive if they know they will want to drive. A driving course need not supply motivation because it can be assumed to be intrinsically motivating. But what makes it intrinsically motivating is the simple assumption that everyone wants to learn to do it. By contrast, trigonometry is more or less the opposite of intrinsically motivating because it can be assumed that hardly anyone feels a natural desire to learn how to do it.

So a course must supply motivation by building on natural motivation. The extent to which this happens in a course can be assessed. To do this we need to understand the natural motivators in a course. Then we can judge their extent. To put it another way, we need to ask, "Why would a student want to learn this?"

There are a variety of reasons that a student might want to learn something (apart from the fact that a course fulfills some degree or certification requirement).

1. Students are motivated to learn when it will help them do something they want to do.
2. Students are motivated to learn when the material is interesting to them.
3. Students are motivated to learn when they are frustrated by something.
4. Students are motivated to learn when they believe there will be some reward for having learned.

Using these criteria, we can judge the extent to which a course succeeds on the motivation dimension by asking if the course relates to an obviously needed skill, is interesting, resolves some frustration, or provides some reward. It might seem that these are still all student-dependent issues, and to some extent they are. What interests one person may not interest another, and the value of any reward might differ from person to person as well. The issue is not the inherent interestingness of an idea or of a course, but the extent to which a course resolves the difference between the absolute inherent interest and an interestingness that makes a course workable. To put this more concretely, we can assume that certain things are simply more interesting than other things on an absolute scale for nearly everybody. For example, sex and death seem to interest everybody while concrete mixing and the sleeping habits of gnats interest very few people. The motivation issue revolves around transforming the inherently uninteresting into the inherently interesting. For measurement purposes, we can ask the following questions:

1. Is the material inherently interesting?
2. To the extent that it is not, does the course provide a means of transforming the material in such a way as to make it inherently interesting?
3. Is the means of transformation natural or forced?

We have written about some of these issues before when discussing goal-based scenarios. The idea is that any course can be made interesting by building upon natural intrinsic interests and using those interests as a vehicle for presenting material that is intrinsically less interesting. In practice, this means that such material can be linked to needs, desires, frustrations, and rewards. The naturalness of that linking is at issue. Math Blaster is a piece of software that fails as a course because it tackles the motivation issue in an unnatural way (tying shooting to math). However, there is a lesson to be learned from Math Blaster. While it is not a good course, it would not score a zero on the motivation dimension because it does get children to use it. It succeeds at doing this because it builds on what is naturally motivating.

Measuring Emotional Impact

Here again, there is the tendency to believe that what is an emotional experience for one person is not for another. But, if you recall, we are talking about courses here, not the emotions of one person toward another. An emotional experience in a course is a fairly predictable thing. Fear, for example, doesn't usually occur in a course, but when it does it can have a huge impact on memory and therefore on learning. Love might be good for memory, but relying upon it for course-creation purposes is probably a bad idea.

The idea is simple. A good course has emotional impact. Some subjects are naturally more emotionally impactful than others, so the problem for a course designer is to reduce the difference by teaching less emotional things in an emotional context. To measure how well this has been done, we need simply check the emotional experiences provided by a course. A typical experience is success. Courses set out to provide a reward (usually a grade—less often a sense of accomplishment), and this can have an emotional impact on the student. Other common emotional aspects of a course are stress, fear, frustration, and so on. What we want are positive emotional indicators. Here again, these need to be tied to learning in some natural way. A course that is one big party might be great fun and have a high emotional impact, but learning might be quite limited in such a situation.

The trick is to count emotional situations that relate strongly to the learning goals of the course. Such a measure is easy enough, although it may seem, at first glance, to be quite subjective. Any good course designer needs to weave an emotional strand into any course. This can be done by recognizing what emotions are, then attempting to evoke them. Typically, people who do research on emotion talk about the following emotions:

Surprise

Fear

Anger

Disgust

Contempt

Sadness

Joy

Shame/Guilt

Envy/Jealousy

Frustration

Love

So one question for a designer, for example, is: How do we make students feel disgust or envy in a course? If you think about it, this is not as difficult as it seems. Envy can be brought about, for example, by playing one student off another or by making a simulated character do better than the student at something. Disgust is obvious, although never pleasant. In any case, to the extent that these and other emotions are aroused, a learner will remember what he or she has experienced.

Measuring Failure

Surprise, according to some researchers, is an emotion, too. But it is a special one because so much of learning depends upon it. If everything goes as expected, it is very difficult to learn. So, a course designer must create surprises. We can measure the extent of those surprises by seeing how often a student fails to easily achieve the various subgoals in a course. A course designer must structure the experiences in a course so that they tend to work out in some way that causes the student to reconsider his or her point of view from time to time. We are not talking about surprising students with a clown or a make-believe Martian invasion. Students will indeed remember such occurrences, but they may not remember anything more than the occurrences themselves. The problem for the course designer is to make the surprises relevant to what is to be learned. This means sequencing experiences so that they tend to reverse the assumptions made from the previous experience. In other words, if you learn *A* from experience 1, experience

2 should teach you the exceptions to A by building on A and surprising you such that just when you were predicting A, B occurs.

Scorecard

Using these metrics, we can grade courses with respect to their value as learning experiences. To see how to do this, let's consider a hypothetical (but typical) lecture course that one might find in college. These seven measures are not equally valued. I suggest that their relative values be as follows:

- Failure: worth 10 out of 100
- Reasoning: worth 25 out of 100
- Exploration: worth 5 out of 100
- Emotion: worth 10 out of 100
- Doing: worth 25 out of 100
- Observation: worth 5 out of 100
- Motivation: worth 20 out of 100

Here is how we might score such a course:

- **Failure: 1 out of 10:** While not a great deal can happen in a lecture that is surprising, some interesting things can happen if a lecturer does his or her job well.
- **Reasoning: 10 out of 25:** This depends upon the kind of homework assignments given; a grade of 10 is assessed on the assumption that there are some real problems that students work on in their homework that require real thinking.
- **Exploration: 1 out of 5:** This assumes that the class has 300 people and that hardly anyone's questions are answered.
- **Emotion: 2 out of 10:** Assuming that this isn't necessarily a bad lecturer, good lecturers can arouse emotion in students by telling good stories.
- **Doing: 0 out of 25:** This assumes that this course consists entirely of lectures.
- **Observation: 1 out of 5:** This assumes the course is straight stand-up lecture with some pictures shown from time to time.
- **Motivation: 0 out of 20:** This assumes that people are signed up for this course for the usual reasons, such as fitting their schedule, completing a prerequisite to something they want to take, or being required to take it.

Now, just in case the reader thinks I was being unduly harsh here, I should point out that I am a professional lecturer and I was thinking of my own talks as I wrote this. (Of course, in one-hour keynote lectures you don't give homework, so the only decent grade I gave out doesn't apply to my own lectures.)

The final grade for a typical stand-up lecture course would be a 15. Obviously this is a rather harsh judgment. Let's look at the opposite side of the spectrum.

Imagine a course where you're learning to fly an airplane using an air flight simulator. (This was the original e-learning course, after all!) Sitting next to you in the simulator is an expert who only talks when you ask for help or when he or she feels that you need to discuss what has just happened. No lectures are given, but an electronic set of experts are available to discuss various situations you might get into and to talk about what they did in those situations. The course designer has laid out an increasingly difficult set of situations designed to cause you to get into trouble and to encourage and help you reason your way out of those situations. Now let's grade such a course:

- **Observation: 5 out of 5:** The course would use many visual images that described previous situations; the bad experiences in the course would provide images as well.
- **Exploration: 5 out of 5:** There is always someone there to help; there is a panel of electronic experts to ask questions of.
- **Doing: 25 out of 25:** The course is a doing course.
- **Reasoning: 25 out of 25:** No situation would be presented that failed to require reasoning, and discussion of that reasoning would occur as needed.
- **Motivation: 20 out of 20:** Anyone who took this course would be interested in learning to fly the plane safely.
- **Emotion: 10 out of 10:** Potential crashes could be very emotional experiences.
- **Failure: 10 out of 10:** Maneuvers that caused difficulties would feel like failure.

Now, I have set this up to make a point. The ideal e-learning course is just like this hypothetical flying course. Naturally, there are many reasons why we cannot create courses like this in every instance. Certainly, the one-on-one nature of the course makes it difficult to replicate in live classroom situations. But, if we are interested in creating virtual courses and we are interested in measuring such courses, then we need to have an ideal to strive for. Next let's consider something in between these two extremes.

We can do this by measuring the finance prematriculation course we built for Harvard Business School and discussed in Chapter 11. As you may remember, the goal of this course is to teach incoming MBA students the basic principles of finance for use in school and in the business world. In the simulations, the student first play the role of junior financial advisor charged with helping clients choose appropriate investment instruments. Later, the student acts as financial analyst who must use several valuation techniques to see if the acquisition of another company makes sense. Now let's grade this course:

- **Observation: 2 out of 5:** It is difficult to use very powerful images in such a course. The students can look at pictures of simulated clients and coworkers, or watch Flash animations introducing the financial system through a living case study. But these images don't create the learning experience so much as they facilitate it.
- **Exploration: 5 out of 5:** There is never a reason that inquiry cannot be done right. Having inquiry handled properly means that there is always available help and there is always a series of experts available electronically. This system includes a large network of interrelated text descriptions and explanations, graphical animations, user help and guidance, and audio expert stories from HBS professors.
- **Doing: 20 out of 25:** While this course might not necessarily pack the punch of the air flight simulator, it does allow the students to feel they really are in the middle of complex business decisions. The students have the same kind of personal interactions and make the same kinds of decisions that normally take place in the financial world. It lacks some of the visuals that take place in the everyday world, however.
- **Reasoning: 20 out of 25:** Students must consider and make complicated financial decisions, then support those decisions with logical justifications. Their reasoning is critiqued by the program and guided by related expert advice. There is no reason that any such course, designed properly, would not require complex reasoning on the part of the stu-

dents for them to successfully make the needed decisions. The students do not have to defend their reasoning, however, and this is also important.

- **Motivation: 10 out of 20:** As incoming MBA candidates, students who take this class presumably want to work in the business world. We like to think that, since the program is designed to look and feel like the real business world, it is compelling enough that motivation isn't really an issue. Of course, if a student isn't motivated by finance, this course may not help that much.
- **Emotion: 8 out of 10:** While finance is not the most emotional of subjects, the life and death of companies and personal fortunes can be. The stories that frame the financial decisions to be made in this course are emotionally urgent and impactful. They cause students the same kinds of emotional stress that might occur in the real-world version of the roles they are playing.
- **Failure: 10 out of 10:** The results of each decision made in this course can be quite surprising, causing students to think long and hard about where and how they screwed up. But be warned that the *surprise* component could also be done rather badly, with every situation in the program being mundane and obvious.

The issue here, of course, is design. It is not my point here to grade a hypothetical course but to point out where the real issues are. A course that is doing-driven will be a very good course if and only if the designers of that course have supplied sufficient expertise to help the doer. Designers must also set up situations such that, in order to complete the task at hand, sufficient reasoning is needed and the situations encountered are unusual and interesting in some way. Thus, there are two real issues.

1. Is the course doing-centered?
2. Has the design allowed for the doing to be memorable?

A course is only as good as its designers allow it to be. Designers must take into account the seven dimensions discussed here. I will leave the particulars of exactly how these criteria are to be measured to others. I suspect this will be a big issue in the future as people demand criteria with which to measure the numerous e-learning offerings that will become available. My point here is to make it clear what needs to be measured and to encourage designers to take such criteria into account when designing new courses.

The age of e-learning is upon us. We must do our best to ensure that e-learning courses are of the highest quality, since it is very likely that we are beginning to lay the groundwork for the educational system of the twenty-first century.

CHAPTER

Postscript: e-Learning Does Not Mean Copying School

Whenever I teach a class, I ask students why they are in college. They tell me things like, "It's a four-year vacation," "The parties are good," "It will get me a good job later," "It's what everyone does, so I never thought about an alternative," and so on. The issue of learning never comes up. No student has ever mentioned it in class, although I ask the question quite often. Why is that? As I said earlier, school isn't really about learning at all. It's about certification. College students attend school to get a degree that they hope will get them something they want. They pick schools on this basis, and they attend school with the concomitant attitude. Students attend college (or any other school) to get a piece of paper, and they try to do well to get recommendations so they can get into the next school or get the job they covet. We never ask a student if he learned a lot, we ask how well he or she did. Evaluation is based on the judgment of others when it comes to "official" learning. Students feel they did well when others say they did well. It is the rare student who says that he or she learned a great deal and thus was very happy with the educational experience.

E-learning offers the opportunity to create some massive changes in what it means to obtain an education. Corporations must not make the mistake of attempting to copy the courses that universities deliver when they build e-learning systems. Those courses were not necessarily built for reasons that bear any relation to the needs of a corporation. To take advantage of the opportunity provided by e-learning, we must change some of the underlying conceptions that shape our very conception of school. We must not assume that professors know what to teach or how to teach it. Copying a well-known professor's course may be a very good idea, or it just might be a very bad one.

Many professors in today's universities are not motivated to provide high-quality teaching. They do not see themselves as providing a service to a paying clientele, and they know students will not act like consumers. Students will not complain if a professor is ineffective, in part because they view effectiveness as the ability to entertain and in part because good grades counteract the potential uselessness of a course. Many a student signs up for a course in college because it is an easy A, or because it fits in his schedule, or because it is required, not because the subject excites him.

It is not irrelevant that it is the parents of the consumer who are paying the bills, making the real service provider's issue one of alcohol policies and dorm room quality rather than of the quality of classes that parents rarely witness and wouldn't deem themselves capable of judging anyway. Since students need the certification and recommendations that universities provide, professors are in a power position, not in a service provider's position. Anyone who can determine your ultimate fate does not consider him- or herself to be a service provider who needs to please the consumer.

Professors understand that they can dominate students and create various hoops for students to jump through in order to get a good grade. They also know that they don't really have to worry about whether anyone has learned anything. In this model it is all too easy to just lecture and use meaningless multiple-choice tests and forget about real education. My favorite example of this comes from the time when we were starting a cognitive science program, and I asked that all professors in that program commit to never giving a multiple-choice test. Now, every cognitive scientist knows that there is no value in such tests; nevertheless, the faculty objected. "Who will grade all the papers that students turn in?" they asked. "We don't have the money for more teaching assistants, and I want to do my research." The idea was dead in the water.

This is all okay with students, as it turns out. There is an implicit gentlemen's agreement about school. Teachers make demands, students satisfy those demands, and those who play the game by the rules win. "You give me the grade, I'll get the degree, I'm out of here." A student once told me that the reason he was a psychology major was not because he liked psychology but because psychology courses always have multiple-choice tests, and he'd found he was very good at multiple-choice tests.

The Nature of the Real University

If we are to rebuild the university, which is in effect what we will do when we build e-learning, it is important to critically assess the basic assumptions underlying a college course. To avoid copying the errors of the existing system, we must understand the following seven things:

1. Why professors teach
2. What professors teach
3. How university requirements get established
4. What students expect
5. How students decide what to study
6. The role of grades and tests
7. The role of certification

Why Professors Teach

There is a certain naivete on the part of students in universities about why the professors who teach them are there. They assume teachers teach because it's their job and that the model of the professional teacher that held in high school applies to the university as well. Nothing could be further from the truth.

Professors at the top universities teach because they feel they have to, or ought to, rarely because they see teaching as fundamental to their life's work. Often, professors who don't get research grants or contribute to the university in other ways are "punished" by having to teach more. The worst professors, that is, the ones who care the least or who have tenure but gave up research a long time ago, typically teach the most courses. A top-notch professor, one who is world famous and brings in lots of research dollars, may teach as little as one course every two years. On the other hand, his or her colleague who has none of these attributes may teach as many as four courses a quarter.

It would be nice to imagine that this is a good system for students, hoping that the nonresearchers happen to be good teachers.

But in fact the opposite is the case. Typically they are burnt-out researchers, resentful of how they fared in the system and with little understanding of how their field has changed in the last thirty years.

The best professors in the United States may or may not be the best teachers. This is actually a complicated idea because the issue of what defines *best* is subject to question, and what defines good teaching is a very open issue. In the competitive world of American universities, *best* has a clear meaning. Universities vie for the services of professors who have the biggest reputations. Top professors get great deals when they are sought after by top schools. These deals include, of course, higher salaries; but as universities can only go so high, other issues matter as well. One of the biggest issues is teaching load. As a result, the best professors have teaching loads of nearly zero and sometimes of literally zero. Clearly, teaching is not valued in such an environment, despite what these same universities say to their prospective students.

In the best schools professors teach because they have to, not because they want to; in the small colleges that are supposed to be very good teaching schools there is a very good chance that a faculty member is teaching something he or she may not understand all that well. Now, this is not true in, say, English literature. In subjects where research doesn't play a big role, where labs are not costly, and where professors don't need graduate students to help with their work, good teachers can be found easily. In fact, those are precisely the fields where there is a glut of teachers on the market. It is possible to learn a lot about English literature at Bard because there are hardly any vacant jobs in that field, so good people find themselves at such places. Even so, most of them would jump to Yale in a minute.

No matter how much professors say they like teaching, and many of them do like it a lot, they all recognize that teaching is not what they were hired for, nor is it what they really do for a living. Professors are primarily interested in the academic issues in their field. They want to write papers and books and communicate with their colleagues. They want to be famous in their fields. They do not get famous for being good teachers. Teaching is low on their priority list.

What Professors Teach

One of the major problems with today's schools is the curriculum. When you tell a professor to teach a class, you might assume this means he or she will teach whatever any other professor might teach in that class. After all, one high school history course is like another, so you might assume that this is true of college as well. But curricula in college are professor dependent. This wouldn't be such a problem if it only meant there was slight variance in how a given course was taught from year to year and professor to professor. Unfortunately, the issue is bigger than that.

Professors teach what they know. There is no standard set of things to be taught in anything but the most introductory of courses. So Introduction to Psychology is pretty similar in every university, as is freshman calculus. But any advanced course is subject to the professor's unique view on his or her field. This is fine because students go to a university to meet interesting faculty and to learn what their view of the field is. Or they ought to. This is what universities have to offer: an opportunity to engage a world expert on his or her own turf to discuss ideas he or she created or is deeply involved with, and for just a few weeks to pretend that you are a world-class economist or sociologist dealing with issues just as professionals in those fields do. This is the ideal. The reality is something else again.

One of the problems with this view is that students by and large don't share it. Most college students go to class expecting to learn the facts. They want to know how economics or sociology works. When I teach a class on how the mind works, students want to know how it works, and I should tell them, please. The difficulty with this view is that most professors don't actually know the answers to the questions students pose. Economics professors don't know how the economy works, sociologists don't know how society works, and I don't know how the mind works. What we all do have are deeply held beliefs about these subjects. We want students to understand the issues in the field, the controversies rather than the facts. And we all fervently want to get students to see things our way, to absorb our point of view, and to understand why our academic enemies are idiots.

Students have no idea that this what they are getting into. They just want to know what is true. They don't want to hear one man's viewpoint. But that is what they get every time (unless the professor is a woman). For this reason, one university is quite different than another, and every course in Artificial Intelligence, for example, is different at every school. This is the fun part of teaching. Professors like talking about their own work and their own ideas. They love trashing their enemies. They love talking about the research they are doing. The question is: *Is this what students came to learn?* It is if they want to become academics, but, by and large, the career of researcher is not what undergraduates have in mind when they arrive at college. Universities deny strongly that they are training institutions. The Harvards and Yales of this world are loath to teach real-world skills. They do not see themselves as helping students prepare for real-world jobs, despite the fact that students believe that the job market opens up by obtaining a degree from an Ivy League school. (Indeed it might, but not because of what a student learned there.) Ironically, the Ivies are very training oriented. They are trying to train students to be academics!

How University Requirements Get Established

With this in mind, we can begin to see how university requirements get established. When I was a graduate student at the University of Texas, I was required to take a course in American Government. I was working on a Ph.D. in Linguistics; I assure you no other school in the country requires a government course in order to get a Ph.D. in Linguistics. So why was this the case at Texas?

It turns out that, because Lyndon Johnson was president and he helped his friends, the Government Department at Texas was very strong. (I don't know if this is still the case. In fact, this is the only Government Department in a major university that I ever heard of.) The department had enough political muscle to get a universitywide requirement passed that made it impossible to graduate from Texas without taking this course. Why would they do that? With all those students taking this class the requirement for extra faculty increased. More importantly, the requirement for teaching assistants increased, and this meant more graduate students for each faculty member to aid his or her research. This was a good deal for the Government Department, and who's to say that a little dose of American Government isn't good for everyone?

At Northwestern all undergraduates must take a math requirement. Now liberal arts students are notorious for wanting to avoid math, so the university has set up a bunch of equivalents. One of these is linguistics, a field with which I am familiar. When my daughter attended the university, I was aghast when she wound up taking linguistics to meet the math requirement and couldn't imagine what she was going to get out of it. She told me the next year that all she remembered from the course was the concept of an *infix*. She remembered this because there is only one infix in English: *fucking*, as in *fanfuckingtastic*. Sounds like math to me.

Requirements get set in a university—from general graduation requirements for a B.A. to Ph.D. requirements in any field—by a committee. This committee represents various interests. When I became a member of the computer science department at Yale, I noticed that in order to get a Ph.D. in Computer Science, students had to take a course in Numerical Analysis (NA) and a course in Artificial Intelligence. I couldn't imagine a bigger waste of time for my graduate students than to take a course in numerical processing by computers when they were trying to build smart machines. One thing had nothing to do with the other. The requirement was there because of a political compromise. No one knew what it meant to get a Ph.D. in computer science, so they simply required a little bit of everything. This could take an entire year out of a graduate student's life for no reason, but no one questioned it. I got rid of the requirement by making a deal with the top guy in NA. His students didn't need to take our courses, and ours didn't need to take his.

It turns out that deals like this are very hard to make in a university. The top NA guy was reasonable, and, more importantly, he was someone whose livelihood was not threatened by such a deal. When professors lose students, they may find themselves in deep trouble. Nontenured appointments can be eliminated, and tenured faculty may wind up teaching subjects they know little about. Unless your subject is very popular, the only way to keep teaching your favorite subject is to make it a requirement. Believe me, NA was not popular; but it was well funded, so the NA guys weren't worried. But there is no way to eliminate the linguistics requirement at Northwestern short of a revolution. Very few students would ever take such courses otherwise. University requirements are about politics, not education.

What Students Expect

Of course, the students know none of this. Students tend to have the view that the university knows what is best for them and that, if they follow the recommended course of study, their lives will work out fine. They expect that the curriculum set forth for them by the faculty is meant to help them get where they want to go after school. This simply isn't true.

In computer science, for example, the skills that will get students jobs include various programming skills that are used in industry. You might think that computer science departments around the country would make sure that all these employable skills are taught in their curriculum; indeed, you would expect them to be the center of the curriculum. Sorry. Most computer science professors are not familiar with the commercial packages that are in use on a daily basis in industry, and even if they happen to know them, they consider them to be of little intellectual interest. So a computer science student will learn the mathematics involved in making calculations about what is computable and the theory of designing programming languages, but not much of what they will ever use in the real world. Computer scientists want their field to be a science, and they want students to attempt to practice that science despite the fact that the students are there because they want jobs in industry.

Why is Introduction to Psychology in every university a tedious survey of every aspect of psychology that no student likes and that no student can avoid? This is a simple question. You can't get around this awful course because, as anyone who has taken it will recall, you are required to be the subject of psychological experiments in order to pass it. That requirement is made by the faculty because they need those subjects for their experiments. Without a course that anyone who wants to take psychology must take, there would be no subject pool. Psychology professors lobby long and hard to make this course required for graduation from the university so that they will have even more subjects in the subject pool. They make sure every aspect of psychology is covered so that any faculty member can teach it, and thus no one hogs all the subjects. A typical student signs up for a course in psychology because he or she wants to understand his or her parents or friends or analyze his or her various personal problems. Universities make sure there is no way you can take courses on these subjects without having gone through other psychology courses that no one would want to take (on visual perception or on statistics, for example). If departments responded to what students wanted, there would only be clinical courses offered, and all those experts in experimental psychology would lose their jobs. When research interests of the faculty fail to coincide with students' course interests, ways are invented to make sure the faculty wins.

This conspiracy is not always supported by the faculty, actually. I once asked some chemists who were very interested in improving teaching in chemistry about the required first-year chemistry curriculum. I asked what percentage of their students were pre-med and got the unsurprising answer of 95 percent. I asked if the first year of college chemistry had anything in it at all that would be relevant to the life of a doctor. They said, "No." I asked if there was chemistry that might be of importance in the career of a doctor. They said, "Of course." So why wasn't the chemistry curriculum revised to include the chemistry that might matter to doctors as opposed to the chemistry they will never need? Because medical schools and various certification boards and publishers had established what courses would be counted toward the requirements for medical school, and there was no changing it. In this case, even the chemistry faculty was frustrated by this, but there was nothing they could do about it.

So, just because you have imitated one of the these courses in a successful e-learning implementation, it doesn't mean that you have done something worthwhile. Many of the courses in a university are there for reasons that are irrelevant in the world of virtual education.

How Students Decide What to Study

One of the serious problems with required courses, standard curricula, and other unchangeables in the current university system is the effect they have on the future of students. It is the rare student who comes to college knowing what he or she wants to be when he or she grows up. Students usually know what subjects interested them in high school, and maybe they know something about the professions of their parents or other people they admire. But those are usually the only guides they have. The fact that the high school curriculum is also unchangeable means that each student is familiar with having taken math, English, history, and some science; so students' first thoughts are often to continue this course of study.

Students want guidance. But the guidance they get is not necessarily what they need. My daughter loved biology in high school and had thoughts of becoming a biologist. When she went to sign up for college biology, it turned out that she had already taken the course in high school. So she was told to take a required chemistry course that was a prerequisite for second-year biology. She wound up hating the chemistry course, didn't finish the full-year course, and had to find a new major. She never got to find out if she really liked biology.

Students are typically directed, either intentionally or through coercion by other students, into the majors that are "in" at their school. At Yale vast numbers of students are English and history majors, despite the fact that there is no call for such majors in the job market. They decide on these majors because it is well known that the faculty at Yale in these areas is first-rate. Students at Yale have absorbed the ethic that a liberal education is what matters, not job potential. The theory behind college education at Yale has not changed much from the nineteenth century. A liberal education means a place to study the classics, not science, or (egad!) engineering or business. Fortunately, the students of the nineteenth century often had Daddy's business to go into. Today, students get the same advice, but find themselves with only law school to attend when they graduate.

The Role of Grades and Tests

Deep down inside this drama is the real villain in the piece: grades and tests. We assume there should be grades and tests because there always have been grades and tests, and school is almost unthinkable without them. After all, without them how will we know who was the best, who succeeded and who failed, who did the work and who sloughed off? How will graduate schools know whom to accept, and how will employers know whom to hire?

Everyone involved in the drama of indifferent education—faculty, students, and administrators—knows that the real role of our universities is certification, not education. You can't certify without grades and tests. Or can you?

Imagine a professor lecturing to a class of 500. How does the professor know if anyone is paying attention? In fact, it is a safe bet that most students are drifting off most of the time. Students know there will be a test and so they try hard to stay awake. No test? Then why fight the hangover? May as well stay in bed. Without tests, the system doesn't work. In an e-learning world, the reasons for these tests become increasingly irrelevant.

Actually, tests are indicative of why the system needs fixing. The problem is that tests and grades are so ubiquitous it is difficult to imagine a school functioning without them. The problem stems from the certification mission of schools. As long as the next school or employer expects that the current school will tell it who is good, the system can't change. But why is the onus of certification on our educational institutions at all? Why shouldn't employers figure out who is good on their own?

As long as tests are the yardstick in school, students will go along with the measure. Students vie for grades and refuse to learn something if it won't be on the test. Students routinely inquire whether they are "responsible" for the material being discussed, and if they are not, they turn off. They cheat, they compete, they wangle their way around, they argue for grades, they whine and complain to teachers about their grades, they stress out, they cram and then forget what they crammed. They do everything but love learning.

The Role of Certification

Universities will never grow out of their certification mission. Too much depends upon it. It's hard to imagine that as many people would go to college as do now if no one really cared about whether you had been to college. No one would fight to go to Harvard if going to Harvard didn't matter. But what matters about it? Not the education. No one asks if you learned a lot; they just assume you are smart because you went there. It is time to rethink this.

We won't get rid of certification, but perhaps we can contemplate new kinds of certification. Students should be certified as having accomplished something or as being able to do something. Like Boy Scout merit badges or Karate black belts or pilots' licenses, the proof should be in the pudding. A student should show his or her stuff; he or she should be able to do something, and the confirmation of the doing should be the certification.

Such changes are unlikely to occur in current universities. It is the rare faculty member who will willingly stop teaching the same old course he or she has taught for thirty years and design a new one that will be more work for him or her to teach because it requires more individual effort. This will not happen unless the venue and the circumstances of education change radically.

Here, then, is why we can begin to have some hopes for e-learning. We can begin to build the courses of the future—courses that might matter to someone who takes them, courses that are about more than certification.

Courses that emphasize doing are a lot easier to design and run on a computer than they are to design and run in a classroom. Classrooms are inherently bad venues for education. No real change can occur until they are eliminated as the normal mode of education. E-learning has a real advantage over traditional schooling: It has no classrooms.

The Role of Explicit Knowledge

In order for e-learning to have a powerful effect on our very idea of schooling, we must abandon the basic model that holds that education means the accumulation of facts. This is because, in a deep sense, education isn't about explicit knowledge; it isn't about getting students to know what happened. It is about getting them to *feel* what happened, to access what happened before to help them think about what is happening now. This, of course, is not so easy to do.

It is very difficult to think about education without thinking about the knowledge we want to impart to students. We live in a world in which knowledge reigns supreme. In the popular culture, games like Trivial Pursuit capture the country's attention; television focuses on Jeopardy, Who Wants to Be a Millionaire, and other "knowledge games" that test who knows what. Far more importantly, school focuses on this same "trivial" knowledge. Schools are driven by tests, and these tests focus on fill-in-the-blank and multiple-choice questions, thereby making success in school dependent upon the memorization of facts. Even in the workplace, companies train employees to do their jobs and then worry how to assess what the employees have learned. The need to assess has focused everyone on things that are assessable. Thus, facts have become "the currency of the educated" because they are so easy to measure.

The problem with all this is twofold. When our institutions of learning focus on test results, it follows that they need to focus on teaching what is testable. The question of what to teach gets perverted by the measurements that are already in place, making curriculum change impossible. But, perhaps more importantly, there is a second problem, which revolves around the issue of our understanding who we are and what makes us tick. As long as we understand ourselves to be a collection of conscious knowledge that we can recite back on demand, we lose an understanding of how we work and of what mental processing is all about. As I have said throughout this book, what we think we know may not be the same as what we actually know.

People have some profound misconceptions about what it means *to know*. Those misconceptions come about because *facts* are what people recognize as what they "know." But we don't really know what we know. We don't know how we learn, how we understand, how we come to feel what we feel or believe what we believe. In fact, all we know for sure are our own sensations, our own thoughts (to a limited extent) and facts.

Most of the really important knowledge people have, the things that enable them to do things and perform and behave in their daily lives, is not consciously known to them. Humans have always had to learn where they were going, how to perform actions of various sorts, how to interact and get along with other people, how to communicate, how to reason, and so on, without "knowing" any of these things. That is, they can do many things without knowing how they do any of them. The knowledge by which they do these things is simply not conscious.

Writers, teachers, preachers, counselors, and others often attempt to make such knowledge conscious. They tell people explicitly what they may or may not know implicitly. Sometimes learning something explicitly in this way, thereby making previously nonconscious knowledge conscious, is helpful, and sometimes it is not. The issue here is whether we can convert conscious knowledge into nonconscious knowledge. If knowledge is only conscious, one can discuss it but it may not be of much actual use.

By consciousness I mean the explicit awareness of what we know or think. This assumption is the basis of our current instructional system and our whole conception of learning. As I have said, while there is truth in the idea that we know a great deal that is quite conscious, the amount we "know" that is nonconscious is far more extensive and significant.

Even so, the current educational system says that students must learn to talk about what they might do rather than actually doing it. When conscious knowledge is portrayed as the *sine qua non* of humanity, or of intelligence, nonconscious knowledge is relegated to a netherworld of knowledge not worth teaching. But as long as we only teach what we explicitly know (because this is in essence what we think of as intelligence), our educational systems will fail.

Instead, we want to teach nonconscious knowledge in our courses because we want our students to be able to *do things*, not just regurgitate facts. The art of e-learning depends upon knowing the difference between what someone tells you he or she wants to know and what you know he or she needs to know in order to do what the knowledge was supposed to enable him or her to do in the first place.

The Future

What will the future be like? When anyone can offer a course to anyone else, people will have a problem choosing the best. Many organizations are building e-learning courses. Who is to say that GE's course in engineering isn't better than Northwestern's? At least GE's engineering course would get you a job at GE.

The line between corporate education and university education will begin to blur. Institutional credentials will become less important than specific course certification. We can already see that with ideas like Microsoft's software engineer certification. In a knowledge-based education system, it matters who gave you the knowledge. Today, Harvard's name counts for a lot, because we all realize that Harvard probably didn't teach you to do anything special. It's an issue of ideas—the folks at Harvard may be reasonably assumed to work on more profound ideas than those at Contra Costa Jr. College. In a doing-based education system, it only matters what you can do. If you can perform at a certain level at a well-specified task, then an employer will want to know that. An employer shouldn't care who taught you or which course you took. There will be doing tests, and those who pass them will be qualified.

Universities were able to thrive in a non-virtual world because location was such a large factor in choosing one. When location goes out the window, which of course it does with any e-learning course, then quality is all that matters. And quality will be assessed by the ultimate users of the product, namely, the students and the employers. There won't be 1000 different economics courses to choose from. Eventually the field of economics, rather than the individual universities at which economists happen to work, will control the content of economics courses. Similarly, corporations that develop high-quality e-learning will be strongly tempted to sell those courses to the outside world and to establish themselves as the leaders in the disciplines in which they build the e-learning solution. Why would Harvard's course in financial management be taken more seriously than GE's course in the same subject? Here again, there will only be a few winners, and it will not be the universities who get to decide who those winners will be.

We are at the beginning of something big. Build a great e-learning course and the world will beat a path to your door. The best e-learning systems of today will form the foundation of the education system of the future.

Bibliography: The Research Foundations of Learning Theory and the "Learning-by-Doing" Method Advocated in This Book

Adams, L.T. and Worden, P.E. 1986. Script development and memory organization in preschool and elementary school children. *Discourse Processes, 9*, 149–166.

Ames, C.A. 1990. Motivation: What teachers need to know. *Teachers College Record, 91*, 409–421, cited in J. Bruer 1993. *Schools for Thought: A Science of Learning in the Classroom.* Cambridge, Mass.: MIT Press.

Anderson, S.J. and Conway, M.A. 1993. Investigating the structure of auto-biographical memories. *Journal of Experimental Psychology: Learning, Memory and Cognition, 19(5)*, 1178–1196.

Bédard, J. and Chi, M.T.H. 1992. Expertise. *Psychological Science, 1*, 135–139.

Bower, G.H. 1978. Experiments on story comprehension and recall. *Discourse Processes. 1*, 211–232.

Bower, G.H., Black, J.B., and Turner, T.J. 1979. Scripts in memory for text. *Cognitive Psychology, 11*, 177–220.

Bransford, J., Franks, J., Vye, N., and Sherwood, R. 1989. New approaches to instruction: Because wisdom can't be told. In S. Vosniadou and A. Ortony, *Similarity and Analogical Reasoning*. New York: Cambridge University Press; Cambridge, Mass.: MIT Press/Bradford.

Bruer, J. 1993. *Schools for Thought: A Science of Learning in the Classroom*. Cambridge, Mass.: MIT Press.

Dennett, D. 1991. *Consciousness Explained*. London: Penguin.

Dewey, J. 1916. *Democracy and Education*. New York: Macmillan Company.

Dweck, C.S. 1986. Motivational processes affecting learning. *American Psychologist*, 1040–1048.

Farrar, M.J. and Goodman, G.S. 1990. Developmental differences in the relation between scripts and episodic memory: Do they exist? In R. Fivush and J.A. Hudson (eds.), *Knowing and Remembering in Young Children*, pp. 30–65. New York: Cambridge University Press.

Fivush, R. 1984. Learning about school: The development of kindergartners' school scripts. *Child Development*, 55, 1697–1709.

Galambos, J. 1986. Knowledge structures for common activities. In J. Galambos, R. Abelson, and J. Black (eds.), *Knowledge Structures*. Hillsdale, N.J.: Lawrence Erlbaum and Associates.

Gallwey, W.T. 1974. *The Inner Game of Tennis*. New York: Bantam Books.

Graesser, A.C., Baggett, W., and Williams, K. 1996. Question-driven explanatory reasoning. *Applied Cognitive Psychology*, 10, S17–S31.

Graesser, A.C., Woll, S. B., Kowalski, D.J., and Smith, D.A. 1980. Memory for typical and atypical actions in scripted activities. *Journal of Experimental Psychology: Human Learning and Memory*, 6, 503–515.

Hudson, J. and Nelson, K. 1983. Effects of script structure on children's story recall. *Developmental Psychology*, 19(4), 625–636.

Hudson, J., Fivush, R., and Kuebli, J. 1992. Scripts and episodes: The development of event memory. *Applied Cognitive Psychology*, 6, 483–505.

Hue, C.W. and Erickson, W. 1991. Normative studies of sequence strength and scene structure of 30 scripts. *American Journal of Psychology*, 104, 229–240.

Kolodner, J. 1993. *Case-Based Reasoning*. San Mateo, Calif.: Morgan Kaufman.

Langer, Ellen. 1990. *Mindfulness*. New York: Addison-Wesley.

McCartney, K. and Nelson, K. 1981. Scripts in children's memory for stories. *Discourse Processes*, 4, 59–70.

Newell, A. and Simon, H. 1972. *Human Problem Solving*. Englewood Cliffs, N.J.: Prentice-Hall.

Read, S.J. and Cesa, I.L. 1991. That reminds me of the time when . . . . : Expectation failures in reminding and explanation. *Journal of Experimental Social Psychology*, 27, 1–25.

Resnick, L. 1987. Learning in school and out. *Educational Researcher*, 16(9), 13–20.

Ross, B.H. 1984. Remindings and their effects in learning a cognitive skill. *Cognitive Psychology*, 16, 317–416.

Ross, B.H., Perkins, S.H., and Tenpenny, P.L. 1990. Reminding-based category learning. *Cognitive Psychology*, 22, 460–492.

Schank, R.C. 1986. *Explanation Patterns*. Hillsdale, N.J.: Lawrence Erlbaum and Associates.

Schank, R.C. 1990, *Tell Me a Story*. New York: Scribners.

Schank, R.C. 1999. *Dynamic Memory Revisited*. New York: Cambridge University Press.

Schank, R.C. and Abelson, R. 1977. *Scripts, Plans, Goals and Understanding*. Hillsdale, N.J.: Lawrence Erlbaum and Associates.

Seifert, C., Abelson, R., and McKoon, G. 1986. The role of thematic knowledge structures in reminding. In J. Galambos, R. Abelson, and J. Black (eds.), *Knowledge Structures*. Hillsdale, N.J.: Lawrence Erlbaum and Associates.

Slackman, E. and Nelson, K. 1984. Acquisition of an unfamiliar script in story form by young children. *Child Development, 55*, 329–340.

Stasz, C., McArthur, D., Lewis, M., and Ramsey, K. 1990. *Teaching and Learning Generic Skills for the Workplace*. Berkeley, Calif.: National Center for Research in Vocational Education, University of California, Berkeley.

Strauss, S. and Shilony, T. 1994. Teachers' models of children's minds. In S. Gelman and L. Hirschfeld, *Mapping the Mind: Domain Specificity in Cognition and Culture*. New York: Cambridge University Press.

Wiley, J. and Voss, J. 1996. The effects of "playing historian" on learning history. *Applied Cognitive Psychology, 10*, S63–S72.

Index

About the Author

Roger C. Schank, Ph.D., is Distinguished Professor of Computer Science at Carnegie Mellon University and the founder and chairman of CognitiveArts, a leading e-learning development firm. He also runs Schank Learning Consultants and is an acclaimed author and lecturer, as well as the inventor of powerful multimedia training tools. He was the founder of the Institute for the Learning Sciences at Northwestern University and the director of the Artificial Intelligence Project at Yale University, where he was also chair of the computer science department. Dr. Schank was also a visiting professor at the University of Paris VII, a faculty member at Stanford University, and a research fellow at the Institute for Semantics and Cognition in Switzerland. One of the world's leading artificial intelligence researchers, Dr. Schank is the author of more than 125 articles and publications. His books include *Coloring Outside the Lines*, *Dynamic Memory*, and *Engines for Education*.